WOMEN WHO LOVE TOO MUCH

Carolyn, Jean, Betty, Jennifer, Amy, Lori . . .

Red-blooded American women whose seemingly successful loves were as good as it gets — except for the one thing they all craved most — the perfect man.

Hungry for love, each woman's single minded determination to *get and keep her man* destroyed lives — in startling episodes of violence that will leave you breathless.

In LETHAL LADIES you will read fifteen shocking and heartbreaking tales of America's most notorious women who loved their men too much . . .

**GOOD VERSUS EVIL. HEROES TRAPPING MONSTERS.
THIS ISN'T FANTASY. IT'S LIFE.
CAPTURE A PINNACLE TRUE CRIME TODAY.**

LETHAL LADIES

GEORGE MAIR

PINNACLE BOOKS
WINDSOR PUBLISHING CORP.

PINNACLE BOOKS are published by

Windsor Publishing Corp.
475 Park Avenue South
New York, NY 10016

Pinnacle and the P logo are trademarks of Windsor Publishing Corp.

First Printing: July, 1993

Printed in the United States of America

*This is dedicated to Steven,
Terra, and Karen.
The three who make everything
I do worthwhile.*

TABLE OF CONTENTS

Introduction
Some Words Up Front . . .   9

Chapter One
Love and Death in the Rockies   19

Chapter Two
The Princess Who Murdered the Queen
for Love of the Prince   40

Chapter Three
The Warmus Love Huntress   61

Chapter Four
The Woman Who Tried to be Perfect   92

Chapter Five
Bambi — The Cop Who Loved a Cop   132

Chapter Six
The Mossler Millionaire Murder   153

Chapter Seven
Sultry, Smoky Southern Murder   160

Chapter Eight
Lucille Miller Wanted Her Man   180

Chapter Nine
The Dumbbell Murder   183

Chapter Ten
The Ghost in the Garret   186

Chapter Eleven
The Tormented Head Mistress   199

Chapter Twelve
Love and Death at Wicky-up   221

Chapter Thirteen
Not Her Sister's Keeper   245

Chapter Fourteen
Semi-lethal Ladies   261

Chapter Fifteen
Erotomania and Murder   289
About the Author   304

Some Words Up Front . . .

In *LETHAL LADIES,* we probe the psyche of women driven to murder because of their obsession with a lover. Since women rarely seek to resolve conflict through physical means, when such violence and murder happens, it leaves the world around it breathless.

Harvard Professor Lee Baer, Director of psychological research at the Obsession and Compulsion Clinic at Massachusetts General Hospital, says there are six million Americans suffering from obsessive-compulsive disorders of the type that could drive a love-obsessed woman to murder. Police authorities claim there are about 450 obsessive murders by women every year.

Dr. Judith Rapoport, a modern pioneer in the study of obsessive-compulsive disorders and other obsessions, says, "Erotomania has long been recognized as a psychiatric disorder in females . . . sometimes known as Clerambault's Syndrome . . . the afflicted women are convinced that the object of their obsession is utterly preoccupied with their love . . . such bizarre preoccupations with another are usually doomed."

Men murder for financial gain all the time. Women, however, rarely murder for money; rather, they murder for the benefit of others or to get the one thing they yearn for more than anything else: love.

It is a theme from the ancient Greek playwright Euripides that is with us today. The woman murderer who kills because of a love obsession. It is Medea, who sacrificed all for her lover, Jason, only to be betrayed when he married a younger woman. It is Clytemnestra who took a lover when her husband, Agamemnon, went to war and had Agamemnon killed when he returned from battle.

It is the Wisconsin Dairy Princess, Lori Esker, convicted of strangling Homecoming Queen, Lisa Cihaski, because of Lori's love obsession with Lisa's fiancee, Bill Buss.

It is Elisabeth Broderick, Amy Fisher, Laurie Boyle and Karen Severson, Lucy Miller, Ruth Snyder, Mary Kay Cassidy, Jennifer Reali, Clara Phillips, Lawrencia Bemenek, Carolyn Warmus, Jean Harris, Dolly Oesterreich, and all the rest about whom we talk about here.

Why do respectable, otherwise law-abiding, women become so controlled, so possessed by the demon of their love that they turn to murder? Women who do not show instability or criminal intent previously. They become consumed by their love, and nothing else matters. So, the respectable lady turns murderess. The woman you had a civilized dinner with last night is plunging a knife into somebody thirty-nine times this morning.

10

Sex is the great gift and the great weapon women use in their relationships with men and, yet, some of the most unhappy women are the ones who have used sex to gain the love and power of a man only to discover that they have gained neither.

Women who become obsessive or addictive lovers and who use sex to feel in control, loved, or to hide their fears of abandonment often are drawn inexplicably to unobtainable lovers who subconsciously reinforce their own feelings of worthlessness.

Those obsessed by love are sometimes said to be suffering from erotomania or a love obsession with another person who doesn't reciprocate the love. Sometimes the person with erotomania fantasizes about the other person sending them signals and messages of his — usually his — love even when the person is oblivious to the person with erotomania.

As Thomas Clavin [*Cosmopolitan*, February, 1992] observes, "Erotomania is a love obsession with a person who does not return the feelings. The delusions of sufferers create havoc in their lives and the lives of the subject of their overwhelming desire."

Erotomania happens to many people and to both sexes. Yet, a significant difference between men and women is that, as in many emotional situations, men tend to express their frustration and anger in an open and violent manner while women tend to repress their feelings and turn them inward.

A classic example of a male erotomanic is Richard Wade Farley who was desperately in love with Laura Black, a coworker at ESL—a defense plant in Sunnyvale, California where they both worked.

Farley constantly stalked Laura, leaving love notes

11

and gifts of blueberry bread, sliced, buttered, and carefully wrapped in foil on her desk every Monday night for almost two months; wrote her 200 love letters; threatened her friends; took pictures of her bending over in leotards at aerobics workouts; and was absolutely certain that she would become his wife even though she refused to date him or even talk with him.

Finally, after four years of this unrequited erotomania, he assaulted ESL loaded with ninety-eight pounds of weapons and ammunition shooting everyone he could hunt down during a five and a half hour siege. In the end, he had slaughtered seven coworkers and wounded Laura critically before the police SWAT squad stormed the place and seized him.

In a less violent example, Dr. Robert Goldstein, director of the New York Forensic Psychiatry Institute, had a case involving a conservative, middle-aged business executive who became love obsessed with a woman he met and talked to on an airplane flight.

He swamped her with phone calls and flowers and, when she kept rejecting him, he believed that it was just her way of testing his love because she was really uncontrollably in love with him. In the end, his love obsession destroyed his own marriage, his family, and his job to the point that he ended up going insane and being committed to a psychiatric hospital.

The same phenomenon includes a variety of celebrity stalkers such as John Hinkley who shot President Reagan to impress actress Jodie Foster with his importance so he could win her love. Linda Fairstein, chief of the Sex Crimes Unit of the New York District Attorney's office who handled the Diane Schaefer case described later, believes that there are a lot more cases of erotomania and love obsession than we really know because many do not end in murder and are handled without it becoming an official police record.

Take the case of an autumn leaves love affair between a divorced, fifty-three year old librarian at a Canadian university who became the patient of psychiatrist, Dr. Murray Stein. She claimed to have been having a torrid affair with a married physics professor when he suddenly had a heart attack and died, sending the librarian into a bewildered depression that brought her to Dr. Stein.

She poured out every detail of the intimacy between herself and her now-dead lover to Dr. Stein including how he dressed, how he looked at her, how he caressed her and made love to her, and their plans to marry as soon as he could arrange for a divorce from his present wife. It was moving and touching. It was also untrue.

The two never had an affair and, in fact, hardly ever spoke to one another. As far as the physics professor was concerned, the librarian was a virtual stranger. But, for her, he was her secret, passionate lover.

Dr. Stein, reporting the case in the Canadian Journal of Psychiatry, described this imaginary affair as a classic case of erotomania which was first identified in detail in 1921 by the French psychiatrist, Gaetan De Clerambault from which it became called Clerambault's Syndrome by some therapists.

Love obsessions come in degrees of intensity as do most human emotions and there is a growing debate about where to draw the line between love and lust. Sometimes the focus seems to be entirely on sex as in the cases reported in June 4, 1990, *Time* magazine.

13

"A woman uses a vibrator so intensely that she ends up in an emergency room. A priest steals money from his church's collection box so that he can pay for prostitutes. A young father of three small children sneaks out at night for anonymous sex in public bathrooms. He contracts AIDS and infects his wife. Both of them are dying."

Some, such as Patrick Carnes, author and academic, claim that sexual addiction is akin to drugs or alcohol and beyond normal control. Other experts challenge Carnes as somebody who is trying to make a name for himself and his theories by introducing a new popular psychology of sexual addiction.

Yet, Richard Salmon, National Director of the National Council on Sexual Addiction, claims that at least a quarter of a million Americans have attended their meetings over some problem in this ill-defined area of love, romance, or sex obsession. Carnes claims that over seven million Americans have one of these addictions.

Writer Maureen Dowd sounded a word of caution, however, about getting caught up in what she calls "Addiction Chic" noting that Americans are getting addicted to getting addicted. Whatever we are caught up in, she warns, we tend to call an addiction and are doomed to end up on an afternoon exposé talk show as in: Next on *Oprah*, "Dwarf Women Shinto Priests Raised in Patagonia Addicted to Raggedy Ann Dolls That Look Like Their Mothers!"

Even so, it is undeniable that people do have obsessions and addictions that affect their lives and that of those around them. In the case of love obsession, women, those who have it agree that it functions like a

14

drug. The pattern is generally the same in every instance.

The pattern starts with finding a male love target or love hostage who eases her yearning for love at the moment. The man soon doesn't give enough attention or enough love or enough sex and the obsessive woman begins to feel more and more insecure. As the relationship goes on, she pushes for more love, affection, and attention, only to be met with the reverse reaction by a man who feels smothered and gasps for more space and air. In the end, the man escapes, leaving the love-obsessive woman abandoned and lonely, again hungry for the self-esteem and reassurance she didn't get as a child.

The sad thing is that no man can give a love-obsessive woman what she wants. The only solid source of self-esteem is from within ourselves. Sociologist Lillian Rubin of Queens College in New York City says that, when women are insecure about who and what they are, they often turn to sex to relieve the anxiety — at least temporarily.

Berkeley, California clinical psychologist Neal King says that sex and love obsession are magnified by inaccessibility, unattainability, and separation. And the obsession is enhanced with a quality and power beyond the ordinary when you have to deal with his dirty laundry and missing dinner at home.

Palo Alto psychiatrist Jonathan Segal reported [*American Journal of Psychiatry*, October, 1989] that, in spite of the fact that erotomania was thought to be rare for a long time, it is far more common than we know. Segal never gives a seminar for other psychiatrists about erotomania without some of them telling him they have patients suffering from the syndrome.

Erotomania persists for years in many patients, but Dr. Segal says, "Often a person retreats, licks her wounds, goes back to her solitary life, and learns to live with disappointment."

But, sometimes it doesn't happen that way. Sometimes the love obsession of a woman turns to murder.

In 1979, Dr. Penelope Russianoff, a psychologist teaching at the New School for Social Research and author of several books and television programs, gave a lecture entitled, "Why Do I Think I Am Nothing Without A Man?" at the YWCA and the response stunned her.

When she investigated the reason for this, she concluded that ninety-five percent of her women patients felt worthless without a man in their lives. She knew, as most of us do, that having a lover and a friend is a wonderfully reassuring feeling for all of us — men and women. However, she was struck by the intensity of the feeling among most women she knew and had as patients.

As she describes the syndrome, "Desperate dependence refers to any woman for whom the major focus in life is a man. The desperate dependent woman pivots . . . round a man who loves her . . . someone who is hers, who cares about her to the exclusion of all other women."

It led to her writing a book of the same name as her original lecture subject in which she investigated the need many women have for being certified as a woman by having a man. It should also be noted that men often do the same thing and are dependent on having a wife. In some instances, such as the Broderick case reported in this book, the man needs a trophy wife to validate his virility and success.

Back in the 1940's, Joan Crawford and Van Heflin starred in the movie, *Possessed*, about a woman so obsessed with her man that she goes insane because he doesn't return her intense love. True to the Hollywood tradition of recycling successful movies, there was more recently the oft-referred to, *Fatal Attraction*, which has now become a generic phrase to describe the kind of murders we talk about here.

Jed Diamond, a San Francisco Bay area psychotherapist and author of *Looking For Love In All The Wrong Places*, identifies the person who typically develops into a love addict obsessed with having a lover:

> She grew up in a home where her needs for security were not met and she felt she was an emotional orphan. Not feeling safe being who she really was, she developed an attractive outer image to draw people to her who made her feel accepted and safe. Inside, she was in turmoil because she was forced to be somebody she wasn't, not because the people who mattered in her life—parents, siblings, lovers—didn't accept her for what she really was. She became increasingly manipulative, desperate, and out of control, trying to get the warmth and security of a true love.

That, as I said, is how, in essence, Jed Diamond describes the love addict. It is also a precise description of Carolyn Warmus, Elisabeth Broderick, and others whose cases of obsession are described in this book.

17

Dr. Howard Halpern, psychotherapist for twenty-five years and author of several books on relationships, defines love obsession in his book, *How To Break Your Addiction To A Person*, as "a compelling need to connect with and to remain connected with a particular person." He also calls it Attachment Hunger: "The feeling that holding on to . . . a particular relationship, is a matter of life and death."

Holding onto a particular relationship for some, can be a matter of life and death.

The tragic truth of that is chronicled here.

One
Love and Death in the Rockies

The cute gamin holding the .45 caliber Colt revolver didn't want to kill Dianne, but her love required it and God approved it.

Dianne Hood was only thirty-two years old, married with three children and a husband plus, unfortunately, the degenerative disease Lupus. Life wasn't all that perfect for her, but she wasn't ready to be murdered as she and her friend Karen Johnson left a Colorado Springs Lupus support group meeting that September 12 in 1990.

She and Karen were walking out of the Otis Park Community Center into the brisk Colorado night air talking about the meeting that had just finished. As the two women walked near some shrubbery on the way to Dianne's car, a threatening figure stepped calmly out of the bushes behind them, wearing camouflage military fatigues and a black ski mask.

In several quick strides, the shadowy figure caught up with the two women and lunged at Dianne's purse. Upon retelling the events of that night, Karen said, "A hand came out and grabbed for Dianne's purse." Rather than resist, Dianne knew the best thing to do was to surrender the purse which she did, throwing it into the face of the intruder and screaming, "Take it!"

The move didn't have the anticipated result. Instead of taking the purse and running away, the mugger pulled out a gun and shot Dianne on the spot. The heavy .45 caliber slug caught Dianne in the back of her shoulder as she turned to run back to the Community Center for help. The impact was like somebody hitting her across the back with a baseball bat and drove her to the ground.

Then, as Karen watched in horror, the mugger deliberately stepped over to the prone Dianne, who sensed what was coming and began begging for mercy. The camouflage-clad assassin took careful aim, holding the pistol with both hands in the recommended manner and fired a bullet through the pleading woman's heart.

Then, and only then, did the mugger race off into the night leaving the dead woman behind and her stunned friend screaming for help.

To the Colorado Springs police there was no great mystery about the crime. After questioning Karen and, more importantly, processing the known facts through the cerebral data bank of their own experience, they quickly labeled the crime for what it was—a cold-blooded, planned murder.

The mugging ruse was patently a phoney set up. A mugger might panic and shoot his or her victim so the mugger could escape. But, no mugger sticks around to carefully execute the victim who is already down and out of play. More significantly, if the purpose of the killing was to prevent being followed or apprehended, why wasn't Karen killed, too?

One of the biggest things going for the police in this case initially was the fact that Colorado Springs, conservative, family-oriented, mostly religious home of the Air Force Academy, isn't that big a town. People know each other and know what is going on behind closed doors and, for that matter, in open pick-up trucks.

Investigators began sniffing around looking for somebody who might be, as Claude Rains said in Casablanca, the usual suspects. These would be people who might have a motive and who might benefit financially or romantically from the murder of Dianne Hood.

In the course of their investigation, the police learned that Jennifer Reali often hung around the back of the florist shop where she worked with a guy in a pick-up truck doing some necking. Probably nothing wrong with that except maybe that they were both married to other people.

Jennifer was a cute, petite Gigi-like brunette with a tomboy haircut, mother of two and married to Ben Reali who was in the Army stationed in Colorado Springs. Her friend in the pick-up truck was handsome, assured 6'4", 215-pound Brian Hood, a local insurance agent and Born Again Christian married with children.

Both Brian and Jennifer had been seen around in other places, too, most notably at Bally's U.S. Swim and Fitness Club where they had both originally met in May of 1990 in the Jaccuzzi.

This bit of information set off a "Bingo!" reaction in the heads of the detectives when they discovered that handsome, charming Brian was also the husband of the slain woman, Dianne Hood. Both Jennifer and Brian quickly found themselves in drab police station rooms, answering a lot of questions about their relationship and their possible involvement in the murder.

Ironically, as it turned out later, Jennifer was the first one to crack and, forty-eight hours after the murder, she spilled out their story of sex, God, love, obsession, infidelity, and boredom.

Both of them, like so many of the modern residents of Colorado, started out in different places. Jennifer started out as a young woman looking for life in Seattle where her father, Keith Vaughn, did well as one of the city's prominent architects. Jennifer was an out-going, adventurous woman who enjoyed rowing on Lake Washington as a member of the University of Washington crew and spent her junior year knocking around France.

In her restless, probing way, Jennifer was also lonely and, because of that, depressed. She thought she would find happiness with Ben Reali, a professional Army officer. So they married in 1984 and began the military musical assignments game of moving from post to post, during which time Jennifer delivered two children in rapid order and realized that hers was not a marriage conceived in heaven.

In fact, she found mixing with Army wives, as she was expected to do, boring. She found military life boring. She found being a mother raising two daughters, Tinneke and Natasha, boring. She found Ben boring. This was one bored lady.

Two things eased the boredom and the more she did them the more she wanted to do them. The first was drinking beer or wine. That relaxed her, depressed what ever anxieties and irritations she had and made her feel good. She liked that.

The second was new and exciting experiments in sex. The way she and Ben had been having sex had produced two kids, but not a whole lot of fun for Jennifer. So Jennifer laid it on Ben that she wanted to try different positions, new erotic stimulants— she wanted to be titillated, teased, tormented, and transported to heaven. Ben, a fairly straight military guy, would be embarrassed to admit later that she had forced him into spanking her to arouse her.

Well, it worked for a while, but didn't last and, by the time they were transferred to a new post at Colorado Springs, their marriage was cracking at the seams with Jennifer throwing tantrums, steak knives, punches, and threats of divorce. The year was 1989.

Meanwhile on another part of the planet, Brian and Dianne had been steadies all through college at Angelo State University in San Angelo, Texas, where Brian, son of a successful insurance man in Houston, was a big guy on campus, playing defensive tackle on the championship Angelo football team, admired by many men and women on campus and overly cocksure of himself.

All that was okay with Dianne because her main

23

plan in life was to marry Brian, have his babies, and make a wonderful, happy home for them all. They married after graduation two weeks before Christmas, 1980, and soon decided to move to Colorado Springs because they liked the atmosphere and the people there and it would let them get away from each of their families while being close enough to visit when necessary.

Brian found Christ in Colorado Springs and became a Born Again Christian with the Fellowship Bible Church while he was a beer salesman. That didn't seem like a proper job for a dedicated Christian in 1986 and his church connections got him a job as an insurance salesman which improved their situation and, in time, Dianne became a Born Again, too.

Then, in June of 1989, tragedy struck the Hood family when Dianne learned she had a debilitating disease, Lupus, that caused arthritis, inflammations, skin eruptions, and kidney problems. Her form of Lupus, however, was not fatal as long as she took care of herself, kept out of the sun and got lots of rest. That was hard with three children, Jarrod, 7, Lesley, 5, and Joshua, an infant at the time the Lupus struck.

This new regime changed their lives, but the Hoods still seemed devoted to each other even though the sex went south and their marriage became mandatorily celibate which was a secret Dianne only shared with her best friend, Darla Blue. Brian was willing to keep Dianne in his life, but he was not willing to lock sex out of it. So, he just got it elsewhere as many men in that situation

24

would. What a perfect moment for the sex-starved Jennifer to walk into.

Bally's U.S. Swim and Fitness Club should actually have been named Bally's Singles Makeout Club because it was reputed to be one of the most notorious singles connection places in Colorado Springs. Most people didn't go there to develop biceps — they went there to develop relationships and one-night stands. So, these two ready-for-primetime-fun-and-loving met and immediately went out on a lunch date.

They continued to see each other for several months and, then, came the incident of the wrinkled shirt. Brian dropped by unexpectedly at the Reali house in May, 1990, while Jennifer was there alone with the supposed purpose of discussing her insurance needs. After a few minutes, she went into the kitchen to get him some coffee and he followed her, grabbed her from behind, spun her around and began kissing her passionately. Sure, "her insurance needs."

She responded in kind and there was a lot of hugging, touching, and frantic groping. When they broke, her first concern was that she had sorely wrinkled his shirt and she asked him to take it off so she could iron it.

The shirt came off, was ironed, and put back on again. They were standing by the washer, dryer, and ironing board with Brian's freshly pressed shirt on when they went and wrinkled it all up again.

Brian unzipped his fly, dropped his pants and, with the sure handling of a man who has done it many times before, hoisted the unprotesting Jennifer up onto the washer and dryer. That's where they made love — pressed shirt and all.

At this moment if this were a play, instructions would say, "God — Enter the Laundry Room Stage Right."

Brian immediately soothed what ever anxieties Jennifer had, and from all indications she had few, by assuring her as a Born Again man who was a personal friend of God's that, "In the eyes of God, we are now one."

This, it turned out was not a tough sell at all. Jennifer was ripe and she instantly fell in love with this exciting and handsome man in her life. And, her love progressed rapidly to obsession with a willingness to do anything he wanted whenever and wherever he wanted it.

Sex was one thing that he wanted, and frequently, and Jennifer was happy to accommodate her man anytime he said during the weeks that followed, meeting him often in the back seat of her Jeep Cherokee.

Again, the trouble with this kind of free-wheeling romance and love obsession is that the man and woman act like they don't care what the world thinks, but the world is watching and that's when trouble comes in. In this case, it was in the form of Jennifer's boss at the florist shop as we saw earlier. He saw them kissing and blew the whistle.

Before that happened, however, Jennifer and Brian were really enmeshed in their love. Jennifer had found heaven and happiness at last, albeit slightly tainted by her husband and his wife. Naturally, between passionate embraces, talk would turn to these dual problems and, equally naturally, Brian found a solution in the Old Testament's Book of Samuel. Jennifer was believing it because she, too, was now attending the Fellowship Bible Church and becoming a Born Again.

In the Book of Samuel it tells the story of King David's love for his mistress, Bathsheba, that was thwarted by the inconvenience of her having a husband. King David solves this difficulty by dispatching Bathsheba's husband into battle and guaranteed death.

As Brian saw it, this was a parallel with the problem of Dianne and he tried to convince Jennifer that killing Dianne would be less of a sin than divorcing her. It was, he assured her, God's plan and, besides, they had already committed adultery and murder wasn't any worse. Even if she was queasy about murder, Brian said that all would be forgiven if she repented before God.

So, on the morning of October 10, Jennifer's love obsession telephoned her and said that Dianne would be out at her Lupus support group meeting the night after next and that would be an excellent opportunity for Jennifer to free her lover. Besides, she was ready to do anything her lover wanted, wasn't she? It wasn't a discussable point. Her man wanted it and her man would have it.

Jennifer knew what she had to do and she wanted to do it right, so, two weeks before the killing, she got her Army Captain husband, Ben, to let her take one of his guns out of his collection and go to a nearby shooting range with her so she could practice with it.

At about the same time Ben and Jennifer were on the target range practicing, Brian and Dianne were off to Sun Valley for three days on a marriage encounter. According to Dianne's friend, Darla Blue, testifying later, Brian met with Jennifer the morning of the murder to break it off.

And, at some point during those two weeks, she bought a black ski mask. On the night of the murder, Ben was working late and Jennifer pulled on a set of his combat fatigues and took the antique gun she used at target practice out of his collection. Then, she drove over to the Community Center, waited in the bushes and, when Dianne and Karen came out, shot Dianne. Running from the scene, she stopped in a nearby alley and stripped off the fatigues and ski mask before jumping into her Jeep and driving home.

Three hundred members of the Fellowship Bible Church gathered soon after the murder to memorialize Dianne Hood and bid her farewell. Nine hours before on that same day, September 15, Brian was arrested for her murder and twelve days later authorities formally charged Jennifer with first-degree murder plus conspiracy with Brian to commit murder.

From the beginning of the legal proceedings, there was no quarrel about who had done what. Jennifer clearly had pulled the trigger, but she would claim that she did it because she had an obsessive love for Brian and he made her do it. On November 16, Jennifer's attorney pled her innocent by reason of insanity and almost six months later, on May 7, a jury rejected that plea and she was

28

ordered to stand trial for the murder.

Jennifer's husband, Ben, decided to bail out and filed for a divorce the day before Christmas, 1990, just a little over three months after the killing. He asked for custody of their two girls. Eight months later on August 28, the divorce would be final with Ben getting the two daughters.

Brian and Jennifer were indicted for murder, but were to be tried separately because Jennifer had made a deal with the prosecution. She would testify against Brian in exchange for the prosecution not seeking the death penalty for her.

Brian's trial was held first in the small rural town of Fort Morgan before Judge Joseph Weatherby because of the hot publicity over the love-obsessive murder in Colorado Springs. Hood's attorney, Richard Tegtmeier, put on a vigorous defense accusing Jennifer of being a self-serving liar who saw the lover with whom she was obsessed slipping away because he was returning to his wife.

Darla Blue testified that Dianne and Brian, "said they were committing themselves [to each other and their marriage] anew. A drugstore clerk, Nancy Bramley, knew about the marriage encounter weekend to Sun Valley and, when Brian came in to pick up Dianne's medications just five hours prior to the murder she asked him about it.

"When I asked him about Sun Valley, his face lit up. He said the trip was like a honeymoon."

Jennifer's ex-husband, Ben, testified that she was a tough woman inclined to violence and Ben's mother said it was ludicrous to believe anyone could force Jennifer into doing anything she didn't want to do.

In the courtroom, Jennifer affected a somber demeanor, wearing modest dresses with Peter Pan collars, pearls, and reading glasses so she looked feminine and vulnerable. On the stand, she shook with gasping sobs as she detailed the killing and how it took every bit of determination to fulfill her lover's orders.

"I didn't want to kill her. All I could remember hearing was Brian's voice: 'She's got to be dead. She's got to be dead. She's got to be dead.' "

Dianne's brother, David Moore, slashed back at Jennifer and the prosecution from the witness box for making their Faustian deal which he charged tainted her testimony.

"I don't believe Brian is guilty. This woman took my sister from me. Now she's trying to take Brian from me. She's ruined our family."

At the end, Tegtmeier decided against putting Brian on the stand in his own defense and rested his case. He felt confident that the jury would not believe Jennifer and that they would acquit his client.

The jury returned to the courtroom two days before Christmas and delivered a dark gift to Brian Hood. It found that, while he was not guilty of first degree murder as charged, he was guilty of two counts of solicitation of murder and one count of conspiracy to commit the murder of Dianne Hood.

In an odd demonstration of remorse for the jury's verdict, the jury foreman, Ron Shaver, sent the judge a letter pleading for leniency in sentencing

Brian. Judge Weatherby pronounced a sentence of thirty-seven years for Brian in the Colorado State prison. He would be eligible for parole in twelve years.

Ben Reali's children were sent to live with his parents in Houston when he was transferred in the service to a new post in Germany. He got rid of his gun collection because he feels somehow partly to blame for Dianne's murder since it was one of his guns that was the murder weapon. And, while he is less a gun collection, he is plus a wife again, having remarried as soon as possible after his divorce from Jennifer.

Jennifer was bound over for trial in March of 1992 in another small town, Glenwood Springs. Attending the trial as symbolic supporters were Jennifer's parents, Keith and Gail Vaughn and David and Angela Moore, Dianne's brother and his wife. The Moores were there to remind people that Dianne was a real, living person—not some legal abstraction—and the woman on trial, Jennifer Reali, deliberately and cruelly murdered her in cold-blood.

The Vaughns had drained themselves financially to try saving their daughter. Initially, they had taken out a second mortgage on their home in Seattle and raised $200,000 with $60,000 going to the defense attorney, Elvin Gentry, and the rest going to defense costs. By early February, the money had run out and Elvin Gentry was about to do the same thing. He filed a motion to withdraw from the case because there was no more money to defend Jennifer.

Gail and Keith Vaughn found some more money somewhere and Gentry agreed to stay on the case. It was a tough case to defend since Jennifer had already confessed to having killed Dianne.

Karen Johnson, the only eyewitness to the murder, saw death in Jennifer's eyes that night.

"There have been a lot of nightmares. I remembered them vividly at one time. I'm told by my roommates that I'm still having nightmares, but I don't remember them anymore."

Karen usually rode with Dianne to the Lupus group meetings and that night was no different. Afterward, she testified, the two of them were walking back to Dianne's car when Jennifer attacked Dianne from the rear.

"That arm had grabbed Dianne and threw her past me. The gun came out of the pocket and was flung right past my head and the first shot was fired right next to my head."

That first shot caught Dianne at the back of her shoulder and the force of it rammed her to the ground as Karen began screaming at the dark assailant.

"She just glared at me. I was six inches from her face when I saw her eyes and they were dark eyes and full of hate. She walked over to where Dianne was lying. Dianne was begging for her life and she took very careful aim and shot her again."

Jennifer's defense lawyer, Elvin Gentry, said she was obsessed by her love for Brian and that she was sexually molested at age six which made her totally dependent on men for her self-esteem; she had been abused and bullied by men all her life,

32

particularly, by her husband, Ben; and, she had been vulnerable to Hood's twisting her personality and controlling who and what she was and did.

Karen rejected Gentry's contention as a bunch of baloney.

"I believe she was totally cognizant the entire time. She had to be. The amount of planning that went into it, the way she stalked us. She had been at the convenience store and chickened out. She knew what she was doing was wrong and yet she did it anyway. She wanted Dianne dead."

The testimony of Jennifer's ex-husband was unexpectedly damaging and cruel, portraying an entirely different woman than whom the defense was trying to project. Captain Benjamin Reali bitterly painted a picture of a violent woman who had abused her own children emotionally. The sparks flew between him and defense attorney Gentry until the tension was almost visible in the already strained trial.

Part of this was because Gentry focused more on Ben's effect on Jennifer's personality than on Brian's manipulation. Ben, according to Gentry, had trapped Jennifer in a loveless marriage and kept her isolated from supportive friends so she was driven in desperation to find love with Brian Hood.

The negative view of Ben was buttressed by Jennifer's women friends, Elena Howell and Jennifer Zavatsky who said Ben was always lurking and acting oddly.

Although he had originally written her a supportive love letter when she was first arrested, as he learned about the details of her affair with Brian and other details of the case, he turned against her and filed for divorce.

Ben testified that Jennifer had told their youngest daughter that she was going to be taken away and her oldest daughter that Brian was going to be her new daddy. He also related several physical attacks she had made upon him, including one wielding a large steak knife.

Gentry struck back by asking Ben if it wasn't true that he had controlled, beaten, and raped his wife? And, wasn't it true that he had rammed the barrel of a pistol up her vagina and asked her to contemplate the effect of his pulling the trigger.

Ben counter-punched with the aplomb of a seasoned soldier under fire and denied all the allegations made by Gentry, claiming that they were complete news to him. Observers generally felt that Ben came off as a very credible witness and hurt Jennifer's case severely.

Ben's sister, Erin Dudley, added to the image of a peculiar personality in Jennifer by testifying that, while visiting her in jail, Jennifer had seemed consumed by a bizarre plan.

"She just talked about wanting more babies. She wanted a baby girl. She wanted to name a baby girl Dianne. It was horrifying. It made me think: Jennifer's not there."

The jury in Jennifer's case was out for almost six whole days which surprised many observers since her case seemed so open and shut. Everybody outside the jury room was anxious as the days dragged on. People in the small town were arguing over the case in coffee shops and stores along the main street while reporters tried to find ways to make the time pass without going too far away so they would miss the verdict. In the local jail, Jennifer waited and quietly talked with her parents and prayed with her pastor.

On the sixth day at twenty minutes to eleven in the morning, phones began ringing and pagers began beeping. The jury was coming in. When it came back at 11:17 on the morning of April 8, the courtroom was witness to the contrasting confrontation between the cool and stoic Jennifer in her Peter Pan collar, pearls, and detached stare and the emotionally over-wrought jury as it solemnly declared Jennifer was guilty of murder in the first degree plus conspiracy with Brian to commit murder.

Curiously, Jennifer seemed surprised that she had been found guilty. No one else in the courtroom was. Judge Jane Looney set sentencing for May 14, one day after Jennifer's thirtieth birthday.

Two people had sustained Jennifer during the long ordeal of her imprisonment and trial, Glenwood Springs pastor James Brown who had been very close to her from the beginning of the trial and Jeanie Brooks, the defensive investigator whose hand Jennifer had clung to throughout the eight-week trial.

"Jen'll be all right. I don't think it's anything she can't handle," said Pastor Brown as Ben Reali blew her a kiss as she was driven away from the courthouse in a police car.

Many observers and, even the prosecutors, felt some sympathy for Jennifer. Prosecutor Bill Aspinwall agreed with the verdict in the Reali case, but didn't think it was right that Brian and Jennifer ended up with different verdicts.

"We've always thought that they should be treated equally. They're both equally responsible for Dianne Hood's death."

The Colorado Springs District Attorney, John Suthers, agreed.

"Our only disappointment and sense of less than full justice in this case is that Brian Hood did not receive a life sentence."

Others thought that the jury must have been seriously divided or it wouldn't have taken six days to reach a verdict in a case where the defendant had confessed to the killing. Defense attorney Gentry had argued that Reali was a sick woman, beaten and brainwashed and out of touch with reality when she murdered Dianne Hood. Obviously some of the juror's agreed with him, but voted for conviction anyhow.

When Judge Jane Looney polled the jury, each of the six men and six women confirmed their verdict of guilt of first degree murder, but four of them were crying when they did. Jennifer's parents listened to the verdict with bowed heads and closed eyes.

Naturally, there was no sympathy for Jennifer from the victim's family and friends after the trial was over. David Moore, who, with his wife, had stayed through the two months the trial went on, gave vent to his unrelenting bitterness.

"The fact is that my sister is dead and Jennifer Reali is alive and Jennifer Reali will be allowed to

36

live out her life at the state's expense, see her friends and family for the rest of her life. I'll never see my sister again."

There was also a bitter reaction at the verdict from Jennifer's ex-husband.

"She gunned down the woman in cold blood. . . . It was a very selfish act. She's a selfish, spoiled bitch."

The jury's foreman, Hunt Walker, a forty-six-year-old public works director in Snowmass Village said, "We examined that case upside down, inside out, and tested every theory. We collectively did the best job possible. My glaring impression is that it certainly was a collection of events that came together that resulted in the death of Dianne Hood and any couple of changes along the way could have prevented this American tragedy. I think that's the most glaring tragedy. We're not talking about a Jeffrey Dahmer here. We're not talking about a John Gotti. And, that's what made this trial difficult."

As for the sentence given Brian, Waler was as unhappy with that as everyone else connected with Jennifer's trial.

"I'm really dissatisfied with the fact that he could get out in twelve years. I think that's wholly unfair."

Jennifer's father formed a Washington State corporation, based in Seattle where Jennifer grew up. All the legal rights to books, movies, T-shirts, coffee mugs, other paraphernalia and the songs that Jennifer has written including the one in which she begs for Dianne's forgiveness belong to that corporation.

The father explained that they had mortgaged their home to pay for Jennifer's legal bills and the corporation is a way of getting the money back plus money for future legal appeals on her behalf.

Others dismiss the commercialization of Dianne's murder as the height of bad taste.

The sympathy that jurors had toward Jennifer was reflected in the sentencing of Judge Jane Looney on May 14. She began by saying that she wished it was within her power as a judge to ease the sentence she was about to hand down, but the law did not give her a choice. The sentence in a conviction of the first degree murder was mandatory.

Then she asked Jennifer if there was anything she wanted to say before the sentence was pronounced. Jennifer quietly looked at Judge Looney and said "No."

Clearly Judge Looney felt as the prosecutors had, namely, that Jennifer was no more guilty than Brian Hood and she was disturbed that each had been found guilty of different crimes with Brian getting the lesser sentence. She labeled the difference in punishments as intellectually unfair and emotionally unfair.

"It seems to me this tragedy is almost like a Greek tragedy. That is, we have a person who is otherwise a really decent person — that being you — of good character, but with some fatal flaw.

"There was no question in my mind that essentially you were carrying out Mr. Hood's plan. He was almost like, in my mind, the embodiment of evil. That is, that he took what we hold most sacred as a society, which are love and religion, and used those repeatedly to influence you.

"I suspect that had you not become involved with and influenced by him, chances are you probably wouldn't have had anything more serious than a traffic ticket or two the rest of your life."

Then, the judge noted that she had gotten many letters urging leniency in sentencing including a number of them from members of the jury, "but I really have no choice about it." So, Judge Looney sentenced Jennifer to life in prison without possibility of parole.

So, Jennifer Reali, a woman obsessed with her love of Brian Hood might be psychically buried inside the Colorado State prison system for the rest of her life without the possibility of parole. The other female victim of this tragedy, Dianne Hood, is physically buried in an unmarked grave in Evergreen Cemetery in Colorado Springs because her family cannot afford a headstone.

Two
The Princess Who Murdered the Queen for Love of the Prince

It was the last place in America you would think passionate murder could happen. The love obsession and murder came right out of "Twin Peaks" with the exception that it happened in real life.

The setting of Birnamwood, Wisconsin, is classically idyllic and Pine Road leading out of town winds and climbs and crests to reveal a pastoral scene of endless fields punctuated by dairy herds and farmhouse clusters riveted to the earth by tall silver silos. It is an expansive, lovely, and lonely countryside.

It seemed to the average traveler a sleepy spot on the American landscape that could hardly harbor intense passion about anything beyond improving the dairy herd and the weather. In the cliche of rural serenity and security, people bragged of their unlocked doors.

Homecoming queen Lisa Cihaski drove thirty-five miles of Pine Road each way every day between home and her job at Howard Johnson's as assistant sales and catering manager, except for

September 20, 1989 when she only made the trip one way. That day had two other significant milestones for her: she and her fiancee, Bill Buss, set their marriage date that morning and she was murdered that night.

Bill got her call earlier saying her new Oldsmobile Cutlass was acting up and she might be running late, but they would still meet at her house and the eagerness in her voice communicated the excitement of a young woman whose life was going well.

Darkness envelopes the long, lonesome reaches of Pine Road at night and ground fog shrouds it in the early morning. When Lisa failed to come home on schedule, her mother searched Pine Road for several miles thinking she might have had more car trouble. Bill waited at the house, but she never showed up.

Morning came across the Wisconsin dairyland and still no sign or word from Lisa. By this time, Kelly Meverden, Lisa's oldest friend, had come over to visit and reported that she hadn't heard anything from Lisa either. The sanguine attitude of everyone toward Lisa's failure to come home or call would later seem strange to some, but her family and friend assumed she had stayed overnight with a girlfriend without calling.

Thinking little about it, Kelly and Lisa's little sister, Tammy, drove to their college classes thirty-three miles away, but had hardly arrived when an urgent phone call from Mrs. Cihaski summoned them back, "Kel, can you find Tam and come home? Just come to our house. There's been an ac-

41

cident. We'll explain when you get here."

Kelly's blood turned cold at the words because it sounded ominous as she and Tammy raced back to the Cihaski house as fast as the car could go. When they arrived, the news confirmed the dread they both had, Lisa was dead. More horrifying, she had not died in an accident—she was murdered in the parking lot of Howard Johnson's.

"The first thing that came to my mind was Lori Esker," Kelly would later report.

Shock swept over the group of small towns around the scene of the crime, Birnamwood, Hatley, and Eland. Settled at the turn of the century by farmers with names like Pietzes, Esker, Szew, and Buss, it is a far-flung, but close-knit region of a few hundred people who shop, worship, go to school, relax, and work together in mostly dairy-related occupations. It's a region with one doctor for the people and seven veterinarians for the livestock.

It is family country where kids and parents work and play together and most attend one of the nine churches together. Young people go to one consolidated high school, go on dates to Chet and Emil's to listen to the jukebox and drink beer and marry young. Birnamwood is the focus of life and, in Lisa's case, death.

Over three hundred came to say goodbye to Lisa at the funeral home on Birnamwood's north end just blocks from where she first went to grammar school. Many felt Lisa's murder particularly threatening and troubling. Clearly, they reasoned, her murderer had been a stranger—a drifter passing through—and people took to locking their doors for the first time and Howard Johnson's started providing security escorts for female employees working late.

The troubling part came from the young woman Lisa had been: gentle in voice and manner, well-behaved and a ladylike, blue-eyed blonde with a very feminine quality about her with not a single enemy in the community. Obviously, except one. She had hoped to leave Howard Johnson's to work with handicapped children and, of course, to marry Bill Buss. But that had been destroyed in her Oldsmobile parked in the Howard Johnson's lot. If she could be murdered, who else was safe?

It took several hours before everyone passed the coffin and dispersed, including Sharon Tinjum.

Sharon and Lisa worked the same shift at Howard Johnson's that fatal night and was with her when she changed clothes after work to meet Bill. As Sharon pulled out of the parking lot, her headlights pinpointed Lisa sitting grimly in her car alongside what appeared to be an "effeminate man with blond hair in a shag cut." She flipped her high beams in greeting, but Lisa made no response and Sharon drove off.

Bill Buss, the unknowingly central figure in the murder, had a reputation for hard work on the family dairy farm often starting at 7:00 in the morning and continuing until 2:00 the next morning. His ambition was to own the comfortable brick house and 440 acres his grandfather had originally settled almost 100 years before.

The solidly built, blue-eyed Bill, with the quiet

43

manner and farm-boy haircut, first encountered Lisa when he was a high school senior and she was in the eighth grade. "Wow. See that guy. Isn't he cute?" Lisa asked her friend Kelly and the impression ripened until Bill became Lisa's first boyfriend three years later.

In 1986, things changed between them. Bill continued to labor toward getting his grandfather's farm and Lisa graduated from high school and went on a six-month travel program. When she returned she needed some time and space for herself and she and Bill broke up. Not that she wanted to leave her roots. She just needed to think and mature and she took a job at the Howard Johnson's in the closest city of any size, Wausau.

Bill continued to be active in Future Farmers of America and, as an alumnus, attended a banquet of the FFA a few months after the break up with Lisa. There he met the current president of the organization, a warm, friendly blonde named Lori Esker and soon became her first real boyfriend.

Athletic and bubbly, Lori saw Bill and knew immediately that's who she wanted for a husband. She went mad over him and, even when she went away to the University of Wisconsin — River Falls, 175 miles from home, she called or wrote him daily and spent every weekend home with him.

Lori grew up with two objectives in her life: a family and a farm. Bill Buss embodied both and she became obsessed with him as the fulfillment of her entire life. It all fit with her life growing up as an Esker whose 315-acre dairy farm on Esker Road had been there for 110 years and whose mother and grandmother and great grandmothers' lives had revolved around the same goals in life. Lori was always filled with optimism and big dreams and Bill Buss was the Prince Charming who was going to make living happily forever after possible.

Lori won farming awards from the 4-H and Future Farmers of America and focused her life on dairy farming including building a herd of cows of her own. Friends report that her college dorm room was decorated with stuffed cows, cow posters, cow mugs, and lace.

The relationship with Bill became very serious and Lori's mother objected that Bill, at twenty-five, was too old for eighteen-year-old Lori. The two responded by Lori moving out of the house to a trailer near the Buss family farm and moving her modest dairy herd to Bill's farm. In the social mores of the region, it amounted to her bringing her dowry to Bill and an open declaration of their engagement to marry.

Life couldn't have been better for Lori at that time as she approached having her man and her family. Then, came the frosting on the cake, she entered the contest for Dairy Princess of Marathon County and won against five other contestants and was crowned, glowing with enthusiasm and happiness, before hundreds of her friends and neighbors at the county fair.

In her bubbly view of life, Lori didn't detect the cooling in Bill's feelings until it became serious and whatever anxieties Bill expressed over marriage she dismissed as a solvable item for later consideration. Others in the community, however, began to notice the stand-offishness Bill had when marriage talk came up and when Lori was around. Some talked about how Lori's vision of the world was not in sync with reality. That she was living more and more in a dream world with Bill as the central obsession.

The end came around midnight on a night in June shortly after Lori had returned from school for summer break. Bill took her home to her trailer and said it was over. Stunned, she ran crying into the trailer, but didn't stay after he drove off. Consistent with her positive and proactive approach to life, she determined to move immediately to get Bill back. Jumping in the white Plymouth Sundance she had the use of as Dairy Princess, she drove to his farm.

There the dagger of his goodbye was plunged deeper and twisted when she pulled up to the farm and her headlights pinned someone coming out of the barn. It wasn't Bill. It was Lisa Cihaski.

Lisa and Kelly had stopped by to visit, they said, and had come out of the barn when they heard a car screeching down the driveway. Kelly described what happened next:

"Lori climbed out, slammed the door and grabbed Lisa by the sleeve. She said, 'You know, you really are a bitch.' But Lisa kept trying to calm her down, kept saying, 'I'm sorry this happened.' At the end, they hugged each other. We thought it was settled."

That may have been what Kelly naively thought, but it would be unlike Lori to let Bill go that easily. She spent much of the rest of that night on the telephone to Bill's best friend, Alan Andrus, crying and begging him to help them reconcile. She blamed Lisa for the break-up and told Alan that she could just kill Lisa for ruining her life.

Ironically, the rekindling of love between Lisa and Bill may have been sparked by haircuts. Mrs. Cihaski cut Bill's hair and he would run into Lisa at the Cihaski house. In time, Lisa began casually dropping by to see Bill for tractor rides or to keep him company during milkings. In time, the old romance with Lisa easily reignited, while the new romance with Lori refused to die an easy death.

Everyone soon learned about the break-up and Lori's desperate efforts to revive it, including trying to get Bill's hired hands to quit unless he took Lori back; emotional breakdowns in public over the loss of what had been the fulfillment of her life's dreams; and, repeated confrontations with Lisa accusing her of letting Bill get her pregnant so she could steal him from Lori.

Lisa wasn't pregnant, but it was clear that she was Bill's girlfriend again.

The pain in Lori's heart was overflowing as anyone who has lost his or her lover knows. It may have been worse than usual in Lori's heart because of her obsession with her dream and Bill as the essential ingredient in its fulfillment. She had no alternatives in her mind. The dream consisted of husband Bill, father Bill, and farm with Bill. Period. So, when she saw Lisa walking out of Bill Buss's barn after midnight, everything in her carefully structured and beautiful world collapsed into a dung heap.

47

One of her friends described how Lori refused to let go of the dream.

"She never was bitter toward Bill at all. She despised Lisa. She kept saying, 'She left him before. She doesn't love the farm the way I do. She'll divorce him and take half.' She referred to Lisa as 'The Bitch.' We felt sorry for Lori. It was common knowledge she wouldn't let go."

Even though she returned to college, Lori continued to brood and drive her friends to distraction with the mourning of her lost dream. When she heard of the formal announcement of Lisa and Bill's engagement that summer, the grief intensified, but would not yield to the inevitable reality.

Lori's cousin called her at school with the news of Lisa's murder and Lori shrieked with surprise according to roommate Anne Tuveson, "We were making dinner. She ran in saying someone strangled Bill's girlfriend."

Later that night she and Anne talked in Anne's bedroom, "She was really concerned about how it happened. She said, 'Well, it's not like she got hit by a car. She was MURDERED.' She didn't cry. She didn't seem sad. She was in disbelief that one human being could kill another in that way."

That weekend Lori went home and Slivers, the 400-pound barmaid in the only bar in Eland said, "All anyone was talking about was who killed Lisa. A couple of guys joked that it was Lori Esker. But we never really believed it. She was in River Falls when it happened."

The detectives assigned to the case knew they had something beyond normal if for no other reason than the intense public attention and clamor for a solution. They tracked every lead they could including the rumors that Lori wanted Lisa dead more than anyone else on earth and included Bill as one of the initial suspects, as well. Even so, the detectives' questioning surprised Lori and she returned to school apparently nonplussed by their suspicions.

Roommate Anne Tuveson later testified, "She kept repeating, 'I can't believe people think I'm that kind of person. Do you think I'm that type of person?'" On phone calls to her friends back home, she continually asked what people were thinking of her.

The detectives persisted in tracking down every clue they could find or think of and one came to River Falls to confirm that, on the morning after the murder, Lori had been working at a campus Dairy Club sale with her friend, Barb Zwiefelhofer. During questioning at River Falls by the detective, Lori reluctantly admitted that she had once been inside Lisa's new car.

She wanted to know if Bill had bought the new car for Lisa so Lori pawed through the glove compartment to see if she could find the registration papers. As soon as she revealed this to the detective, he asked her to come to the police station when she returned home the next weekend so they could get a fingerprint and hair sample from her. She readily agreed because to do otherwise would cause more suspicion, but the decision marked the unraveling of the case.

The following weekend Lori jokingly told her

friends that she had to show up at the cop shop for routine fingerprinting and that police suspicions were ridiculous since she had been at River Falls at the time of the murder. Yet, some friends such as Luke Berglund, who Lori had dated and had confided in almost daily, began to wonder.

Lori appeared at the police station that weekend cheerful and perky in a white denim jacket and wearing feminine, pink lipstick and even agreed to pose for a mug shot without realizing this would be the most dramatically important day of her life.

Detective Diane Krebsbach asked if Lori had any objection to taking a lie detector or polygraph test. At this point, a more sophisticated woman would have insisted on legal advice and been told that the results of such a test are rarely admissible in court and probably would have been advised not to take the test.

But, two things swayed Lori: one, she wanted to allay any suspicions of herself by being cooperative and, two, she learned from Detective Krebsbach that Bill Buss was in the station at that very moment taking a polygraph. The detective even let Lori get a glimpse of Buss in another room hooked up to the polygraph. What she didn't know was that one of the questions the police asked Bill was who would want Lisa dead and he bitterly replied, "Only Lori."

Wise or not, Lori tried to play out her hand and submitted to the polygraph only to fail the test. At that point, the police may have known she was the murderer, but they had nothing they could use in court. Then, the officer running the polygraph began to chat informally with Lori trying to win her confidence in a friendly, understanding way.

The officer told her sympathetically that he was a good Catholic, as was Lori, and the teachings of the church about right and wrong, good and evil governed both of their lives every day. After a time, the officer said that the church understood that good people sometimes get involved in accidents they didn't mean to cause, but couldn't control.

That trigger phrase undid Lori and she began to sob as she said, "You said it was an accident and it really was an accident." The officer listened to Lori's halting confession for the next hour and then summoned Sergeant Randall Hoenisch.

Then, and only then, did the police read Lori her rights and ask if she wanted to call an attorney or her family. She tried calling her mother and, when that failed, signed a waiver to her rights to remain silent or to have an attorney present. The whole ugly, jealousy-ridden bile spilled out of her as the police recorded her story.

Her abandonment by Bill had gnawed at her until she couldn't control it anymore because nothing she tried seemed to bring him back. She was sure she was so much prettier, cheerful, sexier, and loyal to Bill than Lisa or any other woman could be. Twice during the months since the break-up, she had slipped into his bedroom at night, stripped down to seductive Teddy lingerie and tried to entice him by dancing for him, kissing, and licking him and trying to have sex with him again. Each time, he had awakened, watched impassively for a few

51

minutes, and ordered her out.

That fateful weekend, she decided she could endure it no more and she tried to telephone Bill or Lisa to straighten things out. Unable to reach either of them, but certain she could make him see the light if she tried one more time, Lori rented a car and drove the 175 miles from River Falls toward Bill's farm.

Enroute, she passed the Howard Johnson's where Lisa worked and, on an impulse, decided to wait outside for Lisa so they could talk it out and Lori could convince Lisa that Lori and Bill should be together again.

According to Lori's confession, after a while she spotted Lisa coming out and she called out to her, "Lisa, can we talk?" Startled and caught off-guard, Lisa tried to remain polite and cool, but felt apprehensive. "Sure, but I got to get home pretty quick. Have you seen my new car? We can talk in here." Lisa opened the doors and got in the driver's side while Lori got in the passenger's side.

Lisa listened to what Lori had to say about Lisa being wrong for Bill and that if they both loved Bill, they should do the best thing for him, namely, let him marry Lori. Besides that, Lisa had her chance and had dumped Bill and might do it again. It wasn't fair for her to come back after leaving him and it would be even worse if she left him after marriage and took away half of the farm he had worked so hard to build and preserve.

At that point, Lisa interrupted and warned Lori not to get mixed up in her relationship with Bill. They were engaged and going to get married and that was that. "You're not going to get involved again," cautioned Lisa.

Then, Lori pulled out her trump card and implied that she was pregnant by Bill, "I went off the Pill and things happened that shouldn't have."

Apparently, this revelation set Lisa off, who had listened longer than she wanted to, had Bill and her mother waiting for her, and would not let her rival take Bill away from her. According to Lori, Lisa grabbed Lori's throat.

"It was scary. I thought she was going to kill me. Or, really hurt me."

Reacting, Lori pushed Lisa back against her seat as Lisa screamed and squirmed to be free and called Lori a bitch, a whore, and a slut for trying to seduce Bill in his bedroom. Lori realized that Bill had told Lisa about her nocturnal visits and they probably both laughed or ridiculed her which drove up Lori's rage.

"I'm not that kind of person . . . She was so terrible and so mean."

At this point, Lori said she grabbed a leather belt that had been lying in the back seat and wrapped it around Lisa's neck as Lisa continued to struggle and claw and pull at Lori's hair and neck. The furious battle in the cramped confines of the front seat continued for several minutes until suddenly Lisa went limp.

Frightened, Lori dumped Lisa's purse onto the front seat and snatched open her compact to push the mirror against the still girl's mouth. No sign of breath.

Continuing her confession, Lori said she thought

to herself, "Oh, my God, I killed her. I don't know what I'm going to do . . . I didn't mean to hurt her. I know Lisa knows that. I don't know if her family will. They're going to think I did it on purpose."

For sure, Lori wanted to get away from there right away, but, before leaving the dead girl in her new car, Lori slipped off the ring she had on her finger.

"Well, gee, maybe Bill gave it to her. Maybe I'll just take it with me."

For the next three and a half hours, Lori floored her rented car back to the River Falls campus. She returned the car, went home to her room, and went to sleep. The next morning she threw Lisa's belt into the dorm incinerator and the ring into the trash on the way to class.

What happened in the weeks following Lori's confession was a bewildering maelstrom of questions without answers, characterizations without sense, and feelings without explanations as the triangle of Birnamwood, Eland, and Hatley transformed from a clean German-Polish dairyland into a terrain of hidden passions and dark emotions. Outsiders came from all over the globe with their cameras and their microphones and their judgments and their cynical evaluations, to trample the lawn outside the courthouse and the sensitivities of the people of Marathon County, Wisconsin.

The word of Lori's confession spread with a speed and incredulity that defied imagination and hundreds jammed the courtroom, the corridors, and the space around them three days later when the harried police escorted her inside to become the first woman ever indicted for murder of another woman in the history of that county.

For hours beforehand, she had sat in her cell getting herself ready with the help of make-up and a curling iron in violation of normal jail rules. Corrections Officer Deborah Rix recalled that day at the jail.

"It seemed so sad. She looked just like she was getting ready for a date. That really bothered me. She seemed more concerned about how she looked than being booked for murder."

Her appearance in a pastel sweater over a floral dress held the hundreds of watchers mute except for the motorized whir and clicking of cameras. Then, from somewhere in that packed sea of staring, unbelieving eyes a pre-indictment snapped across the heads of all, "Murdering bitch!"

Inside, the judge ordered her held for trial on the grounds that a crime had been committed and sufficient evidence existed that she may have been responsible. What had been an unhappy love triangle turned into a love obsession and had now become a matter of life and death for at least one person and possibly two.

The gauntlet from the courtroom to the jail now reversed with the anxious police nervously eyeing the crowd for any sign of attack and Lori Esker walking erect and as pretty as the day they crowned her Dairy Princess before most of these same people.

Kelly Meverden pushed forward to the outer edge and stared right into Lori's face a few feet away as she passed and screamed in anguish, "Why?" Why, Kelly wanted to know, why? Why did a woman she had known all her life kill Kelly's best friend?

It would be twelve months before Lori Esker would be tried, but three days after her indictment, defense attorney Stephen Glynn, arranged her release on $100,000 bond secured by her parent's family farm.

The terms of her release required her to always be in the presence of one of her parents and she could not leave the premises without six hours advance notice to the sheriff. And, Glynn told the local press that the authorities had exploited and tricked Lori because she was naive.

Yet, the people of the community had come to their own way of processing the events as they always do. Sides were taken and judgments already made as the community fragmented over the case with some townspeople reveling in the attention brought by TV camera crews and reporters and movie producers and book publishers. One movie producer's main concern centered around, "Are the two girls pretty?" God forbid Hollywood should make a movie about obsessive love involving ugly women!

Some blamed Bill Buss for leading on the two women and pitting them against each other. Bill Buss himself withdrew into isolation. Others claimed it must of been an accident because neither woman could have committed cold-blooded murder—not the daughters of Marathon County. Still others saw it as premeditated murder by a headstrong woman never willing to accept rejection at anything she tried.

And, the sick jokes began. At a Halloween party at the River Falls campus, one girl dressed up as the strangled Lisa while bumper stickers warned that if Wisconsin dairy cholesterol didn't get you, the Dairy Princess would.

In the year of trial preparations, both the Cihaskis and Eskers, families who had known each other and tilled the Wisconsin soil for over a hundred years, withdrew from community life and from any contact with each other until the day of the trial. Then, ironically, they were forced into direct contact when the crush of press and spectators which resulted in their sitting side by side in the front row of the courtroom.

Lori Esker came into the courtroom to face the judgment of a jury of her peers that had been transported in from a logging town in another part of Wisconsin. This time she did not look made-up for a date in a pink sweater and flowered dress. Her attorney saw to it that she had no make-up, acted subdued and serious and wore a conservative cardigan and skirt.

Attorney Glynn knew the image he had to present of his client: deep remorse for the accidental death of Lisa in a fight over the love of Bill Buss. She had already admitted the murder and Glynn needed to show it in the context of her obsession with Buss. "You need to understand what the abandonment by Bill Buss did to her."

Glynn knew that Buss's testimony would be harmful to his client because he would reveal intimacies that would embarrass or taint Lori for her

57

love obsession. Objecting to some of the testimony Buss had given to police, Glynn and his client had to listen to the judge reading the testimony out loud in open court, but with the jury not present.

"She then said that every time she drives by and sees me on my tractor, she gets all wet."

The impact on the silent townspeople was electric. No decent woman would say that to a man. Lori's parents sat directly behind her in the breathless, packed room with her father frozen immobile, staring uncomprehendingly straight down at his boots.

The judge admitted the jury to the courtroom and cautioned Bill to be careful in his choice of language. Bill related how Lori continued to pursue him including the two seductive, Teddy-clad visits when she tried to stimulate him to erection by dancing and climbing on top of him. The image of the sex-flaunting Dairy Princess became reinforced in the jury's mind.

The prosecutor, Greg Grau, paraded fifty-eight witnesses before the jury to establish that Lori's trip home from school that night and her confrontation were premeditated. The prosecutor wove Lori's every act from renting a car to learning Lisa would be working late into a tapestry of cold-blooded, carefully planned murder of a love rival.

One witness, Lisa Steebs, related a jailhouse call from Lori telling her how the murder had left Bill distraught and her reaction, "She said she didn't feel sorry for him because he deserved it. If he wouldn't have hurt her, she wouldn't have had to do it."

Grau, a brand new prosecutor on his first major case, ended his summation by saying it took at least two minutes for Lisa to die with Lori's arm pressing down on her throat. He paused for an agonizingly long two minutes to give the jury the full impact of how long Lori had strangled Lisa. Then, he abruptly concluded.

"She told Alan Andrus, 'I could kill her.' And she did. Do justice."

The defense lawyer summed up the inconsistencies in Grau's presentation and insisted that if the crime was premeditated, Lori wouldn't have rented the car in her own name and come to meet Lisa unarmed. She would have been prepared to kill instead of become entangled in a clawing, grabbing, hitting tangle in the cramped front-seat of a car. Yes, he said, Lori killed Lisa. There is no denying that sad fact, but it was an accident — not premeditated murder.

"She's not mine anymore. She's yours. You will reach the verdict you are comfortable with and I ask you to be comfortable with it, because it is going to last a long time."

Hours later at midnight, the jury filed back in the box and rendered the verdict it found comfortable: first-degree intentional murder.

Police instantly rushed Lori out of the courtroom fearing some disturbance as someone in the Cihaski family seated next to the Eskers screamed and the Eskers sat stony silent and still.

Outside the courtroom, the press mob pinned principals against each other with their breathless and insistent questions. Lisa's father spoke bitterly that Lori Esker always had to be number one, but her mother more empathetically said, "There are no winners here tonight. We're all losers."

Pressed by the media for a message to Lori, the stone-faced Bill Buss pushed his way through the crowd and said simply, "I don't give a damn about her."

Eleven weeks later, Lori stood before Judge Michael Hoover and publicly apologized for what she had done to Lisa. "I'm so sorry for all the pain and suffering I've caused. If I could trade places with Lisa, I'd do it in a minute."

Judge Hoover thought her apology insincere and sent her to Taycheedah Correction Institute where the Dairy Princess will be eligible for parole in the year 2003. In Taycheedah, she would meet another woman convicted of murder, Laurie "Bambi" Bemenek.

The mark of Lisa's murder, however, will never be erased from the minds of Birnamwood. Lisa lies in the local cemetery under a simple, gray, granite headstone with only her name and dates of birth and death inside a heart — murdered because of something inside a heart.

Three

The Warmus Love Huntress

Could the hands of love also be the hands of death?

Could the hands deftly unzipping Paul Solomon's fly in lustful eagerness in the car parked in the darkness outside the Treetops Bar & Grill be the same hands that three hours earlier pumped nine slugs from a .25 Beretta into the flinching body of Paul's wife, Betty Jeanne?

Carolyn Warmus was the first child born to the family of Thomas and Elizabeth Warmus in the well-to-do community of Birmingham, Michigan. Another girl was born into the family a year later, Tracey, and the two sisters would grow up in an endless rivalry with each other with Tracey usually winning out as the prettier and more popular. It set the tone for Carolyn's life.

Thomas Warmus rose from insurance salesman to founder of American Way Insurance and possessor of a substantial fortune that gave him estates in Michigan, Florida, New York, and Arizona, along with fifteen cars, eight private jets, and two yachts.

But, the wealth came from his total concentration on work, letting his family fend for itself emotionally.

From her earliest romantic stirrings in junior high school, the well-to-do Carolyn had locked in on male love targets like a heat-seeking missile and followed their every twist and turn until she scored a bullseye. In one example that reporters would later ritually repeat over and over again, Carolyn paid a classmate $100 to arrange a date with a boy she wanted and it developed into a long relationship.

She never fell in love casually. It was always the love affair of the century for Carolyn and, once fixated on it, she clung with the tenacity of a pit bull.

For parlor psychologists, the explanation was relatively easy. Carolyn was a woman desperate for the love of a father who was distant, self-consumed, and unresponsive to her emotional needs. His life revolved around becoming an insurance mogul and earning millions to support the wealthy lifestyle he treasured more than the role of a father. In 1974 when Carolyn was fifteen, he dumped his dowdy wife in a bitter divorce and acquired a younger trophy wife with enormous breasts and cheap, brassy taste with whom Carolyn competed for her father's attention and love.

He had dumped Carolyn emotionally long before. She performed in every way she knew how to gain his favor, from getting perfect grades to doting on his every wish. Sadly, his main wish was to be left alone and so she became obsessed with gaining the love of older, unattainable men.

The pattern was clear in her romance with Paul Laven, a graduate student, who she met at the University of Michigan in 1982. Almost with the first date, her life focused on doing and being whatever he wanted, coupled with mounting pressure on him for marriage. Whatever she was and whatever she did, her question of friends was always, "Do you think Paul will like it? Will Paul be pleased? Will it make Paul happy?"

When the romance broke up six months later, Carolyn went crazy and tried everything to get Paul back which drove him even further away and, ultimately, into the arms of Wendy Siegel.

Carolyn followed the couple constantly, beleaguered them with phone calls, and repeatedly disrupted the classes Paul was teaching with emotional outbreaks. Five months after the breakup, she left a message on Paul's car:

P. — I'm 2¹/₂ months pregnant.
CALL ME!!! PLEASE!

She seemed devoted to turning Paul and Wendy's life into a nightmare until they got a court order keeping her away. Even then, they feared Carolyn would crash their wedding or threaten them with bodily harm.

She wrote to Wendy, boasting that she had a deeper tan and a better body than Wendy and that Paul would ultimately come back. Her desperation over Paul brought her to the verge of suicide, according to college friends.

In spite of or because of her behavior, Paul and Wendy were married in a ceremony that was very private to avoid Carolyn knowing about it and interrupting it. Even then, Carolyn would not accept Paul's rejection and cast about for some explanation why she wasn't pretty enough, sexy enough, adequate enough.

In 1985, Carolyn graduated, ironically with a degree in psychology, and moved back home to her father's house in Franklin near Detroit and took a job as a waitress at a notorious singles pick-up joint, The Jukebox, in nearby Royal Oak, where waitresses danced provocatively on the bar and easily connected with male patrons.

She quickly became part of the hedonistic party scene and everybody thought she was attractive and fun to be around. Here again, she made a quick connection and commitment to Brian "Buddy" Getter who was a single businessman at the time. She immediately pressed him for marriage and he dropped her after three weeks.

With that rejection, the Warmus pattern kicked in again with the incessant telephoning and following and leaving notes on his car and at his apartment.

Buddy was doing all he could to avoid her, including paying bartenders and hosts to warn him when she showed up any place he was. She offered to pay Buddy's best friend generously if he would help her get him back in her life. Nothing worked for Carolyn. She was rejected once again by a man who was older and unattainable.

At some point during this period, she decided that one of the men she was chasing was rejecting her because he was Jewish and she was Catholic.

In either event, the religious barrier to her being attractive to her man was solvable and she began a five-month conversion program under Rabbi David Nelson of the Congregation Beth Shalom in Oak Park, Michigan. She studied and ultimately renounced Jesus Christ and embraced Judaism at the ritual immersion ceremony or mikvah. Rabbi Nelson remarked later that the whole experience was odd because she did it entirely alone and no one was ever present to support her during those five months. Carolyn adopted the Hebrew name meaning "gracious lioness of God," Chana Ariela.

Again, when the full court press failed, Carolyn dropped everything and moved away—this time to New York where she enrolled in Teachers College and soon fell in love with a married bartender at a Ramada Inn located in New Jersey. It was the same movie all over again: some delicious sex and a bitter goodbye followed by the round-the-clock harassment at work and at home. Once again, Carolyn was willing to pay money for help in getting her man.

She hired a rotund, bald Manhattan private eye, Vincent Parco, who advertised in the Yellow Pages that he specialized in "unusual and difficult investigations." It was the summer of 1987 and Carolyn wanted Vincent to disrupt the bartender's life and destroy his marriage so Carolyn could come in and pick up the pieces. Several tries failed to produce any significant results so Parco's sidekick, Joe Russo, suggested faking photographs showing the bartender cavorting with a scantily clad woman. Carolyn agreed enthusiastically and volunteered to be the lingerie model for the photos.

Russo came to her apartment and was greeted by Carolyn wearing a pink wig and a silk Chinese robe under which, Russo quickly discovered, she was dressed only in sexy, see-through lingerie. For the next couple of hours she posed in a variety of seductive stances on her back, on her knees, draped over furniture stripped almost naked or in a body stocking and red camisoles, playing with her breasts, doing a lot of tongue shots, and generally enjoying her role.

After he had shot a thirty-six-exposure roll of film and was packing up his gear, Carolyn sidled up to Russo and asked if she excited him. When he matter-of-factly said, "No," she turned vicious and rammed her knee into his crotch. It was another rejection for Carolyn. How could she have offered herself in these lingerie poses and not gotten a man turned on? It hurt her.

Unfortunately, matching these shots up with photos they had of the bartender didn't work because the result was so obviously faked. Even so, Carolyn continued to come around the private eye's office a couple times a week, often going to lunch with Parco. Russo suspected they were doing sex together, but it was none of his business and he didn't care because he wanted to get out of there and start his own investigation agency, which he did in February 1988.

Russo and Gabe Laura set up All-Tech Investigations with an office over the historic Roseland Ballroom where men paid women to dance with them. Russo never expected to see Carolyn again, but he was wrong. She came around before long, looking for a bodyguard for her rich father, claiming a short woman with brown hair was trying to kill him.

On subsequent visits the story shifted to Carolyn needing protection herself from this same mysterious woman. Mysterious at the beginning, but later Carolyn told Russo, "I know who the woman is. I've seen her where I teach. Her name is Betty Jeanne." Parco would later testify that Carolyn said Betty Jeanne was an ex-mistress of her father's.

Betty Jeanne "B.J." Torrey was born in 1948 in New England, but her family moved south and from age seven on, she grew up in the section of New York State around what would become the Tappanzee Bridge and was always regarded as a very open, happy, and helpful girl.

At the State University of New York in New Paltz, B.J. met, dated, and ultimately married in 1970 an intense, controlling man of English-Lebanese descent, Paul Solomon, who was very conservative and studying to be a teacher. Right after their marriage, Paul joined the Air Force and the couple moved to Alaska for most of his three-year tour of duty during which their daughter Kristan was born.

Returning to the New York State area in 1974, they both got jobs in Westchester County. He as a teacher in Greenville Elementary School in Edgemont and she at the National Bank of Westchester. They bought a condominium in Greenburgh and geared into a very busy life with her civic activities and his teaching, coaching, and playing basketball, golf, and bowling. It was a life of microwave meals, notes on the refrigerator, and brief visits home to change clothes.

Like most marriages, the Solomons's had its good times and its rough spots. Betty Jeanne—Paul had long since forbidden anyone to call her "B.J." anymore—had confided to her mother and her sister, Joyce Green, several times over recent years that she was thinking of leaving Paul. She hated his controlling ways, but didn't suspect there might be other women and, besides, they did have their good moments and she didn't want to break up the home until Kristan was older.

Meanwhile, Carolyn had become a prim, respected sixth-grade school teacher at Greenville school in the fall of 1987 right after the bartender affair ended. It was at Greenville that her next romantic quarry surfaced. Paul Solomon, thirty-eight, sixth-grade teacher fourteen years older, had a classroom across the hall from where Carolyn taught youngsters how to use computers. Paul, with his busy personal and school life, fit right into Carolyn's classic pattern of the older, attainable man.

Soon they were lovers meeting sometimes in her

duplex apartment over the Manhattan east side club, To Catch A Rising Star, or in a car or motel nearer to Paul's place such as around the Brunswick Bowling Alley in Westchester County.

Paul's regular commitments included bowling most Sunday evenings. Soon after meeting Carolyn, he began penciling her in for Sunday nights after bowling.

And, he wrote her a letter that may have changed the course of her entire life:

Carolyn,
I'm falling deeply in love with you. I'm afraid of losing you. I feel guilty demanding certain things, but I don't apologize for it. We both bring a certain amount of baggage to this relationship. With work, we'll be able to dump that baggage and be what we really are.
I just held you and kissed you and I miss you already. There are times when I feel like I just make you unhappy. If you're really smart, you'd do one of two things: turn away and never see me again, save yourself pain and hurt. Or keep loving me and take the risk of you and I having something together forever. It's a big risk for both you and me. I love you.

Carolyn made one of those two choices and it was the wrong one, and the decision did change the course of her life.

For Paul it was Sunday nights, but for Carolyn it

was the rest of her life. She ingratiated herself into Paul's family life so that, before he realized what was happening, Carolyn had made friends with his wife Betty Jeanne. Betty Jeanne told friends that she thought Carolyn was a bimbo, but pleasant and friendly to their daughter to the point that she had taken Kristan on a skiing trip during Christmas vacation in 1988 and began casually dropping by the Solomons's apartment.

Paul, on the other hand, continued to be aloof and exploitive, breaking dates with Carolyn at will and always putting his family ahead of her. She took it all and begged for more—anything, as long as it kept her in contact with him and fostered her dream that he would leave Betty Jeanne and marry her.

The lethal climax came with Carolyn's twenty-fifth birthday on January 8, 1989. Playing the love game as he had to do in order to get the sex he wanted, Paul agreed to take Carolyn out to celebrate, but stood her up when something with Betty Jeanne intervened.

Angry and hurt, Carolyn demanded Paul make good on the date. One observer said that what happened was "an aching, enraging reminder of the father who overlooked her at similar emotional milestones in her life, and the final, undeniable evidence that, as far as Solomon was concerned, his wife's needs would always eclipse Warmus's own."

The next Sunday, the fifteenth, Paul and Betty Jeanne woke up and made love. They spent the rest of the morning watching old movies on TV and going over a brochure for a retirement community they were thinking about investing in. At 1:30 Carolyn called to talk to Paul and upbraid him again for breaking their birthday date. Paul ended up trying to make amends by offering to take her to dinner at 7:30 that night after his bowling date.

It was a long, drawn-out call, but most of Carolyn's were and, apparently, Betty Jeanne didn't think much about it. Without realizing the significance of it, Paul mentioned that Kristan had gone skiing for the weekend. That meant Betty Jeanne would be alone at the condo. Paul then told his wife he had to go bowling with his team at seven o'clock.

He left the condo at 6:30 p.m. and drove to the Brunswick lanes on Central Avenue, the main shopping street through Westchester, and spent about fifteen minutes chatting with the others and excused himself. Outside, he got into his car and drove over to the Treetops Bar & Grill at the Yonkers Holiday Inn to meet Carolyn.

According to the prosecution, Carolyn waited until Paul left his apartment and then she rang the bell and went in to confront Betty Jeanne. The two women exchanged a few words before Betty Jeanne became alarmed and, when Carolyn produced the gun, Betty Jeanne leapt for the nearby telephone and dialed 911. It was 7:15 p.m.

In their New Jersey community of Greenburgh, there was no 911 service and the call automatically switched to a regular operator who did not record the call and only heard, "He is trying to kill me" or "She is trying to kill me" before the line went dead. The operator wasn't sure if the first word was "he" or "she."

Somebody, the prosecution claims it was Carolyn, was at that moment pumping nine bullets from a .25 caliber Beretta into Betty Jeanne as her body spasmed involuntarily with the impact of each lead slug slamming into her. Carolyn denied all of this.

Whoever was right, it was agreed that half-an-hour later, at 7:45 p.m., Carolyn and Paul met at Treetops. The waitress at Treetops said Paul arrived at 7:25 p.m. The Solomon condo is a ten to fifteen minute drive from Treetops.

The two settled in with vodka collins for Paul and champagne for Carolyn, eating oysters, and talking about their futures. The restaurant manager said they seemed to be arguing over something.

They may have been arguing or just having a vigorous discussion depending on one's viewpoint. In fact, Paul was subtly giving Carolyn the big kiss off.

"I'll be happy to dance at your wedding."

"What about you, Paul? Don't you deserve some happiness?"

"If anything happened to Betty Jeanne and me, I'd never get married anyway. If Betty Jeanne and I were ever to get divorced, I'd probably never get married again."

At 10:30 p.m. they adjourned to her Hyundai parked in a dark, remote portion of the parking lot. There they kissed and fondled each other and

Carolyn asked Paul if she could do what she liked to do best with him. He gave his permission and she deftly and eagerly unzipped Paul's pants and did for him what she was very good at and what he relished immensely, oral sex.

Aglow with sexual release, Paul slipped out of Carolyn's car, walked to his own, and drove home. As he approached his condo door at 11:40 p.m., he heard the TV blaring, which didn't seem natural and he quickly opened the door to see what was wrong. The door swung open and the stunned Paul discovered the rigid, cold body of his wife of nineteen years soaked in a pool of her own blood.

Initially, after the Greenburgh police arrived at the gory scene and found the fully clothed Betty Jeanne crumpled on the floor, soaked in blood from nine slug wounds in her legs and back, they took Paul into custody for questioning. One of the reasons was that they could find no sign of a forcible break-in or robbery. They concluded that Betty Jeanne either let her murderer into the condo or the murderer had a key. That made Paul a prime suspect at first.

For almost twelve hours they grilled him about their life together, their marriage, other affairs, financial problems, his movements that night, and other possible motives for murder, but they couldn't come up with anything that was a concrete lie or contradiction and decided his alibi of having been at the bowling alley with friends at the time of the murder was good enough that they couldn't charge him.

Oddly enough, the police didn't test his hands for gunpowder residue which would establish if he had fired a gun in the previous twenty-four hours.

Five days later, Solomon, Betty Jeanne's sister, Joyce Green, and 350 mourners — friends, co-workers and family — said goodbye to Betty Jeanne for the last time at a church in nearby Scarsdale. It was a bitter cold January day and Paul, respected by his peers as a teacher and coach, had sunk into a quagmire of depression repeating to everyone, "I really did love her. I really did love her."

His sister-in-law sensed that there was something a lot more wrong with Paul than only the loss of his wife. She smelled a deep guilt as if some terrible secret gnawed at his insides, but she never believed that he had it in him to commit murder.

The entire community of Greenburgh in New York's Westchester County was stunned by the murder because Betty Jeanne and Paul were so involved in everyone's lives. He was the school teacher and coach, as well as president of the teachers' association. Betty Jeanne was deeply involved in civic activities; supporting their fifteen-year-old daughter, Kristan, on the girls' basketball team; and, working as an executive at a collection agency in a neighboring town of Harrison where she had moved after leaving the job at the National Bank of Westchester.

Of course, not everyone liked Paul because his numerous affairs were known to at least some people in town. One of Betty Jeanne's colleagues said, "She was a great person. He was a slime ball and, because of him, she is dead."

At the trial that would rivet the community months later, one woman reporter summarized the feelings of women toward men like Paul Solomon when she said that the bastards lie to the wives and they lie to their mistresses. The sum total is that the man gets a life and a half and the women each get half a life.

Paul, visibly depressed and lethargic after Betty Jeanne's death took leave from his work at school and also from Carolyn. He completely broke off contact with her after the murder and may have suspected she was the murderer. Still, true to his nature, he soon was dating a younger teacher from school, Barbara Ballor.

Once during July, 1989, Paul slipped while Barbara was out of town and visited Carolyn and asked her over drinks if she had murdered Betty Jeanne. She said "No," that she would never do anything to hurt Betty or Kristan. Paul would later say that he didn't remember if he and Carolyn made love that night. In any case, he returned to Barbara and resumed avoiding Carolyn.

Carolyn, also true to her nature, followed Paul everywhere, beleaguering him with phone calls. When he slipped away to vacation in Puerto Rico five months after the murder, Carolyn followed and discovered Barbara was with him. In desperation, she tried to break up the Paul-Barbara romance by posing as a police officer in Puerto Rico and by making intimidating phone calls to Barbara's parents. She also sent a note to Paul and Barbara's hotel room announcing that she was there watching them. Panicked, the two fled back to Westchester.

At that point, Barbara decided the harassment had reached the intolerable point and she got a court order barring further harassment by Warmus. This brought Carolyn to the attention of the police and they began tracking her past history including putting a tap on her telephone.

The investigation had dragged on inconclusively for six months at this point and the new scent of Carolyn brought two Greenburgh detectives into contact with private eye, Russo. When he told them about the New Jersey bartender affair, the roll of intimate photos, and her concern about protection from a woman she knew named Betty Jeanne, the focus shifted to Carolyn Warmus.

Russo told police that Warmus had tried to get a gun from him, but he refused and, later, thought she might have gone to his ex-employer, Vincent Parco and gotten a .25 caliber Beretta Jetfire. At the time, back in December, 1988, Russo notified the New York City police that Warmus was illegally trying to buy a gun, but they dismissed the report saying there was nothing they could do without further evidence.

After talking with Russo, the Greenburgh detectives got a warrant and searched Parco's office and, while they didn't find the gun, they found other ballistic evidence.

Police determined that the ballistic evidence proved that the slugs from that gun killed Betty Jeanne and they pressured a confession out of

Parco that he had sold a gun to Carolyn for $2,500 in December 1988. That was two weeks before Betty Jeanne was murdered.

Parco also confessed that he had sold Carolyn a silencer he had gotten from a Brooklyn machinist, George Peters. The detectives searched Peters's shop and found shell casings that matched the nine slugs pulled out of Betty Jeanne's legs and back.

About this time in the summer of 1989, Carolyn telephoned a college friend, Ryan Attenson, with whom she spoke occasionally. During Thanksgiving, 1988, she had called to tell him about her affair with Paul and her certainty that she and Paul would end up married and having a family. In the August 1989 call, Ryan said she told him that the woman who had been standing in their way was now no longer a problem. She expressed her love and obsession to Paul in fifteen letters including one declaring, "You are the most important thing in my life."

The next step for the Greenburgh detectives was to search Carolyn's apartment, but they waited until November to do that and, when they finally made the search, they found an unmailed letter to Paul. In it, Carolyn says she would kill herself because she could not "take the pressure anymore." She had, in fact, suffered an emotional breakdown a few months before in August and spent a week in the Metropolitan Hospital.

The curious twist in the letter was that she loved Paul and wanted him to tell her how he had killed Betty Jeanne. The idea, she said, was that Carolyn would commit suicide and leave a note confessing to the murder as her last great sacrifice on the altar of her love for him.

February 2, 1990, the Westchester District Attorney got a second degree murder indictment against Carolyn Warmus.

Three days later, Carolyn Warmus was arrested and jailed overnight until her father's lawyer, David Lewis, arrived and posted $250,000 bail. The blonde heiress protested her innocence with a kind of naive unawareness of a woman who has spent her life trying to please men and bewildered why it should get her in trouble.

Immediately the typical press feeding frenzy began about this true life version of the movie, "Fatal Attraction," and reporters and camera crews were swarming all over Westchester getting shots of the death condo, the Treetops Inn, the Greenville Elementary School, and anything and anybody that would stand still.

Carolyn had immediately dropped out of sight and steadfastly refused interviews, so the media turned to public officials, coworkers, relatives, friends, and anybody who had ever been in the same room with Carolyn. When a college friend was asked to describe Carolyn, she answered simply, "Rich." The man she paid a mutual friend in high school $100 to arrange a date with and who went with her for several months before bailing out said, "I was glad to get her out of my life. She was a very, very unhappy person. She told me she had no father, no love, no affection." He said she frequently contemplated suicide as a way to end her unhappiness and constant rejection.

Writers for *People* magazine translated this into pop psychology that may be close to the truth: "Warmus's [sic] hopeless pursuit of unattainable men was a displaced attempt to capture the most unattainable man in her life: her father."

In the sensational trial that followed before a White Plains jury of eight women and four men, Attorney David Lewis defended Carol and attacked prosecutor James A. McCarty's case which was based entirely on circumstantial evidence.

McCarty charged that Carolyn had "a consuming desire to possess Paul Solomon for herself and Betty Jeanne Solomon stood squarely in the way."

Lewis retorted that it was true that Carolyn loved Paul and had hoped that, someday, he would marry her. Then, leaning into the feelings of the predominantly female jury gently added, "It's not such an odd dream for a young girl."

At pretrial hearings Carolyn did not present herself as a naive, innocent young girl. Although she would not give interviews, would not testify or give statements, she did make a statement in her dress and demeanor. She showed up in tight black dresses with lots of decolletage on display.

Mindful of the messages his client was sending out, defense attorney Lewis put Carolyn through a makeover and had her hair trimmed into a pageboy, she appeared at the trial wearing big glasses, sensible shoes, and bulky knit sweaters and long skirts. Lewis wanted her to look like a conservative school marm and not some harlot who stole other women's husbands.

As the trial of the People of New York began against Carolyn Warmus, defense attorney Lewis became attack attorney Lewis, boring into the testimony of private eye, Vincent Parco, and bereaved husband, Paul Solomon.

Beginning with Solomon, Lewis tried to paint the portrait of a sleazy, betraying husband who had as much reason to murder his wife as anybody else had. Lewis obviously thought it strange and unfeeling of Paul to have continued living in the same condo where his wife had been brutally gunned down. Unless, of course, he was an insensitive brute who really wasn't bothered by the slaughter of his wife and the mother of his child as Lewis implied.

Lewis thought it was the depth of greed and crassness that Solomon had sold the movie rights of the story of his wife's death to HBO for $175,000 with the working title of "The Paul Solomon Story." How low can a so-called bereaved husband sink, Lewis wanted to know?

Finally, didn't Solomon engage in a series of illicit and adulterous love affairs, lying to his wife endlessly to conceal his infidelities, Lewis asked? Solomon had lied to his wife, his daughter, his friends, his colleagues and the police about his affairs, so why should anyone on the jury believe that he was telling the truth now on the witness stand?

But that may have been off-set when he pulled

in a bizarre coincidence in his true-life reflection of the movie, *Fatal Attraction*. The police asked Solomon to provide them with a photograph of Carolyn and he gave them one taken in her computer classroom that reeked of the grotesque boiled bunny scene in the movie. He gave them a color photograph of Carolyn posed with a group of pet rabbits.

Lewis also made a lot of the fact that Solomon had refused to testify for the district attorney until he was granted immunity from any prosecution in connection with his wife's death. Why, Lewis, pointedly wanted to know, did Solomon require immunity if he was innocent and hadn't been charged with any crime?

Lewis scored again when he brought up the visit Solomon had made to Warmus months after the death of Betty Jeanne. Did Solomon have sex with Carolyn that night—sex with the woman he claimed to believe murdered Betty Jeanne? When Paul nervously replied that he didn't remember, Carolyn hastily scribbled a note and handed it to Lewis. Smiling inwardly with the assurance of a hunting dog about to tree his fox, Lewis turned on Solomon and demanded if he remembered talking with Carolyn that night about how his underwear matched his clothing?

Next on Lewis's hit list was private detective Parco. The macho Parco wasn't as wimpy as Solomon, but Lewis worked him over on the stand, including getting him to admit that he cheated on his own wife and twice turned down Warmus's offer of sex. Beyond that, he said that he continued to do work for Carolyn after Betty Jeanne's death checking on Barbara Ballor.

A telling point on Parco's credibility came when Lewis got the admission from Parco that he had lied to the police three times about selling Warmus a gun, but finally changed his story when he was promised immunity from prosecution.

In short, Lewis was mincing the prosecution's witnesses and arguments. One major national magazine speculated whether or not the jurors understood in the end who was actually on trial or if they remembered that somebody had been murdered.

The jammed courtroom was filled with reporters from everywhere and local citizens who couldn't believe this was happening in their town. One senior citizen spectator told the *Los Angeles Times*, "I've never seen anything like this, never in a million years." Another commented, "Everybody knows that men cheat on their wives, but this is all so messy. It's the kind of thing you expect actors and musicians to do. Not nice people from Westchester."

Curiously, a similar trial took place in this community ten years before: the murder trial in which another school teacher and principal, Jean Harris, was convicted of murdering her lover, Dr. Herman Tarnower.

The trial went through eleven weeks and forty-seven witnesses in the high rise White Plains courthouse and was interrupted several times by unexpected events. There were two bomb threats and one false fire alarm that cleared the courtroom. Early in the trial, Carolyn was photographed unexpectedly by a media cameraman and it upset her to the point that she began sobbing. The next day, she ran a very high temperature, began vomiting, and was rushed to the hospital.

In the end, the prosecution's case focused on a phone call Warmus was supposed to have made to a New Jersey gun shop on the day of the murder. Initially, the prosecution introduced Carol's MCI phone bill to prove she made the call in question.

This bill showed that a call was made from Warmus's residence at 3:02 p.m. on Sunday, January 15, 1989 to Ray's Sport Shop in North Plainfield, New Jersey. Testimony next established that a woman came to Ray's Sport Shop later that afternoon to buy fifty rounds of .25 caliber ammunition. She showed a driver's license identifying herself as a Liisa Kittah.

Prosecutor McCarty produced Liisa Kittah who testified that her driver's license was missing, lost or stolen in August, 1988 during which time she had been working in the same room with Carolyn Warmus.

However, once again Lewis rose to dazzle the courtroom waving a piece of paper in the air and announcing the prosecutions evidence was a forgery and that he had Carolyn's *REAL* MCI bill for January 15 which she had received in the mail. He announced dramatically that it did NOT show any calls to Ray's Sport Shop on that day.

Moreover, the bill *DID* show a call made at 6:44 p.m. to Carolyn's mother. This placed Carolyn at her home half-an-hour before the murder and at a distance that would be impossible for her to cover to the Solomon house to gun down Betty Jeanne.

So, obviously, one MCI bill or the other was a lie, but which one was it? Lewis thought we might ask that question and he had a plausible answer. Since one of the things Parco admitted he could do was slip into people's computer files, Lewis thought it possible he had invaded MCI's computer files and altered Carolyn's telephone records.

Thus, when the prosecutor had a copy of the records printed out, the copy conveniently had the call to Ray's Sport Shop and no record of the call to Carolyn's mother. Lewis charged the prosecution was engaged in creating fraudulent evidence.

Now, Assistant District Attorney Douglas J. Fitzmorris put MCI executives on the stand to tell the jury which bill was the *REAL* bill. They testified that all their bills for January, 1989 had a slogan printed on them, "Communications For The Next 100 Years." Because the copy the prosecution had carried that slogan and the copy the defense had did not, the MCI people said the defense copy was the phony.

Yet, under the strong cross examination of defense attorney Lewis, the MCI executive admitted that he could not absolutely say the defense phone bill was phony beyond a reasonable doubt.

Countering that, MCI financial-systems analyst, Michael Yeager, said that the MCI internal computer tape showing what the prosecution claimed was the correct bill was triple protected and difficult to penetrate and alter. With that to support him, Assistant District Attorney McCarty flung the charge of tampering with evidence back at attorney Lewis implying that Carolyn Warmus had created a fake MCI bill on her class computers.

To substantiate Carolyn's inclination to commit forgery, the prosecution tried to introduce a letter it claimed it could prove had been forged by Warmus to clear herself from involvement in a car accident on June 14, 1987. However, Westchester County Court Judge John Carey refused to admit the evidence and the prosecution continued to base its case on entirely circumstantial evidence.

The strongest coup the prosecution could produce near the end of the trial was school nurse Patricia January who revealed Carolyn had told her she had bought a gun from a private detective for her own protection in January, 1989. The nurse said she hadn't mentioned it before because she thought it was common knowledge around the school that Warmus had a gun.

Up until then, the only one who could connect Carolyn with a gun was the detective Parco whose testimony Lewis had discredited because the man lied for a living and was trying to cooperate with the police to avoid losing his license.

Characterized as "a blustery and brilliant defense lawyer," by the *New York Times,* Lewis had ripped witnesses, dazzled and bewildered jurors, and generally raised hell in the courtroom while the Assist-

85

ant District Attorney, James McCarty, didn't seem to do as well, according to some observers.

When the trial came to the summation, the prosecution ruefully knew it had troubles because it had no physical proof to connect Carolyn to the murder. There were no witnesses making the connection. They never found the gun to make the connection. There were no fingerprints or skin, hair, blood, or fiber bits to make the connection.

In his three-hour summation, Lewis emphasized the presumption that Carolyn was innocent until proven guilty beyond a reasonable doubt. He cited the parallel with the witch trials at Salem saying that women were put to death then because that presumption did not exist in trials.

Lewis concluded by saying he believed that Parco had not only not sold Carolyn a gun, but that he had been hired by Paul Solomon to murder Betty Jeanne and pin it on Carolyn. That way Paul, faced with a threat of divorce by Betty Jeanne, could keep the condo, have custody of his daughter, and be rid of his troublesome wife who had been unfaithful to him for nine years.

He reminded them that one defense witness had testified he overheard Parco and Solomon talking about the murder and setting a price of $20,000 for it on the night that Betty Solomon was killed.

In trying to prove Carolyn guilty beyond a reasonable doubt, the prosecution was on shaky terrain, but Assistant District Attorney McCarty concluded that Carolyn Warmus was not some prim school teacher with her hair up in a bun teaching farm kids the three R's.

McCarthy characterized her as a tough, determined woman, "She is intelligent. She's cunning, opportunistic, and she's manipulative." And, while he didn't like using Parco as a key witness, "Sometimes you have to get together with a sinner to get at the devil. The devil in this case is the person who killed Betty Jeanne Solomon."

In the end, the jury deliberated over the 7,000 pages of evidence and 400 exhibits longer than any murder trial jury in the history of Westchester County. After ten days of deliberation, the jury sent the judge a note saying it was deadlocked. Judge Carey refused to dismiss the jury and urged it to continue.

Mid-afternoon of Saturday, April 27 — the twelfth day — the jury sent another note to the judge saying it was still hopelessly divided on a verdict. Carey sent a note back asking if they could resolve their impasse within a reasonable time. His note came back with a bold *NO* written on it.

When the jury first voted, six favored conviction, four favored acquittal and two were undecided. The final deadlock was eight to four in favor of conviction. One juror, a twenty-seven-year-old insurance man, Robert Smith, said some who held out for acquittal couldn't believe that a woman could be brutal enough to pistol whip another woman as had been done to Betty Jeanne. In addition, all the evidence the prosecution had was circumstantial and the four didn't believe that was strong enough to convict.

Juror Rosalind Serber, who was for conviction, said, "I felt very comfortable with their evidence. I couldn't link the [idea of a] frame-up to any of the evidence. I linked it all the way down the other way—to guilt."

Gina Fortugno, another juror, agreed and also voted for conviction.

All of the jurors agreed that the copy of the MCI phone bill Lewis presented was the forgery, but the four against conviction weren't convinced that the bill alone was enough to prove guilt.

On the other side, Fred A. Esposito said he didn't see any big, gaping holes in the prosecution's case, but there were lots of small doubts—enough doubts to keep him and three others from going for the guilty verdict.

But, the nightmare for Carolyn and Paul wasn't over. Assistant District Attorney McCarty announced that he would seek a new trial as soon as possible. It took until July tenth before he could get a new indictment approved by the court and then it all began all over again.

The second trial of Carolyn Warmus, this time with Bill Aronwald as her defense attorney, went much as did the first trial with Carolyn taking copious notes and ultimately filling twenty stenographic notebooks.

One major difference in the trial was a new piece of evidence that was introduced after the first trial had begun and never used because the prosecution didn't have it then. Paul Solomon came forward and claimed that he had accidentally discovered a single black knit glove in a box in one of the closets of his and Betty Jeanne's apartment.

The glove had been seen in a photo of the crime scene lying near the body in January of 1989, but had since disappeared. Now it suddenly reappeared.

When it was tested, microscopic traces of blood were discovered, but apparently it was not possible to identify the blood.

The prosecution seized upon the glove as proof linking Carolyn with the crime scene. It produced credit card receipts from Filene's Basement showing that Carolyn had purchased a pair of black knit gloves the same as or very much like the one found originally near Betty Jeanne's body.

The prosecution charged that this put Carolyn at the scene of the murder at the time it happened. The defense attorney countered that the glove was just like millions of others and couldn't be specifically connected with Carolyn.

However, in his heart, Bill Aronwald had a sinking feeling that the glove was the one deciding piece of proof that would sink the case for his client of everything else shown during the four-month-long second trial.

When the jury came in with the verdict on May 28, 1992 in the sixteenth floor courtroom of Westchester County, Carolyn Warmus was alone. There was not a single member of her family—not her father, her mother, or her sister—and not a single friend to stand with her at her moment of judgment.

When the jury foreman announced the verdict as

"Guilty," Carolyn slumped in total disbelief and muttered, "I can't believe the jury convicted me." There was a smattering of applause from the spectators.

One juror later interviewed by the Associated Press claimed that the glove was not the deciding piece of evidence. It was, said the juror, the entire body of the evidence taken together.

On June 26, 1992 the woman who had once been poised, confident, dressed to the nines in heels, tailored suits, and expertly applied make-up stood haggard, beaten, and sobbing before New York State Supreme Court Justice John Carey in faded jeans, white socks, blue sneakers, and a University of Michigan sweatshirt.

"Your honor, I am innocent." It came across barely audible in an anguished whimper. "I don't—want—to—spend—time—in—jail," she sobbed haltingly, "for something I didn't do."

"I didn't make a phone call to Ray's gun shop. I never bought the gun. I never received it from Vincent Parco. I never bought a glove at Filene's Basement. I had absolutely nothing to do with it. I was nowhere near the apartment on that day. I stand before you devastated. I can only ask you for leniency because I'm innocent.

"If I'm guilty of anything at all it would simply be to believe the lies and promises of Paul Solomon."

Nothing she said cut any ice with the normally restrained Judge Carey who unleashed a tirade against what he saw to be a heartless slaughter of an innocent woman in cold blood, planned and carried out with merciless precision and premeditation. He castigated Vincent Parco as a horrid man of evil influence and, then, dwelt on the terror that the defenseless victim endured in the last moments of her life.

Carolyn Warmus had robbed Betty Jeanne Solomon of 40 years of her life with a painful and unjustified murder and a price must be paid for that. The sentence Carey handed was the maximum sentence he was permitted to impose by law, but you had the impression that he would have made the sentence even stiffer if he could have—twenty-five years to life in prison.

A woman obsessed by love believed the promises and lies of Paul Solomon, who not only wasn't there for her when she needed him, but testified against her to put her in prison. He comes away with a bundle of money from selling the story to HBO and CBS. She comes away with a bundle of bitter memories and twenty-five or more years in prison.

Ironically, Jean Harris had been sentenced to fifteen years to life in this same courthouse a decade before for murdering her betraying lover.

Four
The Woman Who Tried To Be Perfect

Betty Broderick was the perfect wife and mother ready to do and be everything her fast-track San Diego lawyer husband, Daniel T. Broderick III, wanted her to do and be. Except for the one thing she couldn't be—young again and, so, naturally he had to leave her with her broken dreams and a haunting obsession.

It was a classic college 1965 romantic weekend with much rushing around, crushes of people, new faces, new opportunities and frenetic pleasures. Effervescent, blonde Betty Bisceglia, an eighteen-year-old freshman from College of Mount St. Vincent in New York City arrived with two friends at Notre Dame to see the Irish play the University of Southern California.

In the swirl of the weekend, she met a dashing premed student who fancied himself a latter-day Rhett Butler, except his name was Dan Broderick. He introduced himself to the cute blonde by writing his name on the tablecloth as "Daniel T. Broderick III M.D. (A)" with her pen. The ploy did what he wanted, whetted her curiosity.

"What's the "(A)" for?"

"I have just been accepted to med school. (A) is for M.D. almost."

Betty laughed and Dan knew he had her. One of the cardinal rules of making out with women he had learned early in life was to make them laugh within the first minute. This time it was important because, as he bragged to his fraternity brothers after that weekend, "I've met the woman I'm going to marry."

He had to finish his senior year at Notre Dame while Betty was in New York, but he had been accepted to Cornell Medical School which meant he only had a few more months before they would be in the same city. He filled the months with a few telegrams that Betty refused to answer and, then, handwritten letters which she did answer. They made a date to meet at the Biltmore Hotel, but she didn't show and, undaunted, he called and made another date.

Betty grew up in a big, comfortable Catholic family similar to that of Dan's in the tony New York suburb of Westchester County. Her objective was to find a man to marry, love, and have children with.

When he came East to Cornell Medical School, Betty was finishing up her education degree, knew the town, and had the money while Dan was the struggling young medical student. They dated and his controlling streak began to surface when he upbraided her for making any plans or decisions without clearing them with him first. Instead of this being a danger sign, Betty embraced it as the

93

mark of the confident, take-charge man she dreamed of having.

He was romantic beyond her dreams, a driving, ambitious doctor-to-be and she became the first in her class to marry in April, 1969. In many ways being the first in her class to marry was a greater achievement in Betty's eyes than getting her degree.

He hadn't finished medical school and there was the fun of the cramped dormitory room at Cornell with the bathroom shared by the students next door. The mutual hardships were taken in stride even as Dan took charge of Betty's life, money, and dictated her every decision, because the end of her rainbow was within sight. She became his devoted and conscientious wife with her entire world revolving around whatever he wanted and whatever he was. Even when he dropped out of medical school and switched to Harvard Law School and a prolongation of the Spartan graduate student life, it didn't matter to Betty. Her world centered on Dan.

She put up with it even when he was out late with the boys or gone for unexplained reasons and came home drunk. To Betty that was just the way men were and her role as a woman and, as the mother of their two daughters was, in her words, to be Dan's slave.

Besides Betty wasn't feeling well after the wedding and she was working all the time. She either taught third grade or, during off times, sold nurses' uniforms in the store next to the medical school. Her education about reproduction was skimpy at best which is why it took a while for the bulb to go off in her head that she wasn't sick — she was pregnant. She had gotten pregnant within the first four weeks of the wedding probably while they had been honeymooning at a private house on St. Thomas in the Virgin Islands. Their first daughter, Kim, was born in 1970 and, while they lived in modest quarters, her rich parents saw to it that Saks Fifth Avenue provided the baby's layette.

During the time Dan was finishing medical school, he demonstrated his fashion plate inclination by wearing tailored uniforms and monogrammed shirts. That surprised Betty given their tight financial circumstances, but it didn't surprise her as much as Dan's decision to go to Harvard Law School after Cornell.

He decided that the twin degrees would guarantee them a life of ease and wealth and, besides, he was worried that he might accidentally get caught up in the draft for Vietnam. Being in graduate school would spare him that inconvenience. His draft vulnerability was further reduced with the arrival of a second daughter, Lee, in 1971.

They seemed to sail through the turbulent Sixties untouched by the anti-Vietnam demonstrations, antiestablishment movement [they, after all, were working hard to become a part of the establishment] and the feminist surge. Dan's goal was to be rich, powerful, and in control. Betty's goal was to be the best mother in history and Dan's obedient, adoring servant-wife.

Finally, it was 1973, the ordeal of law school was over, another child arrived but died in two days and they drove West for Dan to accept an associate's position with the important San Diego law firm of Gray, Cary, Ames & Frye. They were leaving behind toil and tragedy and he was launching what would become a brilliant law career in medical malpractice law from which the whole family should prosper.

Both worked hard with appropriate rewards including a move in 1976 to a new five-bedroom home on the side of Mt. Soledad in La Jolla. They couldn't afford to completely furnish the house, but Betty got two things she dearly wanted: a washer and a dryer along with a new son, Daniel T. Broderick IV. For Betty it was a blessing after several miscarriages even though it meant money was tighter and she had to work nights as a hostess at the Black Angus restaurant.

For Dan, part of his self-image was that of the powerful, rich lawyer with the attractive, attentive wife and the perfectly behaved children. He took care of the money and the business and it was up to Betts, as he called his wife, to take care of the family side of things.

Dan was a workaholic whose long hours paid off in building a good enough practice that he was able to set up his own office at 401 West A Street in downtown San Diego in 1978 so that he could work even longer hours to spur on his business success. The business success was matched in the opposite direction by a crumbling marriage in spite of Church Marriage Encounter Weekends and counseling. Certainly, Betty and Dan were together enough to launch another child, Rhett, who arrived in 1979. Betty would have one more pregnancy—

96

her ninth—after that, but the doctor warned it was endangering her health so it was terminated and she had sterilization surgery.

In the eighties, Dan's practice started minting money and he became more and more of a fashion plate and spent a lot of time socializing, sailing, drinking, and playing baseball with fellow lawyers and promoting himself in the image of the perfect lawyer and husband with the perfect wife and family. But, things weren't perfect at home because of his lack of attention and lack of involvement in family life and the marriage was slip-sliding down the slope of despair.

Dan insisted his long hours were for the ultimate benefit of the family and that Betty just had to understand and do her part. They had, in addition to the new and bigger house on Coral Reef Drive, a boat and a condo in Colorado while Betty ran up charge bills at designer boutiques to the extent of $37,000 a year.

At a party in 1982 Betty noticed that Dan seemed taken by tall blonde twenty-two-year-old, Linda Kolkena. She didn't think much about it, but it was noted in her subconscious that Dan was sinking into midlife crisis. That tiny bit of data became seriously important the day Dan hired Linda, a little while later, as his $30,000-a-year assistant even though she had no legal or secretarial training.

Linda had actually come to San Diego to be with her boyfriend with whom she quickly parted and started dating the editorial cartoonist of the *San Diego Union*, Steve Kelley.

The summer came and Super Mom Betty took the kids on a five-week camping trip which they all enjoyed even if Dad couldn't make it. The only troubling thing to Betty was that there was never an answer when she phoned home.

When Betty and the kids got back, she sensed trouble right away—you can't be married to someone as long as she had been to Dan and not know it when things aren't right. Particularly when the maid, Maria Montes, reported finding strange women's bathing suits in the house.

Betty pinpointed the trouble quickly as being Linda Kolkena. When Dan came home one night driving a brand new red Corvette, Betty knew that midlife crisis had also come to their house and she demanded that he fire Linda. He refused.

Betty counter-attacked with a crash course on men's midlife crises and a complete makeover for herself. She went on a rigid diet, let her hair grow shoulder length and laid in a new wardrobe designed to tempt, tease, and titillate her man. "I wanted to be perfect, absolutely perfect for Dan Broderick."

But, the pain didn't stop. He didn't come home in time for a special dinner on her thirty-sixth birthday. So, she fixed dinner and put the kids to bed. With the house quiet and lonely, she lay down in the spare bedroom, swallowed a handful of pills, and slit her wrists. Dan arrived in time to save her and begged her forgiveness while swearing nothing was going on with Linda.

A couple of weeks later, for his thirty-ninth birthday, Betty went to Dan's office to surprise him with champagne and a plan to drive to the beach to watch the sun go down in the Pacific together. Her planned surprise turned into ash-filled humiliation when she learned Dan had gone to lunch with Linda earlier and the two never came back to the office. She stayed in his office waiting for him until finally the Pacific sun sank below the horizon like a metaphor of her marriage.

Stunned, Betty left the office and drove home through the evening traffic with her insides thrashing in the embarrassment she endured. At home, she tore all his custom made suits out of the closet, marched out to the backyard and piled them up before dousing them with barbecue starter fluid and burning them.

Dan later explained he and Linda had spent the afternoon taking dispositions and, again, swore they were not lovers while urging Betty to seek psychiatric help. Then, he went out to the yard to survey the charred remains of his wardrobe and went in to bed as if he had just been outside looking at the moon. The next day, he ordered an entirely new wardrobe.

And, with his income skyrocketing, Dan decided they needed an even bigger and better house which they found on Calle del Cielo in La Jolla Shores. First, they wanted to fix up the Coral Reef house to make it more saleable and also to repair a foundation crack in the building.

In September, 1984, they moved into a rental house while structural repairs were being made to their home, but nothing could be done about the structural repairs their marriage needed. February

28, 1985, they got into a fight, Betty almost hit Dan with a bottle of champagne and Dan said he was out of there. Unwilling to remain with Betty, Dan chose to move back into the family home. He would rather put up with the inconvenience of the repairmen and sleeping on a mattress on the floor than the torment of his deteriorating family life.

Being a single mother to the four children and seeing her husband of fifteen years slipping away into the arms of a tall blonde was more than Betty could endure and she began dropping the kids off at Dan's for him to look after. Soon the children were all living with Dan and Dan was openly having an affair with Linda. Her network of "friends" kept her breathlessly informed of every lunch, dinner, and party where Dan and Linda surfaced.

Shifting all the kids to Dan and the Coral Reef house had been a ploy by Betty to impress Dan how much he needed her to take care of the four kids, but it backfired. Dan adjusted his schedule and his life while hiring live-in help to take care of the children. He quickly established that Betty was not only emotionally dispensable, but physically disposable, too.

Now, the anger of betrayal and abandonment began to bubble up in Betty and she took to making guerrilla raids on the Coral Reef house where her husband, her children, her family, her life were living apart from her. Once she smeared Dan's bedroom with a Boston cream pie she found that Linda had made. Another time, she came in while everyone was gone and broke windows, smashed the stereo and sprayed paint all over the walls, cur-

100

tains, and fireplace. Ironically, the police refused to do anything because she was one of the legal owners of the house.

When that was all over, Dan got her the house on Calle del Cielo and he moved to a big home on Cypress Avenue in the exclusive and small neighborhood of Marston Hills near Balboa Park and his office downtown. All the children came to live with him because Betty, to them, had turned into a volatile shrew.

By this time it was over. The marriage was dead. All that remained was to make the funeral arrangements.

In September, 1985, Dan filed what should have been an ordinary divorce action, but turned out to be the most bizarre domestic case San Diego would see in years—one that would drag through the courts and the press for four years and one that is still the focal point of public attention.

Being an ace lawyer and president of the San Diego Bar in 1987, Dan knew all the moves and had all the friends and contacts in the San Diego legal establishment. Betty found that nobody wanted to touch her side of the case. Everybody owed Dan something, expected to owe Dan something, or were afraid of those lawyers and judges who did owe Dan something. She finally had to go 225 miles north to Beverly Hills and hire attorney Daniel Jaffe to represent her.

The tight-knit, incestuous legal establishment in San Diego was aligned against her. Between them, Dan and Betty had three houses. Her house on Calle del Cielo, his house on Cypress Avenue, and the last house in which they had lived together on Coral Reef. Dan was determined to sell the Coral Reef place and get out from under that financial burden, but Betty regarded it as their home and selling it would be physical proof that the marriage was absolutely over and she would never get her former life back.

There were several sales deals made for the house over the months in 1985, but Betty succeeded in torpedoing every one of them. At one reconciliation meeting to work out the details of selling the house, she came to the building where the meeting was to take place, but refused to come inside and be in the same room with Dan. She stayed in the parking lot and her attorney had to shuffle messages and documents back and forth between Dan in the meeting room and Betty in the parking lot. In the end, she rejected making another deal for sale of the Coral Reef place.

Dan counter-attacked by getting a court order giving him the right to sell without Betty's approval. A deal was made and closed in early February, 1986, with Betty's lawyer being notified a few hours before. Betty didn't hear about it until it was over. She was so enraged that she drove over to Coral Reef and tried to set fire to the house without success.

Frustrated and blindly angry, she drove over to Dan's house on Cypress Avenue and demanded her share of the money from the sale of Coral Reef. Dan told her she had ten seconds to get off the property. She got off the property, climbed back in her Chevrolet Suburban, and pulled away from the house. Then, she swung around, pointed it at the front door and floored the accelerator.

Daughter Kim and one of her brothers were in the kitchen when the car rammed through the entrance and everybody started running—the kids hid in the backyard and Dan and daughter Lee ran to the battering-ram car and Betty. Dan ripped open the front door and tried to pull Betty out as she brandished a butcher knife and Lee jumped in to separate her parents without effect. Then, Dan let loose a haymaker and decked Betty.

Minutes later, the police arrived, Betty was cuffed behind her back, put into the backseat of the patrol car and hauled to the San Diego County Mental Health Hospital. She was kept there and, then, in a private facility for three days.

Tempers cooled, but the bitterness had not. Betty's anger showed in her personal care and she began putting on weight until she had gained over sixty pounds. She got a job in an art gallery, was trying to find a new attorney because Daniel Jaffe had quit in disgust and found what she claimed was a platonic friend in a fencing contractor five years younger than herself, Bradley T. Wright. They spent nights together and went on trips together, but Betty insisted nothing romantic was involved.

The divorce was moving forward and Betty said she needed community property money to live and for her share of the divorce legal fees, but Dan thwarted her at every turn. She vented her wrath on his answering machine because he refused to talk with her directly.

Eventually he had to lock his answering machine

in a closet so the children couldn't know that she had called them over and over again leaving messages. When Linda left an announcement message on the machine, Betty started leaving obscene messages calling Linda a cunt and Dan a fuckhead. Dan played the messages for the court to prove she was mentally unstable. The judge didn't buy that and Linda was banned from using the machine as the hatred between the two women escalated.

To Betty, Linda had taken her place. The young exstewardess was openly living with Dan in his new house along with her children. She had Betty's husband, house, children, cars, friends, and position in the community. Suddenly, "I wasn't Mrs. Anything," she said after friends urged her to drop it and get on with her life.

The mark of Dan's influence in the San Diego legal community was blatantly shown in July, 1986 when Betty was served with papers about another court hearing. This was a bifurcation or split proceeding which was rarely used in divorce cases and Betty wasn't even in the courtroom when it took place. She still didn't have an attorney and had asked that the hearing be rescheduled. Unbeknownst to her, it wasn't.

The action the court took that day was to grant Dan a divorce with complete temporary custody of the children. It left the issues of permanent custody of the children, finances, and alimony to be settled some other time. Betty would later characterize it to a reporter as a "way legally to fuck your wife and your girlfriend at the same time." Dan agreed, however, to pay Betty $9,000 a month until the divorce was completely settled.

However, he deducted "fines" from that every-time Betty left an obscene message on his answering machine and she did that regularly besides doing everything else she could think of to get back at Dan and Linda, including cruising by their house many times a day and coming in one day when they were gone and taking their dog. In November, Dan informed Betty he wasn't going to send her any more money because of her harassing behavior.

That brought Betty storming over to the Cypress Avenue house to confront Dan because she didn't have any money if he cut her off. Dan and Linda were getting ready to go to a formal Bar Association dinner called the Blackstone Ball. Dan was wearing his top hat and cape as befitted the newly elected president of the San Diego Bar Association.

When Betty roared up to the house, Dan immediately ordered her off the property and, when she refused to go, he called the police. The police arrived and ordered her to leave and, when she refused, arrested her. So, the children and the world witnessed the bizarre spectacle of the president of the Bar driving off to a formal ball with his girlfriend while his handcuffed wife was hauled off to jail in a police car.

But, now, Linda—who still hadn't gotten Dan to marry her—began her own little campaign of venom. It started with an envelope arriving at the Calle del Cielo house containing a picture of Dan and Linda living it up at the Blackstone Ball. The unsigned message that accompanied the picture said, "Eat your heart out, bitch."

As is usual in the acrid atmosphere of divorce, the grown ups act mostly like children and the children are the innocent and battered pawns. Dan, Linda, and Betty were all trying to preach, plead, and indoctrinate the children that their side was right and moral while the other side was evil or, at least, unseemly and rude. The children were being bounced back and forth between the two sides emotionally and physically.

It was a no-win situation where the driving emotions were hatred, pain, and vengeance.

Betty finally got a good lawyer who wasn't marbled into the San Diego law establishment, Tricia Smith, who won her $16,000 a month temporary alimony at the beginning of 1987. It sounded like a lot to ordinary citizens, but Dan was earning over $1.2 million a year and the mortgage payment on Betty's Calle del Cielo house was $5,000 a month. And, she had lived an extravagant life style during her last years with Dan including spending close to $40,000 on clothes in 1986. In fact, as her fortieth birthday approached in November, 1987, she spent $10,000 for clothes and jewelry.

Both Betty and the children began to get into therapy during the long and trying waiting period of the divorce because everybody's life—not surprisingly—was getting distorted. The boys, Dan and Rhett, were in therapy and the older sister, Lee had gotten into drugs, dropped out of school, and was disowned by her father for a time.

Betty, too, was in therapy on and off, but continued to rage against Dan and Linda on the phone and in two other ways, one very private and one very public.

In the very private way, she was confiding to a diary that she started keeping in about 1985. In a very public way, she started lecturing and campaigning for divorce reform at women's groups around Southern California. Beyond giving speeches, she buttonholed the media at every chance and anybody else who would listen. It was a campaign that she was not waging alone since many other women felt the lash of unfair divorce in their lives including some of Betty's closest friends.

Then, Dan struck the final blow.

At a popular San Diego restaurant, he proposed marriage to Linda in a very public and open way that caught everyone's attention including the press the next day. With a great flourish noticed by the other diners, he sank to one knee and asked for Linda's hand in marriage. She smilingly accepted on the spot.

When Betty heard and read about it, she went ballistic. The last possible hope of restoring her shattered life with Dan, if it still existed, had a white oak stake driven through it. The Broderick's divorce wasn't yet final, but the end had come.

The final courtroom and legal paperwork was started the last week of December, 1988 and finally concluded in April, 1989. Custody of the two minor children, Dan and Rhett, was awarded by Judge William Howatt to Dan. Betty got half of what came from the sale of the Coral Reef house, some of the personal property, and alimony of

$16,100 a month.

The judge once again issued an order that Betty stay away from Dan and the house on Cypress. It had all the effect of spitting on a hot grill. As soon as she could, Betty sneaked into the Cypress house when everybody was gone and stole the list of guests invited to Linda and Dan's wedding set for the front yard a few weeks later. Naturally, she immediately started calling the guests and warning them to stay away from the wedding for their own safety.

The engaged Linda became, once again, the enraged Linda who struck back at her deposed rival by talking her way past the maid at Calle del Cielo while Betty was out and stealing Betty's diary.

Now, each side was notching up the ante.

Betty proceeded to buy a gun in the most open and obvious way possible. First, she bought the five-shot .38 openly and with a legal permit. Next, she told everybody she knew, including her children, that she now had a gun. Then, she showed the gun off to anybody who asked to see it.

Frightened of what Betty might do, Linda urged Dan to wear a bullet-proof vest at the wedding. He rejected that out of hand because it would mar his splendid appearance on this important occasion. The wedding came off all right in the front yard with the reception in the backyard by the pool. In the end, friends of both Betty and Dan conspired to keep Betty busy and in sight all of April 22nd. One of them, Helen Pickard, stayed with Betty and secretly was ready to warn a confederate at the wedding by beeper if Betty started over toward Cypress Avenue.

After Dan and Linda got married, Betty asked Linda to return her wedding china since Linda had gotten a complete set of her own when she and Dan married. Linda refused and began flaunting her new status as heir to all that Betty had been.

The friends of both women were getting tired of hearing daily reports of the most recent injustice or outrage and many wished both women would put a cork in it for a while. Steve Kelley was an exception because he always had time to listen to Linda, but he also was a good friend and concerned about where the endless battling might lead.

It was Steve who warned Linda one time, "This is the kind of woman who could get a gun and shoot you."

Betty was angry, frustrated, and desperate. "I feel like Linda is living my life."

In the summer of 1989, Betty got lucky with the lawyer situation and finally located another attorney who would handle her attempt to get custody of the two boys, Dan and Rhett, back from their father. Dan responded by stalling maneuvers to delay any court hearing as long as possible and to wear Betty down even further.

Betty was not even allowed to care for her own children when Linda and Dan went on extended vacations. Then, more legal papers were served on her threatening punishment if she didn't stop leaving filthy messages on Dan's and Linda's answering machine. She read through the legal papers and felt the overwhelming futility of her life since Dan had left her.

On Saturday, November 4, 1989, she had Danny and Rhett over for a visit and they went to dinner with Betty's friend, Brad Wright.

Early the next morning before the sun streaked the eastern sky, she got up and went down to the kitchen. Over coffee, she sat and reread the legal papers threatening to find her in contempt of court for harassment.

"It was an absolute rewind of the hell of the last years. I knew I was not going to wake up another morning in the same position."

She thought back that Dan had put her in jail three times, a mental hospital once, taken her children away from her, and sold the Coral Reef house without her permission. Suddenly she had to get out of the house to think.

In the car, she decided to drive to the beach for a walk, but on the front seat was a set of keys belonging to one of the children and it had a key to Dan and Linda's back door. Lying next to the keys was Betty's purse which contained a pistol. Impulsively, she decided to settle her life trauma once and for all. She would go to Dan and Linda and show them what they had done to another human being and, then, Betty said she would "blow my brains out right there in his bedroom, so everybody would know what he'd done to me."

Later, she would say, "I wanted to kill myself in front of him and splash my brains all over his damn house. I wanted to die. There was no plan. I wanted to die."

Twenty minutes later, Betty carefully unlocked the back door of Dan and Linda's Georgian man-

110

sion—the kind of mansion Rhett Butler would have had—and slipped up the curving stairway into their bedroom. What happened next is confused, but the one undisputed fact is that Betty fired five shots—not into her brain, but into Dan and Linda.

Two slugs tore into the sleeping Linda's head and lung, killing her instantly. After he had taken one of the hollow point bullets, Dan apparently wrenched his body to the right and stretched out his left arm in a desperate attempt to grab the telephone. The other two slugs burrowed into the wall and bedside table.

Betty ripped the phone out of the wall and fled the house in her Suburban heading back to her house on Calle del Cielo ten miles away near the Scripps Institute of Oceanography. Then, she pulled off Highway I-5 in Clairemont to call home. She was afraid the police might already be at her house frightening the two boys. Instead, she first called Dian Black who was a close friend also going through a bitter divorce. She told Dian that she thought she had shot Dan and Linda.

Dian told her to stay at the phone booth and then Dian called Betty's house to talk to Brad Wright who was there with the boys to alert him to what was going on and ask him to watch over the boys.

Meanwhile, Betty called her eighteen-year-old daughter, Lee, at her house on Sapphire Street in nearby Pacific Beach where she was living with her boyfriend, Jason Prantil. It was a little after 7 a.m. and she was hysterical. Lee told her to come over immediately.

When Betty got there, Lee was shocked at her mother's distraught condition as, between crying and vomiting, she confessed what she had done.

Meanwhile Brad called a lawyer friend of his, Brian Forbes. Brian called the police and the paramedics, but for some reason, they didn't believe his report of a double murder. So, while Brian's wife, Gail, came over to look after the two boys, Brad and Brian drove over to Dan's house.

When nobody answered the door, Brian broke through the screen of the open laundry room window and climbed in over the washer and dryer, calling out as he did so he wouldn't be mistaken for an intruder. He let Brad in and the two searched the house and found the two dead bodies. They went out to Wright's car to use his cellular phone when a patrol car pulled up.

Meanwhile, Betty had called friends and family before she surrendered to the police which she knew she had to do. She talked to her daughter Kim in college at Tucson, Arizona, "You know I had to do it. I couldn't let him live. It was one or the other."

While Betty was telephoning, Lee and Jason went to the house on Calle del Cielo to get Betty's address book and keys and to check on the boys. While they were there, they encountered some uniformed policemen lurking in the bushes next door who came out and questioned Lee about where her mother was. She said she didn't know and she and Jason left.

Back at Sapphire Street, Betty was now on the phone to Patti Monahan, another divorcee friend of hers to tell her what happened. Patti later told her boyfriend that Betty had said she shot Dan five times, "He was gurgling in his own blood. It's true, they really do shit in their pants."

Betty's next call was to her parents, Mr. and Mrs. Frank Bisceglia, in Eastchester, New York. She was talking to them hysterically and sobbing as Lee and Jason walked back in.

Betty hung up and gave her diamond necklace, earrings and watch to Lee. Then, Jason and Lee drove her to a restaurant parking lot where Dian Black was waiting for her with another friend, Ronnie Brown, and the three of them drove to the police station. Betty was going to go in and give herself up, but Dian had been arguing with her all the way not to do it without a lawyer. In front of the station Betty finally agreed and they drove to a pay phone and called a lawyer.

After Betty left, Lee and Jason went over to a condominium that Betty was buying and had moved some of her stuff into. They wanted to get some files that Betty said she might need, but police were waiting for them there. This time, they arrested Lee and Jason and took them back to the Sapphire Street place where they confiscated a tape from the answering machine with Betty's recent message on it saying.

"It's 11:05. I have an appointment with an attorney at eleven-thirty. We're going there. Don't worry, sweetie. Everything will be okay. I hope you're okay. Thank goodness you have the machine on."

At the Sapphire place, the police also took possession of Betty's big leather purse that she had left behind. In it, they found a .38 caliber revolver.

A few hours later, Betty, with attorney Ronald Frant, surrendered to the police.

The word of this double murder and the history of the love triangle soon seeped into the consciousness of news editors around the country who marked this as a notorious case worthy of their precious ink, space, and air time.

In fact, the first open confession of the crime by Betty came during a pay telephone interview from San Diego County jail to the *Los Angeles Times*.

In her confession as reported in the March 28, 1990 *Times*, Elisabeth Anne Broderick claimed that she didn't plan the killings in advance and that they were "a desperate act of self-defense from a controlling ex-husband who was ruining her life."

As evidence of the unpremeditated nature of the act, Betty said she had bought $400 worth of groceries the day before that included fresh veal and swordfish. Obviously, she maintained, no woman would do that and then kill somebody the next day because all that food would go to waste.

After turning herself in, Betty pled innocent and was arraigned and held without bail at the San Diego County jail in Las Colinas. The investigation and legal maneuverings took months before it was possible to get ready for the trial. Throughout the preparations and the subsequent trials some felt there was the undertone of a legal establishment outraged at the murder of one of its own and the subtle determination to make Betty Broderick pay the heaviest price possible.

In March, there was a preliminary filing of documents by both sides and a two-day hearing. The District Attorney, Edwin L. Miller, Jr., picked one of his best assistants to prosecute the case, Kerry Wells. She said it was a premeditated, cold-blooded murder by a vindictive, obsessive, scorned woman who deserved to be sent away for the rest of her life without possibility of parole.

Defense attorney Jack Earley responded that Betty did not go to the Cypress Avenue house where Dan and Linda were sleeping with the premeditated idea of murder. Rather she went to confront Dan over the contents of the legal papers she had been served and had only read for the first time that Sunday morning minutes before she drove to the Cypress Avenue home. The emotional effect on Betty of Dan's using the legal system to brutalize her brought her to the edge with a severe case of post-traumatic stress disorder common to prisoners of war.

"He took my home, my kids, my money. His was the white-collar way of beating you. If he had hit me with a baseball bat, I could have shown people what he did and made him stop."

When word surfaced in August that Betty had kept a diary that her Defense Attorney Jack Earley had kept in his possession, Deputy District Attorney Kerry Wells immediately moved to see it. Earley argued that the diary was filled with irrelevant material.

The diaries were voluminous and in the less than three years she had been writing them—February, 1985 to mid-1988—Betty had filled up ten volumes. Several volumes appear to be the rough draft of a proposed book, "What's a Nice Girl To Do?: A Story of White Collar Domestic Violence in America."

In any case, Judge Thomas Whelan ordered the defense to turn over the diaries to the prosecution two months before the trial began on the grounds that it was possibly important evidence.

The trial opened Monday, October 22, 1990, a few days short of a year from the morning of the murders and each side immediately staked out their positions. Both sides agreed that Betty had shot Dan and Linda to death in their bedroom. From that point on, however, they diverged sharply.

The prosecution, led by Deputy District Attorney Kerry Wells was straight forward in charging the murders had been committed by a woman obsessed with a hatred that had "become the absolute focus of her life."

Wells described the driving emotion involved as greed. "She had married him because he was going to be a moneymaker. When he finally began making big money in the mid-1980s, but then began the process of divorcing her, she felt she was being gypped. As for Linda, Betty felt Linda had what Betty still felt belonged to her and only her and she hated her for it."

The prosecutor added that she would show Betty had threatened to kill Dan just two weeks before the morning that she shot him and Dan "essentially was left to suffocate in his own blood and die."

Defense attorney Jack Earley saw Betty as much a victim of events as Dan and Linda were. She felt, "every emotion a person could probably feel — fear,

116

depression, anger, and hurt. What you see is a person who hurts, with no self-esteem, no way of dealing with problems, someone who was acting on emotions thrust on her."

Earley's version of what happened was that Betty came into the house that morning to talk to Dan and straighten things out since he had previously refused to do that and, instead, had harassed and humiliated her.

She came into the bedroom with a gun that morning intending to either talk with Dan or to kill herself. When he woke up and yelled, "Call the police," it startled her and she panicked and started pulling the trigger without aiming.

Predictably, the courtroom was filled with some 100 spectators including representatives of a movie company, a journalist planning on doing a book, and a writer for the *Ladies' Home Journal* crafting an article on the ordeal of being an older woman.

As the trial wore on, there was intense community interest and one TV station, KNSD, tried in vain to get permission to broadcast the entire case live. It was permitted to air segments, but not gavel to gavel. A dicey moment came when Betty's daughter, Kim, talking through her tears, testified against her mother.

"I don't want my mother to suffer or to die in prison, but I think she should be punished. My father didn't deserve to die."

The high point of the trial, however, was Betty's own testimony which was also punctuated by sobs. She began by telling of their early romance and marriage that brought them to San Diego where, after sixteen years of marriage, nine pregnancies, and four children, Dan Broderick had dumped her for a younger woman.

In the process, she claimed that Dan had used his power as a prominent attorney to seize control of the family money and custody of the children while trying to convince Betty that she was mentally unbalanced.

"Dan's opinion of me was really all I cared about. I didn't care what anybody else thought." That's why it hurt when he began telling her she was old, fat, ugly, boring, and stupid and he wasn't having any fun in life anymore.

The key issue that the defense attorney Earley tried to establish is that the killings were not premeditated. That, in fact, Betty had tried suicide before and, on the morning of the shooting, had originally planned on killing herself. To literally, "splash my brains all over his house." She said she came into Dan and Linda's house dead, defeated, and unable to fight any more.

Psychiatrists for both the prosecution and the defense agreed at least on one thing, that Betty was not psychotic, but that she did have severe depressions. Psychologist Katherine DiFrancesca was an expert defense witness and she put it in a way that most people who knew Betty and Dan understood and agreed with, namely, that Betty had no identity of her own—whatever she was came as a spin-off from Dan. She wasn't Betty Broderick, she was "Mrs. Daniel Broderick, III." When that identity was stripped away from her, she became desperately lost and bewildered.

Explaining what happened in the darkened bedroom that fatal morning as her children and two aunts sat in the courtroom crying, Betty said she doesn't really remember shooting. "They moved, I moved, and it was over."

· When Deputy District Attorney Wells cross-examined Betty, she uncovered some glitches in her story, but Betty basically stuck to her tale of Dan's betrayal and bludgeoning her into submission with horrid lies, closed and unusual court proceedings, and intimations that she was insane like something out of the old movie *Gaslight*. She admitted to vandalizing Dan's home and leaving vulgar messages on his answering machine, but that was only out of her justifiable frustration.

In answer to Wells's probing, she denied telling anyone that she was going to murder Dan or that her children believed that.

The trial titillated San Diego, with people divided into Betty-backers and Betty-bashers with the latter seeming the more numerous. This sharp division would become more significant in the lives of all the principals before many more days had gone by.

Mary Kaye Miller writing to the *San Diego Tribune,* voiced the Betty-backer side, "Betty Broderick's life was hell on earth. She worked hard to help send her husband through medical school and law school. How did he reward her? He traded her in for a younger model."

A San Diego State University sociology professor assessed the community reaction and believed that the strong interest by women is due to shared values and experiences. Many women, he said, have endured the same treatment from men that Betty did and they sympathize with her. In a sense, the Broderick case is a modern day morality play about love, loyalty, betrayal, and vengeance.

The trial ended with what some reporters characterized as fiery summations marked by vocal gymnastics and dramatic gesturing. Wells said it was an ambush and double execution by an obsessive woman whose intent from the beginning was to blow Dan and Linda away. She said:

"The killings were the culmination of years of planning and a smoldering, constant hate for her exhusband, prominent lawyer Daniel T. Broderick, III.

"You don't point a .38 caliber gun loaded with hollow-tipped bullets at two people lying in bed early in the morning and fire without intending to kill them."

Earley, on the contrary, painted Betty as a woman consumed with anger, rage, and depression who saw Dan and Linda together in bed for the first time and fired the gun in an uncontrollable emotional explosion.

"Her act was one of craziness, one of emotion, one that should never have happened."

Almost anticlimactically, Judge Whelan instructed the jury of its five options: First or second degree murder, voluntary or involuntary manslaughter or, finally, not guilty. The jury chose a sixth alternative instead.

After four heavy days of deliberation, the jury reported that they deadlocked ten to two for murder and the judge had to declare a mistrial. Betty would not comment, but her attorney said he wasn't surprised and was willing to talk about a plea bargain with the prosecution, but District Attorney Miller waved that aside while he pondered whether or not to pursue a second trial.

Kim Broderick, Betty's twenty-year-old daughter and a student at the University of Arizona was angry at the outcome. She had testified against her mother and said she wanted the whole mess behind her.

Steve Kelley drew an editorial cartoon showing Betty's Chevy Suburban van driving over Dan and Linda's graves.

Four months had passed and Betty Broderick was still in jail awaiting her second trial for murder, but she passed the word to the outside that jail had done wonders for her. The press naturally reported this because Betty had now become a combination *cause celebe*, curiosity, infamous celebrity and anointed "news-maker" by some strange ritual unknown to any but the news media who are slavish devotees of the concept.

"It's been wonderful. Just what I needed. No responsibilities, no bills, no gardeners to worry about, no dishes to do. Just rest and relaxation. I'm very slowly, but steadily, turning into a human being that functions again."

She was losing the excess poundage, getting 250 letters a month, granting selective interviews on the phone from her Las Colinas jail and, at this point, talking about making a deal with the prosecutor to avoid a second trial. Deputy District Attorney

Wells, responded to the interview with the *Los Angeles Times* by saying she was ready to review any proposals.

The March 1991 *Ladies' Home Journal* published an article about the Broderick case entitled, "Hell Hath No Fury," in which writer Kathleen Neumayer made it sound like Betty had committed justifiable vengeance. Betty reacted that what really happened was that Dan was trying to rob her of the children she loved and the money she helped make it possible for him to earn. She sacrificed through all the lean years of medical school, law school, and the early work years and, now, she was entitled to her half.

"That [the *Ladies' Home Journal* article] was the kind of thing that everybody wanted to believe . . . but that had nothing to do with it. Leaving me for a younger woman . . . had nothing to do with what happened. I have never been jealous of Linda Kolkena for a moment in my life. Ever."

If she had been jealous or seeking vengeance, Betty says she would have tortured them to death.

Six months later, a plea bargain could not be agreed upon, and on Friday, September 20, 1991, the jury selection for the second trial began. As with the first trial, the key issue to be settled is that of premeditation. Did Elisabeth Broderick slip into Dan and Linda's house on Cypress Avenue the morning of November 5, 1989 with a gun in her hand and a preplanned determination to murder those two sleeping people?

The second trial was a lot different than the first trial.

Kerry Wells opened by charging Betty with being a cold-blooded killer who gunned down two helpless people in their sleep and left her dying ex-husband gurgling in his own blood.

Wells dug into Betty about her past abortions with Earley leaping to his feet and almost screaming objection after objection. It had been agreed before the trial by both sides that Betty's abortions would not be brought in. Yet, Judge Whelan allowed the evidence and did not order any of it stricken from the record.

Recounting her story from the stand the second time Betty again said the first time she had read the legal papers threatening her with criminal contempt if she didn't stop harassing Dan and Linda was that Sunday morning of the murders. It was, she said, "more than I could handle."

So, despondent and beaten she drove all the way from La Jolla to Dan and Linda's home near Balboa Park intending to confront Dan and to kill herself.

"All these thoughts just kept churning in my head, like my eyeballs were turned backwards. It felt like the whole world was inside my head. It felt like hell, actually. I went to the house intending to splash my brains all over his house."

Betty testified that she couldn't remember all the details of what happened. "I was like a slide show with a lot of slides missing." She thought this time she heard Linda scream for Dan to call the police and Dan grabbing for the bedside phone.

"Then, I screamed, 'NO!' I fired the gun and this big noise went off and I grabbed the phone and ran out of there. I felt like I let out a huge scream. But I don't know if I even made a noise. It was all sensation . . . this huge sensation."

At another point, Betty described what happened this way.

"I was in a totally altered state of consciousness . . . I walked into the room. I've testified that it was dark. It appeared that way to me. I moved, they moved, the gun went off . . ."

After the cross-examination by Wells, Earley again complained to the judge about Wells's demeanor including glaring at the defendant on the stand and throwing her pencil in disgust during her cross-examination. Unjustified theatrics, but Judge Whelan was letting them happen.

Moving much more aggressively against Betty than she had in the first trial Kerry Wells probed Betty's suicide attempts and things she had said in confidence to her marriage therapist that indicated she was going to kill Dan. Betty's defense was that she was an "absolute basket case" at the time and the thought of having to raise her children alone terrified her.

The change in prosecutor Wells's tone was noted by reporters who had covered both trials. Michael Granberry of the San Diego bureau of the *Los Angeles Times* noted.

"Wells, who was criticized for not being aggressive enough during last year's trial, pounded away relentlessly on Thursday."

Granberry also commented on the change in the Judge's conduct of the second trial.

"Bench conferences have come to dominate the

trial of Broderick. . . . Courtroom observers say these conferences illustrate that Superior Court Judge Thomas J. Whelan is cutting a different figure from the open, media-friendly judge of last year's trials."

In the view of the defense, the changes in Whelan's handling of the trial hurt the accused's side by barring needed testimony and witnesses for the defense. He put severe restrictions on the testimony of family therapist Daniel J. Sonkin who believed Betty's husband, Dan Broderick, abused her physically, sexually, and psychologically. In fact, Judge Whelan's restrictions were so crippling on Sonkin's testimony that he decided not to testify.

Whelan also would not allow evidence of Dan Broderick's alcoholism and drunk driving convictions. Also, not allowed at the second trial was a lot of evidence admitted in the first trial such as Betty's wanting to get her tubes untied so she could have another child by Dan in order to keep him with her. Nor, was Earley allowed to introduce testimony from a man claiming to have been almost hired by Dan to murder Betty.

"Dan Broderick was even thinking of killing Betty if he had to. He was going to try to make it so she was penniless. He told a number of people that it wouldn't be over until one of them was gone."

Testimony that was allowed, however, was that of a jailhouse deputy, Maria McCulough, who said that Betty had no remorse about the killings and returned to jail after the first trial elated with her own performance on the stand.

"One day she came back and said, 'I had such a good day at court today. I had the jury eating out of my hands. I think my crying had a really good impact on the jury. They ate it up.' She was excited like a child would be."

Jail psychiatrist William A. Robinson met with Betty in the Las Colinas lock-up on Monday, November 6, 1989, within twenty-four hours after the killings and testified that he didn't think she was either suicidal or remorseful.

"She appeared happy, outgoing, quite coherent, and relieved. She did not have the attitude of guilt—she had the attitude of anger. People who are angry do not kill themselves. She said that pressure had been taken off her. She was just happy."

The seven-week-long second trial of Betty Broderick ended on Monday, December 2, 1991, almost exactly twenty-five months since the morning of the death of Dan and Linda Broderick.

The jury came back and rendered Betty Broderick guilty on two counts of second degree murder. The defendant seemed to accept the judgment and the polling of each juror with composure.

But, the jury certainly had not reached the verdict in composure.

It was a divided and agitated jury that began deliberations on the Broderick case just as the first jury had been. After much debate over the four days they pondered the case, they agreed on only two things. First, Betty was guilty of either manslaughter [the defense's position] or she was guilty of murder [the prosecution's position]. So, they would focus on the exact definitions of each of those crimes to see which definition fitted what happened.

Second, they agreed that they would not give up until they had reached a verdict of some kind. They would not be an indecisive hung jury as the first one had been the year before.

Even given this agreement into the jury room, they were still twelve troubled people. Jury foreman George McAlister said of their task.

"It was an American tragedy. We had to get this out and then go beyond being human beings and focus on the issue. At any point in time, it was possible to have a hung jury again, but we decided as one group to pull together and leave the jury room with a verdict. That was our responsibility and we owed it to the victims.

"We all had some sympathy for her. We felt it was a tremendous tragedy. But, we saw so much aberrant behavior. Her reactions weren't something a normal, reasonable person would do."

With that, McAlister and several others began pushing the group to vote for a first degree murder conviction, but the others wouldn't be pushed. McAlister tried to keep them focused on the legal definitions writing on the blackboard to clarify points. So, before long, most of them agreed to compromise on second degree murder. That still wasn't acceptable to everybody and a few were holding out for manslaughter.

McAlister favored the toughest penalty he could get out of this jury of seven men and five women and pushed for that all the way. In the end, he told everybody on the jury that he thought they could and should reach a compromise on second degree murder.

Still, there were several not comfortable with that and they tried to stall to give others time to waver and reconsider. A long lunch break was decided upon to give people time alone to think it over.

It had not been easy as juror Maurizio DiMartino said, "It's been quite a load for a person like me, a simple person like me. I've lost a lot of sleep over it. My emotions were touched many times. Like many of the jurors during deliberations we laughed and we cried, but we did come to a conclusion and I'm satisfied with it."

One of the women jurors, JoAnn Phelps, tried to understand how what happened twisted everyone's lives.

"I sympathize for her. I sympathize for the family, for the kids. It's just that human response. Still, I just don't think we can let our emotions and our sympathy get in the way of justice."

The jurors had been together for eight weeks and in the early days when the trial was still going on, they spent their off hours Christmas shopping at the nearby Horton Plaza or descending on the snack machine room on the fourth floor of the courts building and snarfing up Snickers candy bars and bags and bags of pretzels.

When the trial was over and they were finally faced with the decision of Betty's severe guilt or milder guilt, each of the jurors tended to pull in and become more isolated from the others. Some complained about stomach disorders caused by the tension.

Nor was the end of the trial greeted with composure by the relatives of those involved. Maggie Kolkena-Seats, Linda's sister from Portland, Oregon, complained that her sister and brother-in-law were unjustly murdered by Betty—particularly her sister. After all Maggie's sister's main crime was that she was younger and more attractive than Betty and loved Dan. For that, she was murdered. Maggie also thought that all the media attention Betty was getting as the poor little abandoned wife was disgraceful.

Dan Broderick's brothers, Terry and Larry, echoed that feeling and were dismayed because much of the time it seemed as if their brother was the defendant on trial and not his murderer.

Judge Whelan accepted the verdict of the jury, thanked and dismissed them and set February 7 as the date for sentencing Betty Broderick on her two convictions of second degree murder.

When that time came, Judge Whelan listened to strong appeals from the relatives of both Linda and Dan in addition to an emotional plea from the prosecutor, Kerry Wells. All urged the harshest of sentences for Betty Broderick.

The Judge agreed and gave Betty the maximum sentence allowed, fifteen years on each of the two counts of second degree murder. He added two years for possession of a gun as the California law allows. The terms are to be served consecutively for a total of thirty-two years which means Betty Broderick will not be eligible for parole for at least eighteen years.

Naturally, a movie for TV was immediately rolled into production based on the story from the viewpoint of Dan's brother and Linda's best friend. Predictably, this epic starring Meredith Baxter depicted all the terrible things Betty did, but somehow forgot to mention Dan's long-term affair with Linda. As usual, Hollywood's version of the Broderick case is Hollywood's version of the Broderick case.

Betty's reaction to the endgame of this tragic scenario surprised many. Not only were many taken back by her stoic acceptance of the verdict when delivered in the courtroom, but they were bewildered by her interview with the *Los Angeles Times* the next day via prison pay telephone. She characterized all that had happened as "the will of God."

She said that the killings, her trial, and pending prison term was in the hands of the Lord.

"This will sound crazy, but I do believe that what happened in that room was the will of God. What happened in that jury room and with the verdict was the will of God. And the sentencing will be the same. Whatever happens, I have to live with for the rest of my life."

"If I could have hugged each of the jurors, I would have. I would have told them it was OK. I wouldn't want them to live under any kind of burden because of me. But I do wish the people who believed it was manslaughter had been stronger."

Speaking of living under a burden, probably the saddest part of the second trial is one that will resonate in some lives for years long after all the rest of the testimony is forgotten. That was the testimony of Betty and Dan's daughter, twenty-one-year-old Kim, and eleven-year-old son, Danny.

The testimony of both was used to convict their mother. One can only wonder in apprehension and sadness what the impact of having helped put their mother in prison will do to their lives.

Five
Bambi—The Cop Who Loved a Cop

Eleven-year-old Sean Schultz's hysterical phone call echoed the terror in his heart as he pled for help from a neighbor at 2:30 in the morning of May 28, 1981 as his mother lay dying in her bed. The neighbor was Sean's mother's lover.

The neighbor was a Milwaukee cop, Stu Honeck, who had been dating Sean's mother, Christine, since her divorce from Sean's father. First, Stu asked to speak to Christine, but Sean said she couldn't speak, she was gurgling.

"Gurgling?" It was a word that conjured up the worst possible circumstances in Stu's mind. It was a word that brought him upright and barreling out of bed, grabbing for his pants and pistol while hollering at his roommate, Ken Retkowski, also a Milwaukee cop.

After hurriedly pulling on his clothes while on the phone calling 911 and barking into the receiver for help, Honeck and Retkowski were at Christine's house in less than two minutes flat.

Arriving at the same time was the first patrol car of a tidal wave of Milwaukee police that would pour into the Schultz home at 1701 West Ramsey Street. This crush of police including Sean's father, Fred Schultz, Jr., who had divorced his mother six months earlier and married a beautiful twenty-one-year-old ex-cop and ex-Playboy Bunny, Laurie Bembenek. There were so many cops surging through the death house that morning that they were literally bumping into each other and, in the process, destroying or contaminating every bit of evidence that could help catch the murderer. It was, in the midst of cruel tragedy, a scene from a Keystone Kop movie.

The entire Bambi case was about cops. It seemed that everybody connected with the case was a Milwaukee cop, was related to a Milwaukee cop or used to be a Milwaukee cop. It was a case about sex, cops, bigotry, cops, drugs, cops, corruption, cops, murder, cops, malfeasance, cops, love, cops, intrigue, cops, greed, cops, drunkenness, cops, and human tragedy. It was also about cops—mostly Milwaukee cops.

Christine Schultz lay sprawled across her bed, a blue and white bandanna gag in her mouth and a ugly large-bore bullet hole in her back and chest.

Sean and his seven-year-old brother, Shannon, had dinner at home that night with their mother and Honeck, who was over for a couple drinks and the meal. He was anxious to have Christine marry him, but was afraid of pushing it too hard and had already earned the hatred of her ex-husband, the philandering Fred. He had gone home earlier and the kids had adjourned to watch TV in their bedroom across from their mother's.

Around two a.m. somebody came into the darkened house and tried to strangle the sleeping Sean who jerked awake and fought back along with his brother Shannon. The intruder seemed to be a large man with a red ponytail, wearing an olive drab army field jacket.

Fleeing from the boy's room, the attacker ran into Christine's room who apparently woke up in time for the boys to hear her plead, "God, please don't do that," followed by a single shot. Bursting out of their room to go to their mother's aid, they saw the dark figure leaping down the stairs three at a time.

They will never forget what they saw in their mother's bedroom. She was face down with a bloody wound in her back, a scarf around her head, and a cord of some kind around her left hand. She was alive, but gagging. Sean ripped her T-shirt and exposed the wound so he could wipe off the blood, but it kept bleeding. That's when he grabbed the phone and called Stu.

In a serious breach of common sense, the Milwaukee police department let Schultz become intimately involved in the investigation of his ex-wife's murder. Because he might be a suspect, detectives asked him to produce all the guns he owned. He produced a .38 caliber Smith and Wesson from home which detectives passed around with their bare hands, sniffing and giving it back to him without noting the serial number. They didn't give Fred a paraffin test to see if he had fired a gun recently.

Laurie "Bambi" Bembenek's involvement in the

case began some time before, because the gorgeous, blonde, slender tomboy was the daughter of an ex-Milwaukee cop, Joseph Bembenek and his wife, Virginia. Laurie's life began as an accident and the accidents just kept happening. She was what is called in some families a caboose—a baby at the very end of the train who was not expected. The next accident was her name which was originally Laurie Ann, but somehow appeared on her birth certificate as Lawrencia.

Joe Bembenek, a staunch Polish Catholic, was a Milwaukee police officer along with a lot of other Poles and Germans, but after three years he dropped out, unable to stomach the regular and routine corruption. He became a carpenter instead.

Soaring to 5'10" with blue eyes, a drop-dead figure, the high cheekbones that fashion models made famous, and long blonde hair, Laurie went out for sports and the band, and dreamed about being something besides the wife and mother her environment seemed determined she should be.

The idea of being a cop appealed to her and she enlisted in the Milwaukee Police Department and instantly became the butt of intense sexism from the men in her department. Being called a "pussy cop" and "cunt" became ordinary terms of address as she worked her way through the police academy. At one point she was charged informally with having smoked pot at a police party and urged to confess and resign. No one seemed interested in what the other policemen were doing at that same party.

She refused and, while other nonwhite and woman recruits were dropping out, Laurie hung in, determined to graduate. Along the way, she picked up the nickname "Bambi" and made friends with another woman recruit, Judy Zess. Finally, on July 25, 1980, Laurie graduated from the police academy with her pride, her dignity, and her feminist beliefs still intact.

What she saw in her time as a Milwaukee police officer repelled her just as it had her father. She saw policemen brutalize minorities and women, drinking on duty, sleeping for hours during their shifts, selling pornography from their patrol cars, and getting blow jobs from hookers.

A month after leaving the academy, Laurie and two other women officers were fired without warning by seventy-year-old Chief Beier for what was vaguely called, "the good of the service." No specific charges or deficiencies were made, she was just turned into history overnight for no apparent reason except that she had been born a female.

The firing knocked the wind out of her emotionally but, always spunky, she decided it was unfair and she was going to fight it with a grievance filed with the police union. During the next months of hearings, filling out forms, waiting to be called for this meeting and that hearing, Laurie got more and more depressed. Then, came the hammer blow.

The investigations forced Chief Beier to release Laurie's file and in it was the sworn testimony of her good friend Judy Zess saying the two of them had smoked pot at a concert. Laurie was never told of the charges, never confronted with an allegation, and never given the chance to respond. She, however, did confront Judy immediately and Zess broke down, crying that she had been forced to sign a confession after hours and hours of cruel interrogation and that she was frightened and confused and didn't know what else to do.

In spite of this, the two women clung together, like two lost souls bewildered in a rainstorm not of their making.

Then, the police union said it was dropping Laurie's case because another cop testified that Laurie had been arrested for smoking pot at that same concert. The fact that there was no arrest record or any other collaborating proof didn't seem to bother the police union. The worst part was that, because of this, the state unemployment benefits department said she had been fired for cause and, therefore, had to pay back the $2,500 she had collected in benefits.

Some in the department were angered by her exposing their bigotry and hypocrisy and responded in quaint and sophomoric ways such as leaving a dead rat on her windshield and harassing her with threatening phone calls.

After the police department dumped her, Bambi got by as an aerobics instructor and working as a Playboy Club waitress at the Lake Geneva Playboy Club. She only worked as a waitress there for six weeks, but the label stuck to her and, from then on every reporter *HAD* to mention she was a Playboy Bunny as if that was the ultimate definition of a woman.

Beyond that was the implication that she was not only a Playboy Bunny, but that she was a Playboy nude centerfold, displaying her naked body to millions of drooling men and, perhaps, the illicit mistress of Hugh Hefner.

In truth, she was never a centerfold, but she did become a mistress, but not of Hugh Hefner. Instead, she became the mistress of — what else? — a Milwaukee cop, a philandering, controlling Germanic type named Elfred O. Schultz, Jr., who she met at the Playboy Club.

At the time, Elfred or Fred, was sleeping around with a lot of women including a friend of Laurie's, Margie Lipschultz, who was also a — guess what? — Milwaukee cop.

At first, Laurie thought Fred was obnoxious and boorish, but as is often the case with love, he started pushing Margie aside and hitting on Laurie. Margie told her Fred was divorced with two kids, and had a insatiable lust for sex. That pretty well summed up all any woman needed to know. She decided to ignore him.

Meanwhile, in late November and early December, Laurie's life got busy. She decided to enlist in the Air Force and was given a February reporting date. She filed a complaint with the Equal Employment Opportunity Commission charging sex discrimination by the Milwaukee Police Department. And, she accidentally got hold of photographs of the Tracks Picnic through her friend Margie.

The Tracks Picnic was an annual affair sponsored by Tracks Bar in a local public park and widely attended by patrons of the bar including many Milwaukee cops. It was notorious for drunken, lewd, and boisterous behavior which was ignored by the on-duty police — some of whom were attending anyhow. The photos showed a number of naked people drinking and cavorting in the park including one man identified as "Fritz" who was actually Fred Schultz. He was standing before a large crowd in the park jaybird naked.

She couldn't help mentally visualizing the man in the picture the next week when she accidentally ran into Fred in a local restaurant. She was surprised at her own reaction noticing how Nordic and handsome he was. He immediately began flirting with her and she agreed to a jogging date along Lake Michigan. The jogging date extended into food and drink and a stunning change in her feelings about Fred.

His commanding, self-assured manner coupled with a wistful vulnerability touched deep into her and she went out with him the next night for an evening of dinner, drinking, and dancing. She realized that she was falling in love and was ready to give him anything he wanted as they swirled around the dance floor.

They began seeing each other constantly from then on and Laurie gradually learned more about this strange, domineering man. For one thing, he was also in contact with his wife, Christine, several times a week and paid close attention to his two boys, Sean and Shannon, and would became outraged if Christine made any major decisions about the boys without Fred's prior permission.

Fred also had a roommate, Stu Honeck, who was, naturally, a Milwaukee cop and dating Fred's ex-wife, Christine. One of the things that Laurie didn't know was that Fred's first marriage broke up because he insisted Christine participate in wife-swapping parties and was known to hang around with ex-felons and drug dealers. It might not have mattered since she was so in love with and obsessed by Fred.

Still, Laurie was due to go into the Air Force in February and that put a finite limit to her affair with Fred even though he was wooing her big time with cards, flowers, constant dates, and phone calls. It all had to come to an end in February or so she thought.

Then, came the call from the Air Force. It had learned about her pending discrimination suit against the Milwaukee Police Department and refused to accept her for training until that was resolved. She could drop it, but the feminist bile within her churned at the prospect of giving up. So, the Air Force could take a hike. Laurie was sad and Fred was glad. Within days, he proposed and they eloped to Waukegan, Illinois, January 30, 1981, to be married.

Laurie was in love as she had never been in her life and couldn't believe her own happiness being with Fred. She really became consumed with him and couldn't imagine life without him. After a week's dreamy honeymoon in Jamaica, they returned to Milwaukee and, to save expenses, moved into one of the Bay View Terrace Condos with Judy Zess. Fred worked the night shift and Laurie and Judy spent most of their evenings together until Judy started dating a body-builder upstairs who, coincidentally, hated Fred. Tom Gaertner, who didn't seem to have any visible means of support, despised Fred because Fred had killed one of Tom's best friends, a cop who was dealing dope.

As if that tension wasn't enough, Fred got another financial blow from his ex-wife that bent him out of shape with anger. The final property settlement from the divorce came down and it gave Christine their house which Fred had built himself plus $746 a month in combined alimony and child support. Fred's anger was vehement with the cursing frustration of a man caught in a trap screaming to heaven over the injustice of his fate. Laurie couldn't understand why Fred had come out so badly and had given in so easily when he cryptically explained in a low and dangerous voice that Christine had him by the balls and could get him fired if she wanted to do it.

The clear implication was that Christine had some terrible secret she was holding over Fred that could ruin his career and, possibly, send him to jail. It was a dark specter that would haunt their relationship well into the future and, probably, never be excoriated.

Laurie's complaint to the Equal Employment Opportunity Commission went through hearings, but seemed doomed to failure while roommates and ex-roommates were getting aggravated with each other. Judy had moved in with Tom sticking Laurie and Fred with her share of the lease and, still-married Stu Honeck was in trouble for violating a Milwaukee Police Department rule forbidding cops from sleeping with anybody but their wives. Somebody had turned him in for sleeping with Christine Schultz — Fred Schultz.

141

Honeck called Fred and Laurie's place and left a brief message on their answering machine: "Fuck you, motherfucker." The date was May 26, 1981.

According to Laurie's description of her activities the next day, Fred and Laurie had rented a new, smaller apartment near her parents house and Laurie had spent the day going on job interviews and then coming home to continue packing so they could move.

Her mother was with her and Fred was sleeping. At eleven p.m. Joe Bembenek came by to pick up his wife and Fred got up to go to work. Fred left fifteen minutes later after asking Laurie if she was going to go with her friend Marylisa to the local hangout, Tropicana, for drinks that evening. She said she was going to go to bed and get some sleep.

Off on his shift, Fred called her three times during the next hour-and-a-half to see if she was all right, but Laurie figured it was because he was jealous and afraid she might be going out. She thought his jealousy was kind of charming given how much she loved him and would never be disloyal to him. Thinking about Fred, she drifted off to an exhausted sleep as she would later testify.

As Laurie told it afterward, the next thing she knew was the phone ringing at about quarter to three in the morning and Fred's excited voice penetrating her consciousness with the startling announcement that Christine had been killed. Laurie said she didn't fully grasp the message in her sleepy stupor and fell back asleep until another phone call from Fred an hour later.

Then, stunned by the news, she said she called Judy Zess and her mother and wondered aloud how she was going to raise those two boys. She put a robe on, made coffee and waited for Fred.

About four a.m., two Milwaukee detectives arrived and asked her about Stu Honeck and Fred. They also asked her if she owned a green jogging suit and a gun and, then, they left.

Another hour passed until Fred came home along with his partner, Michael Durfee. Fred seemed cool as a cucumber and went right into their bedroom and fished out his second gun, a .38 caliber revolver which he handed to Durfee. Durfee smelled the gun and checked it out before pronouncing that it clearly had not been fired recently.

Fred had Laurie come with him and Durfee to I.D. Christine's body in the morgue and stop by the police station while Fred went in alone to confer with another detective. Laurie subsequently said she was amazed at how controlled Fred had been while viewing the bullet-mutilated body of his ex-wife and mother of his children. She marveled at how matter-of-factly he described to her the gag that had been in Christine's mouth and the path of the bullet that pierced her body and then, the soft nose flattened by impact with the tissue and bone, expanding many times its original, entry diameter ripping a huge hole out of Christine's torso. It was a stomach wrenching experience for her, Laurie said later.

The next couple of weeks were spent in morbid and unaccustomed tasks for Laurie such as helping with arrangements to bury Christine, deciding about moving into the Ramsey Street house [something Laurie was against, but gave into Fred on], trying to become an instant mother to two young frightened boys, and continuing to look for a job.

One day while she was working part time at the aerobics gym, two Milwaukee detectives came to see her and asked if she would take a lie detector test. They said they were asking Stu Honeck, Judy Zess, and Fred to do the same thing. She said she'd think about it. Later, Laurie consulted Fred's lawyer and he strongly advised against it on the grounds that the results are often misinterpreted.

Fred took the test because he felt he had to do it and came away from it blown out of the water because they learned about a lot of things he didn't want anybody to know such as his smoking pot in school, hitting Christine, and lying a couple of times on police work.

About this time, Laurie finally got a job she wanted and her life began to straighten out. She was a campus security officer at Marquette University.

Three weeks after Christine's murder, detectives took Fred's .38 Smith and Wesson away from him and ran it through ballistics with the stunning result that it was the murder gun. No one has ever explained the disparity between this finding and the inspection of the gun by Officer Michael Durfee immediately after Christine's killing when Durfee stated the gun had not been fired recently. Of course, somebody might have switched guns during those three weeks.

Six days after that, two Milwaukee officers came

to Marquette and arrested Laurie for the murder of Christine Schultz on the grounds that she had access to the gun and a key to the Ramsey house and hated Christine because of the alimony Fred had to pay her and the secret hold she had over him. It was June 24, 1981.

A hot and muggy September 1, Laurie "Bambi" Bembenek appeared in court for the preliminary hearing to determine if there was enough evidence to charge her with the murder of Christine Schultz.

The scenario laid out by the prosecution painted Bambi as a loose woman who wanted life in the fast lane and saw Christine as an obstacle. The morning of the murder, the prosecution claimed, Bambi put on a green jogging suit and red wig. Entering Christine's house with a key taken from Fred, Bambi tried to scare Christine into moving out of town, but a fight ensued and the gun went off killing Christine.

The case against Bambi consisted of much circumstantial evidence and her attorney, Donald Eisenberg, poked holes in some of it. Sean Schultz had grappled with the masked murderer and said it couldn't have been Bambi. Eisenberg got Durfee to admit that he could not tell if the gun in evidence was the same gun he examined at Schultz's apartment the day of the murder. Durfee also claimed that his police notebook with details from that day had been accidentally thrown away.

However, Eisenberg never asked if Durfee thought that Fred or somebody Fred hired might be the murderer. Bambi said she didn't want Eisenberg to involve Fred and, besides, part of Eisenberg's fee was being paid by Fred. Three years later Wisconsin yanked Eisenberg's license for a conflict of interest in another murder case.

A red wig was found in the plumbing of the apartment building in which Fred and Laurie lived at the time of the murder. Since Laurie was a fitness buff always working out and jogging, the prosecution said she waited until Fred had gone to work, put on the wig and jogging outfit and jogged over to the Ramsey house. Then she slipped in, confronted Christine, and killed her after which Laurie jogged home and pretended to go to bed.

The news media, of course, went ballistic over the story. Here is a sexy Playboy Bunny [a redundancy in the public mind] who is an ex-cop and obsessive woman who is determined to kill to protect and keep her man. A sexy Playboy Bunny who killed so she and her lover could live in the fast lane. It was a classic love triangle and the press just ate it up.

At the trial the manager of the apartment building testified to pulling the wig out of the plumbing drain line. Judy's mother, Frances Zess, got on the stand and rocked Laurie back in her chair by saying that Laurie had said it would pay to have Christine blown away rather than pay all that money to her every month. It happened at a dinner party at her house, she said and others, including her daughter, were present.

Then, Judy got on the stand and collaborated what her mother said. On cross-examination, she contradicted herself first saying she thought Laurie wasn't kidding and, then, saying she thought

Laurie was kidding. Judy also testified that Laurie had asked Tom Gaertner, who Judy had married and was in jail awaiting sentencing for selling drugs, if he knew any hit men she could hire.

Finally, they put Fred on the stand and he did a curious thing. Instead of refusing to testify against his wife, he invoked the Fifth Amendment saying he wouldn't testify until he was granted immunity from prosecution for himself for anything he revealed. The court granted the immunity and Fred gave an emotional description of his life and love with Christine, breaking into tears on the stand to the astonishment of Laurie who remembered his cold-as-ice demeanor at the morgue.

Stu Honeck followed Fred to the stand to relate that Christine had told him several times that she knew Laurie hated her. Later, Sean testified that the murderer couldn't have been Laurie because she always smelled nice and it wasn't a green jogging suit the killer had on like everybody had been saying, it was an olive drab Army jacket.

On October 16, Judge Ralph Fine decided that, while much of the evidence was circumstantial, Christine had been murdered by Fred Schultz's off-duty .38 revolver to which Laurie had access. Further, she had access to a key for the Ramsey house and, of all the other people involved in the case, had a motive. Therefore, he bound her over for trial on the charge of first degree murder of Christine Schultz.

Three weeks later on November 9, she appeared before another judge, Michael Skwierawski to be arraigned, that is, read the charges against her and to make her plea. She and her lawyer, Eisenberg, stood silent in protest of the arraignment so Skwierawski entered into the record that she was pleading innocent to the charge of murder. Ironically, when Skwierawski had been in private practice before being appointed a judge, he had been Tom Gaertner's attorney.

Before the trial began some weeks later, the lawyer decided that Fred and Laurie weren't legally married in Wisconsin. They got married in Illinois, but Wisconsin law said you had to be divorced for at least six months before remarrying and Fred and Christine had not been divorced that long before Fred and Laurie got married. So, they had a quickie ceremony in front of a judge in Eisenberg's office.

On February 23, 1981, Laurie's trial for murder began. It went over much of the same ground covered in the preliminary hearing connecting Laurie with the red wig and green jogging suit. Judy Zess and a group of miscellaneous witnesses testified against Laurie including Fred's former partner, Detective Michael Durfee, whose most amazing revelation, as noted before, was that his log book with the notes he took at the scene of the crime and, later, at Fred and Laurie's apartment had disappeared.

Then, on February 27, Fred was on the witness stand again. He didn't add much to his previous testimony, but at least he didn't cry on the stand. What was added at the very end of the trial were two surprise witnesses: Marilyn Gehrt and Annette Wilson. Gehrt owned a wig shop and testified that

Laurie had bought a red wig from her some time before and Wilson was a security guard at a local shop, The Boston Store, and testified that Laurie had shoplifted a green jogging suit from the store.

Assistant District Attorney Robert Kramer and defense counsel Don Eisenberg spent hours summing up their sides of the case and the jury retired to ponder the guilt or innocence of Lawrencia Bembenek after hearing forty-nine witnesses and looking at 134 pieces of evidence.

On March 9, 1982, the jury came back into the courtroom and none of the jurors looked at Laurie. Eisenberg had a sinking feeling in his stomach because that was a telltale sign of a guilty verdict and he was right. The judge characterized the case as the most circumstantial he had ever seen and the case could have gone either way. Yet, he said he had seen sufficient evidence to judge Laurie guilty. Whereupon, he immediately sentenced her to life in prison at the Wisconsin State Prison at Taycheedah.

A juror claimed they had tried not to convict, but the evidence was too much and five of the women jurors walked into the jury room already convinced of Laurie's guilt. The key issue for most of them was the gun. Laurie had access to the gun that killed Christine.

There was a strong division of public opinion over Laurie's guilt even though the two major newspapers in Milwaukee agreed with and applauded the verdict.

Three appeals followed and were rejected over the next eight years until finally, on July 15, 1990, the slender Bambi squeezed through a basement window at Taycheedah, scaled a seven-foot barb-wired topped fence and fled to Canada with her boyfriend, Dominic Gugliatto, the brother of another inmate.

Popular support for Bambi's run for freedom generated over 12,000 calls to talk radio stations; "Run, Bambi, Run" T-shirts; and, yellow wind-shield cards, "Bambi On Board."

Bambi and Dominic went underground among the orange vinyl booths of the Columbia Grill & Tavern in Thunder Bay, Ontario, Canada, where owner Louis Kebezes couldn't believe his luck in snaring such a beautiful and efficient waitress. As mysterious as it appeared, Kebezes let it alone and so did all the other regulars. It took a tourist to pull the cord.

He called the TV show, "America's Most Wanted," and reported that a woman looking like the missing Bambi waited on him in a Thunder Bay restaurant. That brought Police Detective Ron Arthur into the Columbia to check Jennifer Gazzana's papers. Apparently satisfied, he told Jennifer she "was not the person we want."

Whatever Arthur said, it triggered panic and put Jennifer on the phone immediately. Moments later, a call came back for her and she announced her mother had just died and she had to leave right away for a few days. Hugging a fellow coworker on the way out, she walked out the back door minutes after Detective Arthur had gone.

Quick as she moved, the police moved quicker. As she and Gugliatto threw belongings into their cases and prepared to flee their basement apartment, the police confronted them and announced, "The game is over. We know who you are."

Arrested, Bambi and Dominic fought extradition back to the United States claiming she was framed for the murder. Ultimately, they were returned to custody in the United States.

Meanwhile, on October 14, 1991, Milwaukee County Circuit Court Judge William Haese ordered a new investigation into the case at the urging of private detective Ira Robins and Chesley Ervin, a former Milwaukee County medical examiner. Both men claimed that Bambi was framed and that the bullet that killed Christine Schultz did not come from the gun offered in evidence at Bambi's trial as the murder weapon.

The end finally came December 9, 1992 when Lawrencia made a deal with Circuit Judge Michael J. Skwierawski. She pled no contest to a charge of second degree murder of Christine Schultz and Judge Skwierawski immediately sentenced her to twenty years in prison and released her on the spot for time already served.

Again, not a single media story from the *New York Times* to *USA TODAY* could report the story without saying in the first fifty words that Bambi was an ex-Playboy Bunny. In any case, Lawrencia spurned the entreaties of reporters as she left court and went instead to have a pizza and soft drink dinner with her family and friends. The talk was that she would return to Canada where the people were very sympathetic to her.

Sheldon Zenner, her attorney, thought that was a

good idea and would give her a new life even though he felt, "She'll never be able to get back to a normal life. She is forever tainted by this. It will haunt her forever."

It won't haunt Christine Schultz because she's dead and, at least, Bambi doesn't have to run anymore.

Six

The Mossler Millionaire Murder

Candy was a blond sexpot who used her body when that worked and murder when it didn't.

Born poor as Candace Grace Weatherby in Georgia she figured out very early that, if her family lacked physical assets, she didn't. She found her smoldering sexuality got men to do nice things for her if she played it right.

And she played it right.

Her first important move was to get the hell out of Buchanan, Georgia, where she might end up marrying somebody's idiot son and become a brood mare and drudge. Instead, she got herself to New Orleans and began modeling. She was fifteen at the time.

She made one misstep at the start by letting Norman Johnson talk her into marriage and two kids, Rita and William, before she moved on to bigger things. In 1948, rid of Norman, this Southern Belle with the drop-dead figure made her biggest score marrying Jacques Mossler — a big-bucks Texas operator in banks and oil who moved around in Chicago, Houston, New Orleans, and Miami.

Mossler was twenty-five years older than his new

wife, but she made him feel like a virile young man again. If he had only known.

They had a few enticing, exciting years and, then, they decided to adopt four children, Daniel, Christopher, Eddie, and Martha. The choice was considered somewhat odd because of the business of adopting that many at one time. But this was not the last odd thing to happen in the busy, travel-filled life of the Mosslers.

One time Candy was missing for three days on a car trip she was making alone between Atlanta and Houston and Jacques was alarmed when she failed to arrive on time and even more alarmed when her wrecked car was found without her. A banged-up, barefoot Candy came out of the woods after three days claiming amnesia and recalling nothing about the car wreck.

Then, came another fateful drive with four of her children on the night of June 30, 1964, while she and the family were at their Florida apartment. At one o'clock in the morning she complained of a headache and got all four children into her convertible and went for a drive, leaving Jacques behind. The group drove around until 4:30 a.m. when they returned to the Mossler place and found Jacques dead.

Jacques was more than just dead. He was murdered. Whoever got him smashed his head in and stabbed him thirty-nine times. Their boxer dog was chained up and, according to neighbors, had been barking vigorously for two hours without stopping. For some reason, that didn't prompt the neighbors to call the police although one woman did peek out her door.

Mrs. Peggy Fletcher across the hall heard a loud argument in the Mossler's apartment about two a.m.

Mary Kay Cassidy being
led out of the courtroom
after her testimony.
(JOE AMON)

David Bowers and his
father.   (JOE AMON)

Bonnie McKinley and Ed Hill, Mary Kay's
sister and brother, outside court.   (TONY TYE,
PITTSBURGH POST-GAZETTE)

Lisa Cihaski's flower-covered grave. (WAUSAU HERALD)

Lori Esker, 20, sobs as she is led from the courtroom to the Marathon County jail. (WAUSAU HERALD)

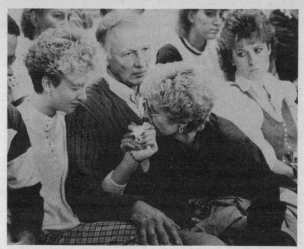

Left to right: murder victim Lisa Cihaski's sister, Tammy; their father, Vilas; their mother, Shirley. (WAUSAU HERALD)

Jennifer Reali (MARY KELLEY, GAZETTE TELEGRAPH)

Carolyn Warmus (PAUL ADAO, NEW YORK POST)

Paul Solomon leaves the Westchester County courthouse after a full day of deliberations in the Warmus trial. (UPI/BETTMANN)

Betty Broderick and her attorney Jack Early listen to Judge Thomas Whelan declare a mistrial. (REUTERS/BETTMANN)

Kim Broderick testifies in the double-murder trial of her mother. (JACK YOHN, SAN DIEGO UNION-TRIBUNE)

Betty Broderick smiles as she is led to a holding cell following her conviction of second-degree murder in the deaths of Daniel T. Broderick and Linda Kolkena Broderick. (DON KOHLBAUER, SAN DIEGO UNION-TRIBUNE)

Death scene at Wicky-Up, Big Tujunga Stream in the San Gabriel Mountains north of Los Angeles, where Michele "Missy" Avila's dead body was found under a log in the water.

Irene Avila holds a photo of her slain daughter. (ROGER W. VARGO, LOS ANGELES DAILY NEWS)

Karen Severson being taken away to start her 15 years-to-life sentence. (BOB HALVORSEN, LOS ANGELES DAILY NEWS)

Laura Doyle, 21, in Glendale Municipal Court (JEFF GOLDWATER, LOS ANGELES DAILY NEWS)

Amy Fisher cries as she listens to her 5-15 year sentence in the shooting of Mary Jo Buttafuoco. (DICK YARWOOD, NEW YORK NEWSDAY)

Amy Fisher (MARY MCLOUGHLIN, NEW YORK POST)

Drew Barrymore stars as Amy Fisher in "The Amy Fisher
Story," an ABC Sunday Night Movie. (AARON RAPPAPORT,
CAPITAL CITIES/ABC, INC.)

Lawrencia "Bambi" Bambenek in court. (AP)

Wisconsin prison escapee Lawrencia Bambenek attends a hearing in Thunder Bay, Ontario, where she filed for refugee status. (AP LaserPhoto)

Candy Mossler
(AP/WIDE WORLD PHOTOS)

Lucille Miller, 42, leaves the
California Institute for Women in
Frontera on parole after serving seven
years of a life term for the murder of
her husband.   (AP/WIDE WORLD
PHOTOS)

Ruth Snyder in the electric chair. (NEW YORK DAILY NEWS PHOTO)

and someone shout, "Don't—don't do that to me," whereupon the dog began his barking. Then she heard a man come out of the Mossler's apartment and walk down the hall.

By the time she peeked out her door, the hall was empty, but she heard someone running on the driveway outside. Other neighbors saw a man and woman drive hurriedly out of the parking lot in a 1959 yellow Dodge. Still no one called the police until a shocked Candy and her children found Jacques's bloody body crumpled on the living room floor between the dark coffee table and the flowered sofa.

Five days later on the fourth of July, the scene shifted from Miami to Houston as the Houston police arrested Melvin Lane Powers, a salesman at a trailer lot bankrolled by Mossler. He was Candy's nephew and sometimes used the Mossler name. What they didn't know at the time was that Melvin was also Candy's lover, but it didn't take them long to find that out. There were some other things they also didn't know and didn't find out for a while. In any case, they charged the twenty-four-year-old Powers with the bludgeoning-and-knifing murder of Jacques Mossler in Miami.

They said Powers flew from Houston to Miami where he got a car, went to the Mossler's apartment and after murdering Jacques, flew back to Houston. The two most telling pieces of evidence against him was his bloody handprint on the kitchen counter in the Miami apartment and a note written by the dead man.

The murder made Candy and her children very rich heirs instantly and, more importantly to her, left her free to openly be with Mel. There was one hitch, however, the note left by Jacques. It seemed to implicate both Mel and Candy in Jacques's death. It read, "If Mel and Candace don't kill me first, I'll kill them."

There was another angle by which Candy was drawn into the crime. Immediately after rushing back to Houston, Candy hocked her jewelry to retain the hottest defense lawyer in Texas, Percy Foreman, to defend the nephew accused of the vicious murder of her husband. It's not the sort of thing innocent, bereaved widows tend to do.

Then came the big surprise. The Florida authorities also indicted Powers for murder as expected and indicted Candy for murder as not expected! The authorities charged that Candy got Powers to murder Jacques Mossler so she could get her hands on both Mossler's seven million dollars in the bank and Powers's body in bed.

The trial began in January, 1966, with Florida Circuit Judge Harvie DuVal presiding. The press couldn't get Powers to talk and couldn't keep Candy from talking. She talked excitedly to anyone who would listen and grandly dismissed the charges as ridiculous in a free country. To complete the unlikely portrait of the bereaved widow, she came to court every day wearing seductive outfits and blowing kisses to everyone in range.

Beyond that, she claimed to know who the real murderer was. All she would reveal was that his name was "Ted" and he didn't want to come forward, naturally, and stand trial. However, said Candy, if things went badly with her trial, Ted would confess and save her. She passed out photos of herself and her children grieving at graveside and gave interviews to any reporter that would treat her story sympathetically.

The trial had everything a desk editor dreamed about in a story: vicious murder; petite, gorgeous, sensual blonde; millions of dollars in inheritance; and, sex — lots of sex not just because Candy radiated sex, but because of reams of evidence about her sexual activities in and out of marriage, in a variety of ways and with a variety of partners including her nephew in various hotels around Houston and even, some whispered, her black chauffeur.

In an exclusive interview with a little-known reporter from the Hearst newspapers, Dr. Joyce Brothers, Candy fingered the killer. Candy didn't name the killer, but she told Dr. Brothers that Jacques was a flaming homosexual who could not or would not perform sexually in bed with her.

Instead, he prowled the low-life districts of whatever city they were in late at night to find a gay lover for the evening. He constantly brought home these sleazy male lovers to Candy's embarrassment.

Candy wouldn't say, but the implication her lawyer, Foreman, let out was that she and the children left the Miami apartment at one a.m. because Jacques had brought home a homosexual lover. He also suggested that, the viciousness of the murder was indicative of a crime of passion. Bashing in Jacques head was enough to kill him — why the thirty-nine stab wounds unless they were from a sadistic, homosexual lover who relished giving pain?

Finally, there was the dog: a powerful boxer who would have protected his master had it not been chained to the door. Clearly, the only one who could chain the dog was Jacques and that meant whoever came into the apartment was not someone he feared.

The prosecutor, Richard Gerstein, had some damning witnesses and evidence. Mossler, he contended, had discovered Powers and Candy having sex and was about to leave her without any money. This forced Candy to improvise a murder plan quickly.

So, said Gerstein, Powers flew to the Miami airport, picked up a car Candy left for him and then drove to the Stuffed Shirt Bar where he got the bartender to give him a giant-sized Coke bottle. Powers then went to the Mossler apartment, was let in by Jacques who chained the dog after which Powers bashed Jacques's brains in with the Coke bottle.

The prosecution had the car with Powers's prints in it and matched the bloody palm print found in the Mosslers' kitchen to Powers. Defense attorney Foreman wisely didn't refute that evidence, but raised the question about *WHEN* those prints had been made. He also charged that the police were shielding the real murderer, an avowed homosexual interior decorator named Fred Weissel who owned a white car.

Then, prosecutor Gerstein produced William Frank Mulvey, a man who had befriended Powers while they were both in prison as Powers awaited trial. Mulvey testified that Candace had originally hired him, Mulvey, to murder Mossler for $7,500, but he didn't do it. Further, while in prison with Mel Powers, he heard Powers bragging about killing Mossler.

Foreman destroyed that testimony by charging Mulvey was willing to say anything the authorities wanted so he could get out of prison. Foreman then produced Mulvey's wife who contradicted what her husband said and, finally, a prison guard who testified that Mulvey and Powers had never been physically close enough for them to have had the conversation Mulvey claimed they had.

He also charged that the police were shielding the real murderer, an avowed homosexual interior decorator named Fred Weissel who owned a white car. When she said she knew who the real murderer was, had Candy said his name was "Ted" or did she say "Fred?"—some people weren't sure.

Then, Percy Foreman cut loose with his favorite strategy. He attacked the victim trying to prove how unworthy he had been and implied the victim *DESERVED* to be murdered. Corny? Yes, but it worked most of the time.

After seven emotion-packed weeks in the courtroom it worked once again on March 6, 1966, when the jury brought back a verdict of not guilty.

Tearfully with gratitude, Candy immediately jumped up, ran over to the jury box and kissed every one of the twelve men who had just saved her from death row. She also thanked them on behalf of her little children waiting at home. Candy was now not only free, but a widow worth millions, but hardly anybody doubted she had been involved with the murder of Jacques Mossler.

Later, Percy Foreman sued Candace for most of his fee of $600,000 for the murder defense. And Candace, the wealthy heiress, disinherited three of her adopted children and heirs, Daniel, Christopher, and Martha, because they had turned into wastrels and bums without proper respect for their mother.

She never married Mel who went on to be a successful and wealthy real estate developer in Texas. Instead, Candy went from lover to lover and finally ended up dead from an overdose of drugs in her suite at the Fountainbleau Hotel in Miami.

Seven
Sultry, Smoky Southern Murder

The South has a mystique unlike that of other regions of the country, characterized by a network of family dynasties of wealthy aristocrats. It permeates all their relationships including those of love, sex, money, and murder.

It is an elite culture that couldn't exist without slavery and, even though on the eve of the American revolution slavery existed in most northern states, it is forever associated with the South.

And, it is one of the great myths of Americana that we fought a great civil war—in fact, the bloodiest war Americans have ever had—over slavery. In fact, the war was, as are most wars, a clash between vastly different religion-dictated lifestyles and beliefs and an economic war fought over business advantages in which the slaves played a symbolic, but not pivotal role.

After the Civil War, those who stayed in the South and became successful went into commerce to produce consumer products the world wanted: the Candlers produced Coca Cola; the Cannons produced towels; and, the Dukes and Reynolds, produced tobacco and aluminum foil.

Both the Dukes and the Reynolds started as small farmers and grew into tobacco giants. The Reynolds of No Business Mountain in the southwest corner of Virginia were descended from Presbyterian Scotch-Irish that fled first the economic depression of the northern counties of Ireland in the early 1700s to religiously tolerant lands of western Pennsylvania and then south along the Blue Ridge Mountains to the cheap and rocky soil of western Virginia and North Carolina.

The founder of the family fortune was Hardin Reynolds who began selling chewing tobacco very successfully throughout the South. The Civil War came and went, but Americans still loved chewing and spitting and Hardin saw to it they had his tobacco with which to do it.

After the Civil War, Hardin freed his slaves and turned most of them into his tenant farmers growing his tobacco. His wife Nancy Jane Cox also gave Hardin his own work force in the form of sixteen children, one of whom would become a giant in the tobacco business, Richard Joshua Reynolds—R.J. Reynolds.

R.J. was an impressive man over six feet tall with a mustache and goatee who went to Emory and Henry College, but pretended to have come from backwoods illiterates rather than the Southern middle class. His travels in several states convinced him that the market for tobacco was limitless in the cities if they could get it to the marketplace effectively. He got his father to back the establishment of new tobacco production in Winston-Salem, North Carolina, which was a rail hub and the biggest city near their home.

The move was a stroke of genius and business boomed as fast as R.J. could bring his various kinfolk in to help him run it. When he first moved to Winston-Salem, R.J. produced 150,000 pounds of tobacco a year. Within a few years they had eighty-seven different brands and were producing six million pounds a year making the Reynolds family one of the richest in the South.

At age fifty-four in 1905 and enormously rich, R.J. married his cousin Mary Katherine, age twenty-five, whom he had been courting many years waiting for her to finish growing up. They quickly produced four children, two of each gender, and, more importantly for the Reynolds family, R.J. went into the cigarette business with the creation of Camel cigarettes in 1913. Within one year, it was the number one brand in America commanding forty percent of the market for cigarettes. Five years later, R.J. died leaving behind a fortune and a tobacco company that produced 100 million pounds of tobacco products a year.

Mary Katherine remarried, but died early—only eleven years after R.J. did. The four children were left one-fourth of the Reynolds estate each when they reached twenty-eight years of age. In the meanwhile, they were technically under the guardianship of their uncle, William Neal Reynolds, whose main interest was race horses and not children. The four children were actually raised as all millionaire heirs and heiress were—by governesses and tutors.

The two daughters lived traditional heiress lives pampered in luxury and travel and each made conventional marriages.

The two boys, Zachary Smith and Richard Joshua, Jr., lived wild, playboy lives as was called for in the Roaring Twenties of F. Scott Fitzgerald's flapper era. And, as the characters in Fitzgerald's novels, the lives of R.J.'s sons and those who shared parts of their lives seemed doomed to tragedy.

For Richard Joshua, "Dick" Jr., excitement and adventure were required so, at age seventeen, he ran away to sea from college and quickly learned he loved the ocean, but not as a common seaman, so, he bought his own freighter. He refurbished it to provide himself with posh quarters and rented the rest out to his father's company to transport tobacco. Since his father had agreed to double every dollar earned over each son's $100,000-a-year allowance, Dick made good money running his luxury freighter.

Beyond that, he had a plane on board so he could indulge one of his favorite pastimes, flying. That inspired him to start his own small airline out of Long Island. He also indulged another love of his, the theater and beautiful women and got a good share of both.

Then, came the accident in 1929. Driving drunk in England, he hit and killed a young man on a motorcycle and ran away from the scene. He was caught quickly and spent seven months in an English prison for manslaughter. He went back to sea for the next few years.

Zachary loved being a rip-roaring playboy using his brother Richard Jr. as a role model. He learned to fly his own airplane, toured Europe, hung around Manhattan's clubs, and dropped out of a genteel, but mediocre Virginia college to pursue "life." He met Anne Cannon on the Virginia college circuit and soon thereafter they were married.

Intermarriage among the Southern aristocracy in the tradition of European royalty was common and one of the storybook romances of the Roaring Twenties was that between tobacco heir, Zachary Smith Reynolds and Anne Cannon. They married in their teens, but the storybook tale had a sour ending.

Anne was nineteen, Zachary was eighteen and it was a match made in Southern heaven. Except that Zachary preferred Manhattan and its steamy clubs and jazz and fast women to a sleepy Southern heaven.

Anne was not to be denied her fun, either. One of the men she dated, Tom Gay Coltrane, a proper twenty-seven-year-old banker from an old-line family who was cut from the same conventional Southern cloth as was Anne. They went to a party April 12, 1930 where everybody got falling-down, blasted drunk. They fit right in and early in the morning Tom brought Anne home and when the sun came up, there was Tom, dead in the neighbor's yard—a victim of bad booze. The death was never explained, but hushed up with typical Southern respect for gentility and discretion and Anne found other men to please her.

A child arrived August, 1930—nine months and one week after they got married—but Zachary wasn't there even though he did send a telegram of congratulations. She divorced Zachary a year later,

164

took $500,000 for the baby and $500,000 for herself and that was it.

The matter of money bothered high-flying Zachary about this time because he was being kept on a close leash with only around $200,000 a year [it varied somewhat from year to year] to get along on. Of course, when he finally made it to age twenty-one, he would come into plenty of Reynolds's money, but in the meantime, he decided to sue everybody and everything in sight demanding more money from the Reynolds trust and estates. His targets included most of his relatives including his in-laws and the Safe Deposit and Trust Company of Baltimore. It didn't work.

Meanwhile, he had been in New York, Baltimore, and Europe as the psychic slave of a sultry female who was the opposite of his sweet Southern belle wife at home. This woman was what fire and brimstone preachers were screaming about when they ranted about sin from the pulpit. She was Libby Holman, smoky sex from across the footlights on the stage and the high-priestess of the blues.

Elspeth "Libby" Holman was a sensual, seductive savvy show business star with bee-sting lips, a luscious figure and a sultry voice created by God to sing blues songs like "Body and Soul." Like the gypsy moth, she exuded a mating scent that brought males from miles around eagerly to circle her sexual flame.

Zachary wanted her from the first minute he saw and heard her in a Baltimore show starring Fred Allen and Clifton Webb in the fall of 1929. He fell insanely in love with her even though she was at first oblivious of him, then amused, and then puzzled by his ardent pursuit. His puppy dog determination in following her all over the world and constantly proposing finally made her consider his pleas seriously.

Zachary, nineteen, had a very close friend from back home, Ab Walker, who was a good 'ole boy who just hung around and helped Smith with whatever he was into. What he wanted to be into more than anything on earth was Libby, but he had a hard time being as witty and bright as the show business celebrities who surrounded her. He also had a hard time competing sexually with Libby's regular lover, Du Pont heiress, Louisa Carpenter, with whom Libby spent a lot of time at Louisa's Long Island home. Libby, in fact, openly complained that men were crude animals and she preferred the softness and sensitivity of a female sexual partner.

It was said that this didn't repulse Zachary or his friend Ab Walker because they both enjoyed sex with each other upon occasion, too, and had since their college days together. Ab was homosexual in his youth, but, in time, he became bisexual as we will see.

In the summers, Zachary rented a home near Louisa's on Long Island and kept dropping by or buzzing the place in his airplane. When the two women went to Europe, he hired private detectives to keep him informed of where they were and he kept showing up.

It was during their times on Long Island that Zachary and Libby finally bedded each other. Libby had not changed her mind about the nature of the male animal, but in a traditional feminine way she also recognized that the theater business was uncertain and she needed something to fall back on. The soon-to-be very rich and naive tobacco heir was a perfect fall-back.

Zachary had come back from an aviation adventure in Europe and a sexual adventure on shipboard with a married novelist, Nancy Hoyt. But, when he landed, Zachary lured Libby to the palatial family estate of Reynolds to impress his power and wealth upon her. All the money gave Libby's eye a new focus on the idea of marriage, but she still didn't accept his now-constant proposals.

The deciding phone call came, ironically, the day after Anne's divorce was granted from Zachary in October, 1931 in Nevada where Anne had been staying at the dude ranch of Cornelius Vanderbilt, Jr.

He was on the phone to Libby adopting the universal and eternally final tactic of unrequited lovers, suicide. He had heard she was having a sexual liaison with another wealthy heir and he told Libby that his life was worthless and meant nothing without her. If she refused to marry him, life wasn't worth living and he would kill himself immediately. Naturally, he lied. He waited and waited before killing himself immediately and five days later, Libby agreed to marry this young man.

He was a minor and it was tacky to get married immediately after the divorce from Anne, so they did it secretly in Monroe, Michigan. Soon after, Libby left on an around the world tour. Alone, Zachary was also on an exciting around-the-world flight filled with adventure, close calls, almost losing a foot, nearly drowning in a Swiss lake, being jailed, catching yellow fever, and being stranded in Afghanistan.

They reconnected in Hong Kong in April, 1932, had another — real — honeymoon unlike the one night they had slept together after they got married. They gambled, danced, smoked opium, and, then, on to a New York engagement where they publicly announced their marriage.

They returned to the Reynolds estate in Winston-Salem, Reynolda, and tried to settle into marriage. It was hard, because her Broadway friends would visit and Libby loved to flirt with the men and women making Zachary uncertain about who would receive her sexual favors that night. And, there were Zachary's "good 'ole boy" friends who hung around as well. This didn't bother Libby because she could flirt with them, too. In fact, some thought there was a sexual thing going on between Ab and Libby.

Then came the big Fourth of July weekend and the pig-picking party that included Zachary's contemporaries from the Winston-Salem area and Libby's friends from the Broadway stage.

The second Mrs. Reynolds reveled in being queen of the great white mansion that dominated six hundred lush acres of North Carolina countryside with its own airport, stables, lake, post office and Presbyterian Church. The king was twenty-year-old Zachary who shared with his brother Dick, a $100 million inheritance built on Camel cigarettes.

The king and queen of tobacco threw a luxurious barbecue or, in North Carolina lingo, a pig-picking on the night of July 5, 1932. It was a huge success with pigs roasted by the score and backwoods white lightning sharing the drinking choices of the evening with champagne. The young Southerners stuffed their stomachs already afloat in liquor, swam in the pool, and played sexual games of flirtation and fulfillment in the woods and in the great house.

The general condition of most participants in the pig-picking that night soon reached drunkenness and, in many cases, typically Southern falling-down drunkenness. Among the victims of the bottle was Libby Holman who was determined to prove herself a regular gal to Zachary's friends. She could drink with the best of them and she proved it with the inevitable result. Late in the evening she gently slipped away from the group to go into the main house.

The celebration among the young women in their long party dresses and the white-jacketed men continued noisily and enthusiastically outside in the hot, humid North Carolina summer night without Libby and, for that matter, without Zachary since he apparently had also gone inside.

Later the gaiety was suddenly punctuated by a sound that instantly stunned the party gaiety. Good old boys in the festive, drinking, singing crowd knew instantly that it was the sound of a shot whipping across the heads of the crowd from within the house. After a moment of breath-stopping silence, several men dropped their drinks and raced toward the great white two-story Reynolds palace.

What they discovered sobered them instantly. The number of male heirs to the Reynolds millions had just been cut in half with Zachary Smith Reynolds sprawled on the cold tiled floor of the sun porch, his brain and his life terminated by the small bullet that made an ugly hole in his skull and splattered blood and brain profusely as head wounds do.

Libby Holman, a bride nine months earlier, had just become an heiress. Four weeks later, Libby Holman also became an indicted murderess.

Libby admitted being with Zachary in the house, but she claimed that the vast amounts of alcohol in her system blurred her brain and all she remembered was Zachary calling her name out loud and a bright flash.

Word was sent to Zachary's brother, Dick, and reached him while he was chained to a tree in Dakar, North Africa in a drastic attempt to cure his D.T.'s from drinking too much whiskey. Freed immediately at the news, he took a motor boat and connected with a ship for Brazil where his trip was delayed by a revolution and he finally arrived a month after Zachary had been buried.

The coroner's hearing was held ten days after the death in the very room where the killing took place with the coffin in the room as was the custom and with Libby appearing as witness and spectator wearing provocative, flimsy gowns. At the beginning of one session she wafted into the room, stood for a long couple of minutes in front of the sun drenched window so that the male members of the coroner's jury could fully enjoy the vision of the ample, silhouetted figure before she sat down. No one objected or commented on this entrance.

The preliminary conclusion that the heir had shot himself was supported by testimony from his best friend, Albert "Ab" Walker. To reinforce the suicide theory, Libby unleashed an explosive revelation — riproaring, party-timing playboy Zachary Smith Reynolds was impotent, he couldn't get an erection. The scandalous news swept through Winston-Salem's high society like a hurricane racing in from the Atlantic coast.

The common theory was that it was easy for a somewhat inexperienced young man like Zachary to make his bedroom conquest of the pliable Anne Cannon, but both he and his penis were intimidated into sexual paralysis by the torrid, sensual Libby Holman.

Why would Libby make this intimate humiliation and reflection on Southern manhood in open court? Because, she went on, whenever Zachary was confronted with his willing and sexually alluring bride and a flaccid penis, he would grab for the revolver he kept in the bedroom and threaten to kill himself.

The male humiliation became a bridge, suggested Libby, to self-loathing and jealous fantasies such as the one Zachary had experienced a few nights before at a drunken party in the Robert E. Lee Hotel when he decided the problem was that Libby found him sexually repulsive.

Then, during the fatal July fifth party, Libby said that Zachary tormented himself with fears that she would run off into the woods with a virile competitor like Ab Walker and lavish her luscious body on him.

There was even a suicide note introduced from Zachary's college days in which he announced killing himself because a girl had rejected him. Still another reason for Zachary committing suicide was suggested by the hearing coroner and would appear ridiculous to a community more tolerant and sophisticated than the Winston-Salem of 1932. However, it was an extremely serious matter there and then and perhaps even eclipsed the scandalous sexual motivation. The coroner said that he knew Zachary had only recently discovered — gasp! horror! shock! — that Libby Holman, his worshipped new bride, was a Jewess originally named Holtzman.

"In addition to being a Jew, Libby was also a Yankee, and a Broadway Yankee at that. Nice Southern girls didn't sing black-rooted blues songs. Libby thus began to appear to the Winston-Salem community as a modern Salome, a designing woman, the epitome of female treachery."

There then were the whispers about Libby carrying on with Ab Walker and going swimming with him in the lake that night around midnight before Zachary was shot.

Talk was that it looked less and less like suicide. There also was a serious problem with the physical evidence. Zachary was shot in the right temple, but was known to be left-handed. Then, the trajectory of the shot made it unlikely that the gun could have been held by the victim.

And, speaking of the gun, where had it been? A suicide victim can hardly hide the gun afterward. Two searches for the weapon right after the shooting found nothing, but four hours later it was found on the floor in plain sight next to where the body had been. How did it get there and who was responsible? So, murder was the conclusion and Libby was the logical suspect.

First of all, she was the main beneficiary so she had the motive. Second, she had been in the house at the same time as Zachary had been. Third, it was said that she was very friendly with Zachary's closest friend, Albert "Ab" Walker and some said they were having an affair.

Thinly below the surface, to Zachary's contemporaries, Libby Holman was a fortune-hunting whore who had invaded and soiled Southern white manhood. Besides which, she would get all that damn money if something wasn't done. It wasn't right in the merchant minds of both the Reynolds and Cannon families. So, something was done.

August 4, 1932, the new heiress was indicted for murder by the county grand jury along with Ab Walker.

They laid hands on Ab right away and put him in jail without a chance at bail. However, hospitality is hospitality and his meals were catered by the Robert E. Lee Hotel.

Libby was trickier to get hold of because she was street-smart enough to get out of town after the coroner's hearing and was in her hometown of Cincinnati. Here she was in a quandary. She was the heir to millions of dollars that her in-laws wanted to cheat her out of. However, she couldn't get any of that money unless she returned to Winston-Salem and beat the murder rap.

Her father hired a tough Winston-Salem lawyer, Benet Polikoff, to defend her and her show business friends hired the famous underworld lawyer, Sam Leibowitz of New York, to help out, too.

Libby Holman was famous and had been feted and celebrated in cities around the world, but never had she had a reception such as she got in Winston-Salem as an alleged murderess. She was dressed from head to toe in black including a heavily veiled face and driven in a big car that was part of a long motorcade of police and others through the streets lined with thousands of silent spectators to the courthouse to surrender. She and Ab were soon released on bail and a few days later, the trial began—and so did a tough quandary for Libby and her opponents in the heir war, the very private, secluded Reynolds family.

The quandary for the Reynolds family was that it hated all this scandalous publicity. They had already gotten a much unwanted dose of it when R.J. "Dick" Jr. had been convicted of manslaughter and spent hard time in the slammer in England. Then, of course, was Zachary's shameless running around and libertine lifestyle while he was married to the very Southern Anne Cannon. Now, the suicide or murder involving Zachary's best friend and a New York Jewish theater Jezabel. It was more than a person could stand. But, it wasn't over.

Libby's attorney, wanting to establish that Libby loved her husband and was incapable of murdering him, wanted to reveal to the court the secret that Libby was pregnant. This would arouse sympathy and put the marriage in a more acceptable light. It would also cool the in-laws anger and determination to push for conviction and deny Libby all that money.

The only problem, of course, was the contradiction. Libby originally testified that Zachary's death was suicide caused by his humiliation over his impotence. Now, Libby's argument for her being incapable of killing him was that she was pregnant. If

174

Zachary was impotent, who was the father of Libby's child?

Well, as usual, pragmatism won out over logic and the announcement of her pregnancy was made in court and set off another wave of cluck-clucking over back fences in staid Winston-Salem. In the Reynolds family it aroused more than a cluck-cluck. It triggered heightened panic at more family scandal being dragged out in public. If there was a trial, more would surely come out. If Zachary couldn't be the father, who was? And, what about Zachary's fathering Anne Cannon's child or did he? It was a red-faced social mess and public embarrassment and would continue to be unless something was done! And, of course, something *WAS* done.

Dick had returned by this time and he cast his vote that the trial should be stopped and the affair hushed up as quickly as possible. He certainly knew what it was to go through bad press.

A letter was sent to the judge and the prosecutor on October 10, almost a year after Zachary and Libby's wedding day, by William Neal Reynolds. The Reynolds spokesman said that the family didn't believe Zachary committed suicide, but it also wasn't convinced he was actually murdered. So, the Reynolds family would be happy if the matter was dropped [and all the public humiliation disappeared].

This being Winston-Salem and being 1932 and the Reynolds' being the Reynolds', the case was dropped and the whole tragedy quietly allowed to close.

Wrong. The heir war was not over; it was just shifting troops and tactics.

175

One of the reasons that Libby married Zachary and returned voluntarily to Winston-Salem under the threat of a murder trial was all that money. Something like $30 million in a day when a million was real money. But that wasn't what the dead Zachary had in his mind or in his will. In his will, now made public, Anne Cannon and their daughter got $50,000 each — peanuts. Zachary's two sisters and brother got all the rest split three ways. And, sensual, luscious, brave, savvy, talented, beautiful little Libby? Zip, nothing, zero, nada, goose-egg.

Libby immediately announced she was suing to break the will and on January 10, 1933, she had a new ally in the suit, Christopher Smith Reynolds, the son of the dead Zachary who only weighed two pounds eleven ounces, but was to be a very powerful influence in coming events.

Meanwhile, Dick was having court and publicity troubles of his own again when Johanna Rischke sued him on some ridiculous fraud charge. She claimed that Dick had fraudulently convinced her to move from Europe to America for her career. Rather than fight it, the family settled out of court for $140,000.

Of course, when there is big money, everybody wants to join the party and get a piece of the action. And, each one is sure that he is the only deserving of the heirs involved in the war for the money.

The gladiators for the Reynolds family were Zachary's two sisters and brother Dick. These three wanted the entire estate for the three of them. Then, the Cannons did something that really angered the Reynolds.

Anne Cannon decided that the $500,000 each to her and her daughter, little Anne, settled on them at the divorce was not enough.

And, there was the Cabarrus Bank and Trust Company of Concord, the financial guardian of little Anne. They jumped in claiming little Anne was a minor and her mother couldn't legally throw her rights away to her father's fortune. So, the bank claimed *ALL* of Zachary's money in the name of his daughter. The Cabarrus Bank was run by Anne Cannon's uncle and this suit split Anne's father and uncle into two such bitter camps that the two brothers didn't talk with each again for years.

Libby Holman stayed in New York City with her infant son and let the Cannons and Reynolds fight it all out.

Finally, everybody realized that what they were doing only made the lawyers rich and they began to talk settlement. At that point, Libby's representatives rejoined the fun. It took three years, but everybody got a pretty good piece of the $30 million pie in the end.

The two children of Zachary's [everybody had stopped mentioning impotence for some reason] got $15.5 million between them with little Anne getting $8.5 million and Christopher getting $7 million. Libby got $750,000 for her nine months marriage and custody of Christopher and his $7 million. The rest of the $30 million went to Zachary's two sisters and brother with the understanding that they would give it to charity which they did.

With Zachary gone and his sisters away from Winston-Salem living their own lives, Dick decided the time had come for him to settle down and take charge of things. On Christmas day of 1932, Dick dutifully got engaged to a genuine hometown Southern belle, Elizabeth Dillard. They married a few months later and moved into the family mansion where Zachary had been killed, Reynolda.

Dick behaved with uncharacteristic dedication and seriousness for the next thirteen years to the point that the citizens of Winston-Salem even elected him mayor in 1941. Soon after, World War II came and he went to sea with the Navy in the Pacific.

When he came back, he was his old self again: in love with the sea. He gave Elizabeth $11 million for a divorce, turned the business over to assistants and started the Manhattan-theater-woman circuit again. He married an actress and that lasted for six years when she announced she was leaving him for the notorious Nicaraguan diplomat and lover, Porfirio Rubirosa. Even though she was leaving him, Dick gave her $2 million.

Undaunted, Dick married a third time one day later to a Long Island society woman, Muriel Marston Greenough, only to have this one go sour, too. He gave Muriel $1 million to leave and she happily accepted it and then came back with her lawyer demanding $6 million more. This was too much even for Dick and a long, long court battle followed with Muriel finishing with the short end. All she finally got was $5,000-a-month alimony.

Obviously, the aging and sick heir of R.J. Reynolds, Sr. liked the idea of marriage and assumed that he just hadn't found the right woman yet. So, he gave it another shot. This time he married Annemarie Schmitt, a doctor of philosophy twenty-four years younger than him, on board a cruise ship in the South China Sea.

Dick Reynolds only lived three years more, ironically dying in 1964 from chronic emphysema. The very day Dick died, Annemarie bore him a daughter.

On Zachary's side of the family, Libby Holman went back on the stage, but never blazed as brightly again. When she was thirty-three in 1939 she married an actor eleven years younger, Ralph Holmes, who died six years later of a drug overdose.

Christopher, the son of Zachary and Libby, did well at a fine Vermont prep school, Putney, and decided to scale Mt. Whitney with a friend. The young men were never heard of again and, are probably locked frozen for an eternity in one of Mt. Whitney's glaciers.

Libby had a deep affair with actor Montgomery Clift who was heavy into the gay life and drugs. After he died of an overdose, she married an artist in 1962, Lou Shanker. She committed suicide eleven years later at age sixty-seven.

Anne Cannon ran away from her money to become a quiet, happily married social worker in Philadelphia and little Anne, Zachary's other child, married the son of her horse riding teacher.

Eight
Lucille Miller Wanted Her Man

Only two things stood in the way of Lucille Miller's happiness: her husband and her lover's wife.

On the night of October 8, 1964, the resident of a lonely San Bernardino, California house near the highway to Newport Beach answered the insistent knocking and yelling at the front door and found a distraught, petite brunette in her early thirties.

Within minutes, the San Bernardino police arrived and their swirling red lights illuminated the charred remains of the Miller family Volkswagen Bug and the burnt cinder that had been Dr. Gordon E. "Cork" Miller, Lucille's husband.

As Lucille tearfully explained, she and her thirty-nine-year-old dentist husband had been driving when the car suddenly burst into flames. Barely escaping with her life, she leapt from the blazing vehicle and ran for help. Her husband, who hadn't been feeling well, had taken some relaxant pills, she said, and seemed unable to get out of the car.

From the very beginning, investigators decided Lucille's story didn't wash. The first clue jumped up at them on the scene of the tragedy. In the back seat of the burned-out VW was an empty gasoline can. Lucille tried to explain it away by saying they carried the can in case of emergency, but something else the detectives found nearby destroyed that innocent explanation.

Just beyond the berm of the highway, they came upon a partly burned four-foot-long weed stalk common to the fields of that part of the inland empire of southern California. It seemed obvious that Lucille had emptied the contents of the gas can over the car in which her husband was passed out from sedatives and used the stalk wrenched from the field as a giant match to ignite the car from a safe distance.

They had the body and the means, but it took some time to develop the motive which was considered essential to get a conviction. Actually, the motive did not so much develop as come forward and reveal itself.

As detectives probed the Millers' private lives in search of a reason for the murder of Dr. Miller, someone else watched police progress. Being a wealthy attorney, Arthwell D. Hayton, tapped into courthouse connections to keep informed of the Miller case. As the sniffing by the detectives moved closer and closer, Hayton got more and more anxious.

To Hayton, Lucille regularly had been a hot roll in the hay, but an enormous pain in the kazoo with her interminable phone calls. Yes, Lucille had performed well for Hayton in two different beds, but that didn't mean he planned to marry her.

In the first bed where Lucille performed admirably, she pleased him sexually better than any woman in a long time and, certainly, better than his dowdy, ailing wife.

The second bed in which Lucille performed admirably contained Arthwell's sick wife, Elaine. Lucille cared for Elaine while Arthwell amused himself with another woman on Catalina Island off the coast of southern California. "Nurse" Lucille doped Elaine up with heavy dosages of Seconal and, when the woman lapsed into helplessness, Lucille finished the job with a pillow pressed hard against her face.

No question about it, Lucille had been pleasurable and useful, but obsessed with the idea that Arthwell should marry her. Arthwell didn't have that in mind and became nervous as the investigators came closer to uncovering their affair.

In the end, Hayton panicked and confessed the affair to the police while insisting Lucille's subsequent obsession alienated his feelings for her. What happened after that, to his wife and her husband, flowed from the insane obsession of a possessed woman and he had nothing to do with it, Arthwell claimed.

Lucille Miller, judged guilty of the murder of her husband Gordon, was sentenced to life in prison and, in the never-never land of our legal system, released to the streets seven years later.

Nine
The Dumbbell Murder

Ruth Snyder was one of the most amazing love murderers in the history of America. Not just because of what she was and what she did, but because of what she wasn't.

She was not, for example, some vulnerable, petite baby doll seductress. Ruth Snyder was a frumpy, peroxide blond dominatrix who loved sex with her lover, Henry Judd Gray, but not with her husband. In fact, Ruth constantly dwelt on sex with Henry Judd Gray and that surprised people because Henry was a wimpy, nervous little nerd addicted to dapper clothes—a classic mama's boy for whom Ruth played surrogate mother.

It may have been partly Ruth's domineering nature that brought the mama's boy out in men because even her husband, Albert Snyder, called her "Momsie." Albert, an art editor for the magazine *Motor Boating*, lived in total ignorance of Momsie's torrid affair with Henry. In time, however, Momsie decided she must possess Henry openly and even more frequently than she had been and this required getting rid of his wife and her Albert.

The night Ruth selected for getting rid of Albert was March 19, 1927, and she wisely ordered Henry to lace up his courage with whiskey and then come to the Queens, New York home she shared with Albert after midnight when she and Albert had retired.

Slipping quietly downstairs after Albert had drifted into sleep, the lightly clad Ruth let in her lover and they both tiptoed up the stairs in the darkness of the silent house. Quietly, they opened the door to a large closet at the top of the stairs and moved into that space as Ruth began kissing and undressing Henry. Her forceful love-making required Henry to fondle and caress her on command and then open his pants to her as she dropped her night dress. Passionate, animal lovemaking followed with Ruth commanding and demanding and Henry complying and obeying until they both lay sensually drained on the floor of the large closet.

Soon, her strength and obsessive determination returned and Ruth rose, dressed and handed Henry a heavy lead sash weight used in those days to raise and lower windows. Opening the door carefully, they stealthily moved to the bedroom where Albert was asleep.

At Ruth's direction, the uncertain Henry hit the sleeping Albert on the head with the lead weight. Ineptly delivered, the blow failed to incapacitate Albert, but instantly aroused him to defend himself. He grabbed at Henry and the two struggled and Albert screamed at his loving wife, "Momsie, Momsie—for God's sake, help!"

Momsie helped all right. She leapt forward, wrenched the sash weight from the bumbling Henry's

184

hand and smashed repeatedly onto her husband's skull until it was crushed into a bloody mess that splattered on all three of them.

The police didn't accept Ruth's tale of burglars invading the house and continued to question her closely until she suddenly collapsed and confessed all, implicating Henry as the instigator. Police arrested Henry and he confessed almost immediately, implicating Ruth as the instigator.

Newspapers plastered the lurid details of the affair and botched murder all over their front pages for days with Broadway columnist Damon Runyon labelling the killing, "The Dumbbell Murder."

The jury returned a guilty verdict and the judge sent the two to Sing-Sing in Ossining, New York, to await execution in the electric chair. Public attention continued on the two — particularly Ruth — with newspapers serializing their biographies and 164 men proposing marriage to Ruth because they longed for her dominance.

On January 12, 1928, a whiney and terrified Henry Judd Gray had the electrodes attached to his bare arms and legs and moments later 12,000 volts surged through him. Ruth Snyder, stoic and stern, followed and, as the blast of electricity involuntarily thrust her hooded body against the restraining straps, a reporter for the *New York Daily News* carefully pulled up his pant leg slightly and remotely triggered the camera attached to his ankle.

This remarkable photo of the instant of Ruth Snyder's death with the caption, "DEAD!" filled the entire front page of the *News* the next day.

Ten
The Ghost in the Garret

The Beverly Hills police broke down the door and found Fred Oesterreich, wealthy apron-maker, sprawled on the floor of his posh living room with three nasty holes in his heart and head.

His wife, a normally stoic woman, was locked in an upstairs closet and was very frightened and upset with apparent good reason. She had been assaulted suddenly and without any warning in the privacy of her home and her husband now lie murdered on the living room floor.

Walburga Oesterreich told the first officers to arrive on the scene that she and her husband had been out and were arguing about a family matter when they came home. Their argument continued as they entered the house and she went upstairs to hang up her coat while her husband, Fred, stayed downstairs to lock up.

Police would later surmise that Fred had unexpectedly encountered a burglar caught inside the house by their return and, in the confrontation between them, had been shot and killed.

Mrs. Oesterreich said that, as she was in her walk-in

closet, she heard yelling and crashing loud noises from downstairs followed by the shot of a gun going off. Startled, she turned to run downstairs and find out what was wrong when somebody slammed her closet door shut in her face and locked it.

She said she had screamed several times and then decided something was terribly wrong and she had better be quiet so as not to attract attention to herself.

In time, she heard the siren of the arriving police who had been summoned by the neighbors and when she thought she heard the police come in the house downstairs, she began screaming for help again.

From the point of view of the police, they had gotten a call from neighbors saying that there had been loud noises and the sound of an argument at the Oesterreich's. Soon, after, the neighbors heard what sounded like shots and decided to call the police.

That was a decision easily made because the city of Beverly Hills encouraged its residents to call the police immediately at the sign of unexplained noises or strangers in the community. The police patrols the city frequently and it is virtually impossible for someone to go for a walk in the city's residential areas after dark without being challenged for identification and an explanation of one's presence within five minutes. That's the way the residents have it and that's the way most of them want it.

So, once the police were summoned to investigate the noisy goings-on at the Oesterreichs, the police were there within minutes.

One officer promptly went around to the back of the house while his partner went to the front door and rang the bell. When nobody answered, the second officer tried the door and, finding it unlocked, cautiously entered with gun drawn.

The first thing he saw in the elegantly furnished living room was the body of Fred Oesterreich lying on the floor. He could see one bullet hole in the back of the fallen man's head and didn't need, therefore, to check if he was still alive. Bullets to the back of the head, most police know, mean the victim is very dead.

Gun still drawn and now very much on the alert for fear the gunman might still be in the house, the officer skirted the body and moved to the back of the house. Going through another room and the kitchen, he opened the back door and let his partner in with a quick appraisal of the situation.

Surveying the death scene, the officers saw that the room was obviously the site of a terrific life-and-death struggle that Fred Oesterreich had tragically lost. The room was in total disarray with the rugs jammed up in a bunch against the furniture, a table covering ripped off and furniture overturned. A chair lay across the dead man's body and the French door leading outside was open with the screen ajar.

Then, came the scream from upstairs which jarred the officers who were already edgy. The open French door suggested that their killer had escaped, but they knew better than to assume that and the screaming for help from upstairs was unnerving. In spite of that, they went up the stairs and found the source of the pleas for help coming from behind a locked closet door. The key, curiously, was lying on the floor in front of the door.

After exchanging identification messages through the door so as to calm the screaming woman and to assure the police who she was, one of the officers opened the door and rescued the near-hysterical, sobbing Mrs. Oesterreich.

Calming her down as best they could while breaking the terrible news of her husband's death, one of the men stayed with her while the other officer called the station to report and call for homicide detectives.

Soon the detectives arrived and began their investigation and so did the legendary police chief of Beverly Hills, Clinton H. Anderson, who always took a very personal interest in serious cases happening in his jurisdiction. He was police chief of Beverly Hills for over thirty years and one of the keys to his longevity was his personal interest in whatever serious happened to any of the residents of his small, jewellike city.

The new widow had regained sufficient composure to take the detectives on a careful search of the house and she confirmed that everything of value seemed to be where it was supposed to be. The only significant property missing, she said, was her husband's wristwatch. This valuable diamond-studded watch had apparently been pulled off his wrist by his killers before they escaped.

There were some things about this case that troubled Chief Anderson, but being a successful cop in a upscale town like Beverly Hills requires a lot of tact and good public relations. Even millionaires are subject to attitudes and problems and he learned to be ginger in his dealings with them. So, he publicly and quickly charged the case off to murder by a burglar and urged the citizens to be double sure they locked up carefully at night while his men vowed to increase their surveillance and patrols.

Beverly Hills or not, however, Anderson was still a savvy cop and he instructed his detectives to keep the case open because of the things that left him and them uncomfortable.

In the first place, most burglars don't carry guns. They don't want to introduce a gun into the burglary situation precisely for the reason of what happened to Fred Oesterreich. Better to be caught in a simple burglary than to go to the California gas chamber for something that got out of hand and turned into murder.

Secondly, Fred Oesterreich was shot three times at close range: twice in the chest near his heart and once in the back of the head. The slugs the coroner pulled out of him was from a .25 caliber automatic. From experience, the detectives knew that the .25 caliber automatic is not normally the kind of gun a man uses. Normally, a man uses a bigger bore gun like a .38 caliber or even a .45 caliber.

Mafia hit men traditionally use a .22 caliber, but they don't get into a physical fight with their victims and they don't confront them in their living rooms. They normally come up to their victims when they are sitting down and put one slug in the back of the head. Clean, simple with no complications. This was obviously no professional hit.

The mess in the living room also conveyed the scenario of a confrontation followed by a physical struggle ending in three bullets fired from the back. Yet, that is a scenario hard to visualize, thought the detectives. Would a struggling man hold still so his assailant could carefully shoot him three times in the back and the head?

Beyond that why would the intruder have shot Fred three times? Fred wasn't armed and any one of the three shots would have at least brought him down and put him out of action and, certainly, while there was no way of knowing the sequence of the three shots, the shot to the head killed him. A normal intruder would have simply wanted to get away and to bring down Fred and escape. The only reason for the intruder staying to shoot Fred three times had been a fear for being later identified. So, that's possible, but it still isn't solid.

Finally, there was the evidence from the neighbor who had called the police in the first place. When questioned, she said that she had carefully looked out her window at the Oesterreich house after she had first been attracted by the sound of the loud argument and then alarmed by the three shots. She said that, after the shots had been fired, she saw a man moving around inside the Oesterreich's living room and, then, somebody turned off the porch light, but nobody came out the front door.

Why would a killer pause to turn off the porch light especially when he wasn't going out the front door. It seemed from what the police found at the crime scene that the killer probably left through the French doors. So, why delay his escape by taking the time to turn off the porch light?

Yes, thought Anderson and his detectives, there is definitely something wrong with this picture, but they couldn't find out what it was. However, all of them knew that, just as it was immortalized by Victor Hugo's detective in *Les Miserables*, Inspector M. Javert, patience is the friend of the police man. So, they sat on the case and waited.

Their break came a year after the killing from a cop in the Los Angeles Police Department, Detective Captain Herman Cline. In connection with another investigation, Cline discovered Fred Oesterreich's diamond-studded wrist watch. However, to the authorities' surprise, Cline did not find it where one might expect such as in a pawn shop or in the possession of some criminal.

Instead, he uncovered the watch in the possession of an attorney. He was, in fact, the attorney who was handling the probate settlement of Fred Oesterreich's estate. The attorney explained that he had gotten the watch from Mrs. Walburga Oesterreich which turned police attention to the still grieving widow.

Mrs. Oesterreich, in turn, explained that she had found the watch in another part of the house several months earlier and hadn't said anything about it to the police or anybody else because she didn't think it mattered at that point and she didn't want to drudge up the story of her husband's murder again to be dragged through the same sensationalizing press that had reported it when it happened. It was not an entirely believable explanation, but Anderson and his detectives continued to see what would develop.

Mrs. Oesterreich may have had a point about the publicity because the discovery of the watch did make all the newspapers in the town and stirred up the old case again.

It did something else, however, and that was what Anderson was waiting for like a falcon poised to drop upon his prey.

Two men, unknown to each other but almost at the

same time, came into police headquarters and confessed. No, they didn't confess to the murder of Fred Oesterreich. They each confessed to being hired by Mrs. Oesterreich to dispose of a gun for her! Now, the case was taking a dramatic new twist, but nothing compared to what would happen soon.

The poised and composed Mrs. Oesterreich met the police questioning about the guns with the cool equanimity for which she was known. They were old guns that she and Fred had kept in the house for a long time, but had never made use of and she decided to get rid of them because they made her uncomfortable after Fred had been killed.

That didn't satisfy the police or the District Attorney and they went hunting for the two guns. The one man who said Mrs. Oesterreich hired him said he threw it into the famous La Brea Tar Pits which are literally prehistoric pits filled with tar into which many dinosaurs and prehistoric animals drowned and were preserved for eons until dredged up by modern day scientists. Just as the scientists were successful, so were the police able to fish out one of Mrs. Oesterreich's guns.

The second gun was buried by the second man under a rose bush in his own garden and that, too, was retrieved by the police. However, both guns were badly deteriorated and the police couldn't use them effectively for evidence.

Even so, the authorities felt they had enough reasonable suspicions to arrest Mrs. Oesterreich for murder and put her in jail. She wasn't in the slammer for very long before she posted $50,000 bail and was back on the street.

The D.A.'s investigators, working with the police, tried to break her story and to find additional evidence proving that she had killed her husband, but it was an uphill fight and they never made it. Certainly, one fact that stymied them for a long time was the fact that the first police officers on the scene found her locked up in the upstairs bedroom closet with the key on the hallway floor outside the door.

Frustrated with that reality, the investigators, the police, and the D.A. finally had to admit they couldn't make a case that would stick. After months under suspicion and indictment, Mrs. Oesterrich's murder complaint was dropped.

Patience. Patience. That was the key in this very unusual case where the key would ultimately be obsessive love, but it would be seven years more before Chief Anderson would find that out.

Most of Beverly Hills had forgotten the Oesterreich case, but not Anderson. It came down to his instinct and his knowing that Fred Oesterreich was not murdered by a burglar and most likely murdered by his wife, but not being able to prove it.

Most cops will privately admit that at least half the murder cases that are solved are not solved as a result of police investigations and police work. They are solved by the police simply *BEING THERE* when somebody who knows the guilty truth finally decides to talk. That doesn't mean the role of the police is less important, it just means it is a different one than a lot of people think it is, but the result is still the solution of many crimes.

So it was with this odd case. The police tried and tried, but never actually were able to solve the case.

They were never able to answer the question of the locked closet door, for example. In April 1930, eight years after Fred Oesterreich was shot down in his own living room, a lawyer who used to represent Mrs. Oesterreich, but didn't anymore, contacted the police. He wanted them to meet Otto.

Otto Sanhuber was a meek-looking man of small stature, horn-rimmed glasses, and quiet manner. He was working at the time as a janitor, but that wasn't what he had been doing for years before.

For years before he had been Mrs. Oesterreich's lover right under the nose of her husband—no, actually it was right *OVER* the nose of her husband. For ten years, Otto had been living in the attic, hiding at night and coming down in the daytime after Fred left for work so he and Dolly, as he called Mrs. Oesterreich, could play house.

Otto became what Anderson would later call, "The Ghost in the Garret," many years before in Milwaukee where he had been a mechanic fixing sewing machines in Mr. Oesterreich's apron factory. He and Dolly met and he became friends of the family and, soon, Dolly's lover. Fred didn't catch on right away, but after he did, he ordered Otto to get out of his house, out of his factory, and preferably, out of his town.

Dolly, who by this time, was crazy in love with Otto who was a better lover and more fun than stuffy old Fred, came up with the solution to the lover's problem. She installed Otto in the attic of their Milwaukee house and began their up and down relationship.

The routine seemed to work out all right for Otto and Dolly loved having her lover so convenient and devoted. After Fred left for work, Otto would come down from the garret and play the perfect husband/ lover. He helped with the housework, cleaning, making beds, preparing vegetables for dinner, and making love with Dolly.

In the evening, he would climb back into the attic and spend the evening reading by candlelight and sleeping. Sometimes after Fred had gone to sleep, Dolly would creep up into the attic to be with Otto for a while.

Her obsession with Otto meant that he would live hidden in the attic for years through seven moves between four houses in Milwaukee and three houses in Los Angeles even though he was getting tired of the arrangement by 1918 when they all first moved to Los Angeles and he thought he wanted to cut out and join the Army. Dolly had her man, however, and she was damned if she was going to let him go. And, astonishingly, Fred never knew.

The two lovers repeatedly talked about their unusual arrangement and repeatedly agreed that, at some point, they would probably have to get rid of Fred. Since a divorce under their circumstances would have left them penniless, the solution was clearly something that would make her a widow. Of course, they could have solved the problem by ending their affair, but that wasn't going to work for Dolly who wanted her Otto.

The climax came unexpectedly, but both Otto and Dolly set up the circumstances so that the end was inevitable. The only thing undetermined was the moment. That came the night Dolly and Fred came home arguing vehemently.

Otto, who was the one who owned the two guns,

heard Fred and Dolly come in fighting loudly and, then, there was the sound of a struggle. Alarmed that something was seriously wrong, Otto came downstairs holding one of his guns and witnessed Fred knocking Dolly down.

Suddenly, Fred looked up and saw a man he had suspected was sleeping with his wife ten years before and who he had ordered out of their lives long ago in Milwaukee standing on the stairs. With an incredible sense of betrayal engulfing him as he stood between his faithless wife and her banished lover, Fred Oesterreich must have felt the stake of treachery driven through his heart an instant before Otto pulled the trigger and shot Fred three times.

Quickly improvising a plan now that their long anticipated murder of Fred was done, the two messed up the living room to simulate a struggle and, then, they went upstairs and Otto locked Dolly in the closet. Climbing back into his attic retreat, he remained absolutely silent until long after the police left.

The next morning, Otto and Dolly resumed their unusual romantic lifestyle and, a few months later, he gave Dolly his guns to get rid of, which she did.

Given this amazing story of a love affair that resulted in Fred Oesterreich's murder, the police arrested both Mrs. Oesterreich again and Otto Sanhuber.

Under oath on the witness stand, Otto changed his story and claimed his earlier confession was a lie told to protect Dolly from being accused of doing the shooting. In reality, Otto now said in his new story, Fred *WAS* killed by an intruder. It didn't matter, the jury convicted Otto of manslaughter.

And, that in turn didn't matter.

Otto had been convicted of manslaughter by a jury uncertain whether the killing was premeditated [murder] or spur-of-the-moment action [manslaughter] and it gave Otto the benefit of the doubt. However, the statute of limitations on manslaughter was seven years in California at that time and the jury convicted Otto of manslaughter *EIGHT YEARS* after the crime. Therefore, Otto didn't spend a day in jail after his conviction.

On the other hand, the trial of Dolly Oesterreich was a different matter. She was charged with being an accessory to the murder of her husband with her courtroom defense being handled by the famous celebrity lawyer, Jerry Giesler. He tried to convince the jury that she was merely an innocent witness to Otto's shooting of her husband.

In the end, the jurors were confused and divided and the trial ended in a hung jury. In reviewing his options, the District Attorney threw up his hands and said he really didn't have enough to insure a conviction or to justify a new trial. So, Dolly was set free, too.

Their love affair soured by the murder trials—not by the murder—Dolly spent the rest of her life living in an apartment over the Beverly Hills supermarket she opened and ran. Otto Sanhuber dropped out of sight and has not been heard or seen since.

What is left of the story is one of the strangest love affairs and murders in Beverly Hills history.

Eleven
The Tormented Head Mistress

It was the most singular and prophetic incident in their fourteen years of love, devotion, betrayal, sex, denial and death.

Who would have believed a distinguished cardiologist and the reserved mistress of the most exclusive girls school in America would go on a 1977 TV game show together? Those who knew the egomaniacal Dr. Herman Tarnower—a perennial suck up to the rich and powerful for acceptance—understood he would do it, but Jean Harris—the rigid and frigid mistress of the Madeira School in Virginia? It didn't make sense. In fact, it was the most public demonstration in the tragic history of these two that she had transformed herself from a self-assertive, confident modern woman into an obsequious, deferential slave woman because of this powerful, chauvinistic, ostrichlike male.

So, in a metaphor of their decade-and-a-half together, they dutifully stood together on the now-defunct quiz game, *What's My Line?* as Bennett Cerf and Arlene Francis probed their professions.

The most telling clue that the two spoke was, "I tend rich people's bodies" and "I tend rich people's daughters."

Jean Struven was born into an affluent life in which servants, private schools, and vacation homes on the lake were routine as was having a bigoted, manic-depressive civil engineer father with a hair-trigger temper ready to erupt over the most trivial incident from a burned-out light bulb to a misplaced sock. His Venusian rages cowed everyone in his family and neighborhood. Jean learned early to stick with her mother and to do without question whatever the dominant male in the household demanded.

Along with her two sisters, Jean constantly strove for her father's love and approval and never got it. The groundwork was being laid for the classic kind of love obsessive woman that Carolyn Warmus would also turn into. Ironically, the two Midwestern women, Harris and Warmus, ended up in the same prison on the bank of the Hudson River for the same reason: murder.

As a young woman in Cleveland's Laurel School—the best private school the city had to offer—Jean Struven turned herself inside-out to excel at everything. Classmates recall her even to this day as quite attractive, smart, well-mannered, popular, and always achieving—class or school offices and honors, recognition, and with excellent grades. Jean wanted to be accepted. She wanted her father to notice and appreciate her. He never did, but she never gave up her search to find him and be accepted by him even if he had some other name.

In December, 1966, she found him while she was living in Philadelphia and employed as Director of the Middle School at Springfield. Jean was a forty-three-year-old divorcee, pretty, intelligent with a very modest income of $12,000 a year, and very little experience in the real world of sophisticated professionals.

Her friend Marge Jacobson invited Jean up for a holiday weekend dinner party to the Park Avenue apartment Marge shared with her interior decorator husband. She had a man she wanted Jean to meet—an urbane cardiologist bachelor just perfect for Jean. His name was Dr. Herman Tarnower.

With Herman Tarnower there was one thing people *didn't* agree upon and there was also one thing people *did* agree upon. People didn't agree on his competence as a physician. People did agree that he was a smooth, practiced, devastatingly successful skirt chaser with technique and charm that left his female prey breathless. That is the universal testimony of friend and critic alike, including many of his mistresses.

It is important to some that we note here that we are talking about his technique and manner as a *chaser*, as a *wooer*, as a *suitor*. For women it is the chase that delights and intrigues. For men, it is the *sexual conquest*, the reward for all that effort, the bedding and not the wooing that counts.

The attentive, tender nature of the chase bespeaks love and caring which is what women seek from a relationship—it is particularly what love obsessive women such as Jean Harris *must have* from the relationship. The sex is only what must be endured as part of the bargain for women.

Tarnower's male friends gleefully referred to his sexual physical endowments from what they personally saw in the locker room of Scarsdale's Century

201

Golf Club. Clearly this was a man with an enormous penis, a man who was the envy of his brother males.

Yet, his lovers did not give him high marks in bed even though they acknowledged the size of his instrument was intimidating. One ex-mistress referred to Tarnower as "The Elephant" while another claimed that he was large, but not potent and had to be sexually stimulated extensively to perform. She finally gave up, saying that she didn't like working that hard in bed.

So, here was this tall, aging, bald, despotic bachelor doctor sitting next to Jean Harris at a chic Manhattan dinner party courtesy of her good friend Marge.

It was like staking out a tender, naive lamb in the forest as bait for the ruthless, hungry puma. Jean Harris didn't have a chance.

First, he overwhelmed her with his masterful presence of self assurance, wisdom, and artful charm. She was hypnotized. This was followed in the weeks afterward with the occasional note, a gift book, and, then, a letter. Not a mundane letter saying "hello and how are you" from suburban Scarsdale. No, no, no. This was a letter from his safari camp in the wilds of Kenya, "Is there any day you might be in New York in March?" it asked.

You know that there would be a day in March that Jean would be in New York for the beguiling doctor no matter what it took.

The expert pursuer Tarnower picked up the tender and ready morsel Jean at her hotel in a limo and whisked her away to a trendy secluded restaurant to dine on a menu he had ordered days before. Then, it was off to the Pierre for an evening of dancing and drinking Manhattans and whiskey sours before he deposited her back at the Barbizon-Plaza Hotel.

And, it was here that the penultimate skill of Hi Tarnower, the woman tracker, was displayed in all its powerful subtlety. At this point in the game, Tarnower had in his mesmerizing power a woman willing to melt into his arms and reward him with whatever he wanted. But, he did nothing. There was no sophomoric groping, no pressure for sexual intimacy, no demands for further pleasure. He simply bade her an affectionate and respectful goodnight and left.

Of course, the roses came the next day.

The roses were followed by what became a parade of affectionate, caring phone calls. Then, the master stroke. Tarnower proposed that Jean come to Manhattan and, then, his home in Purchase for a happy weekend *with her two sons!* He wooed the woman *and* the mother in the same grand gesture. The man was a virtuoso!

The cascade of dinners, weekend visits, flowers, parties, lunches and love notes drenched Jean in a warmth of amorousness she had only dared dream of before.

> *Darling,*
> *I love you very, very much. How can I tell? — I miss you and want to share so many things with you . . .*
> > *More love,*
> > *Hi*

The ardor culminated a few months after they

had first sat next to each other at Marge's dinner party when Hi proposed marriage and sealed it with an emerald cut diamond ring that Jean later learned was worth $10,000 — almost as much as her annual salary at the Springfield school.

It was a storybook, whirlwind romance with only one discordant denouement. Jean was about to make an incredible mistake that would destroy the fairy tale and at least two lives.

Jean did something that no single woman would do, but many mothers would. A single, childless woman would have pressed for a wedding. Like the successful fly fisher, a wise single woman knows that hooking the trout is only the first step and the game is not over until he is safely gaffed and in the fishing creel.

Instead, caring, thoughtful, logical *mother* Jean Harris said that she *couldn't possibly* marry Hi for a year or more because she didn't want her sons to have to change schools once again.

Like most men of his experience and reputation, Tarnower had already felt the secret twinging of the wedding whim-whams in that enigmatic organ buried deep inside most bachelors. She was giving him an excuse to postpone the wedding while still enjoying all the pleasures — physical and psychic — of having a steady woman around.

Given the moment, he seized it — not in person, smart bachelors never perform romantic surgery in person — with a telephone call to Jean three hours away in Philadelphia. He called and confessed with mock self-deprecation polished on a figurative artisan's wheel that he "couldn't go through with it." He knew he was terrible, but he couldn't control himself. It was something buried deep inside over which he had no control. It had seized him in its not-to-be-denied grip and forced him to renege. Most men know this is bullshit in its most unadulterated state.

However, most men also know that the biggest thing they've got going for them is women's gullibility. Never was that more evident than in the person of Jean Harris. A self-reliant, strong, achieving, independent *MODERN WOMAN* except in affairs of the heart! She had sought the love and acceptance from Hi that her father had denied her and, now like her father, Tarnower had turned on her.

She should have run, but her emotional feet couldn't move as she crumbled into a helpless rag of defeat and despair. Having lost what she dreamed of, Jean Harris suddenly knew she would have to settle for whatever she could get on whatever terms the male tormentor dictated.

A few months later, Jean wrote her letter of surrender:

"I do know that for a little while you were a wonderfully strong, loving, desiring, and desirable male animal and as . . . honest loving female I found every moment with you satisfying and good. . . . As far as never seeing you again . . . I won't let that happen however much you protest. I have to know how you are . . . [It was beautiful] having you love me—even for a such a short time—"

In describing Jean Harris's condition at this point, her biographer and friend, Shana Alexander spoke from the mystic place she shares with Jean since they are both women who grew up at the same

205

time, in the same environment, and molded by the same forces.

"Jean Harris accepted the men's attitudes toward sex and power. . . . Jean tolerated other women in Herman's life because that is what the other wives did . . . and Jean never thought like a mistress, she always thought like a wife. . . . All her life, Jean Harris had been blind to her own worth. She *was* a good teacher, a beautiful woman, a warm, devoted, responsible parent, a dutiful daughter, a staunch friend and a Japanese mistress. But what she wanted most of all was *to be wanted*."

She felt most wanted when she was in Hi's arms in the bedroom of his estate in Purchase even though she would often find other women's lingerie and personal items lying around. She even once found a nightgown of hers smeared with excrement by one of Hi's other women who, along with a terrifyingly mysterious caller, resented Jean's even limited access to the nirvana of Hi's embrace.

Herman Tarnower was the first generation American son of Russian immigrants who worked hard and whose cap-maker father died of a heart attack at fifty-four while Herman was studying under a post-graduate fellowship in Europe. With $5,000 from his father's life insurance, Tarnower began his medical practice in Westchester County, New York, after getting his degree from Syracuse and finishing his World War II service in the Pacific.

He was keenly devoted to every convenience and need of his wealthy Scarsdale clients—always available as a doctor; advisor; and hunting, fishing, golf, or card-playing companion.

He wouldn't go to the movies or take trips out of

town for fear of missing a chance to serve and be available for both the social and medical whims and needs of his rich patients. And, certainly these were the powerful and rich who worked in Manhattan and lived in Scarsdale and whose names as financiers, publishers and the like were household words. Loeb, Lehman, Sulzberger, Rothchild, Knopf, Bronfman, and Schulte were just some of his clientele.

His practice prospered and grew sufficient to create a small Scarsdale Medical Center to the envy of some other physicians among whom he was not highly regarded and who thought his bedside manner and social charm far exceeded his medical knowledge and skill.

As the charming bachelor doctor, Tarnower developed a reputation in Westchester County as a good sportsman, ardent and successful ladies' man, and gourmet host. His dinners were regarded as a treat with excellent wines and cuisine leavened with high octane guests, each of whom was impressed by the other guests and the man who brought them together. He made it a point to focus attention on his guests and was immensely popular with them for doing so.

For years Tarnower had been handing out a one-page, mimeographed sheet to his corpulent coronary patients about how to lose some pounds. The rules were not very complicated: cut out fats, salt, and booze and eat lots of fruits and vegetables.

In April, 1978 the Sunday *New York Times* carried a story about this "new" diet that Dr. Herman Tarnower of Scarsdale had developed which had well-known people losing more than a pound a week without being hungry.

Three months later under the guiding hand of Oscar Dystel at Bantam Books, *The Complete Scarsdale Medical Diet* hit the market, and was number one on the *New York Times* best seller list for thirty-one weeks selling some 711,000 copies and making Herman comfortably rich.

And, he had the trophy women to certify his wealth and success. They were many and varied, but in the final years they essentially came down to Jean Harris and her chief rival, Lynne Tryforos, the doctor's medical assistant and a woman almost twenty years younger than Harris.

Still, it didn't matter or maybe it did. From prison Jean Harris would later write that the happiest days of her life were when she was with Tarnower no matter how outrageous, thoughtless, and cruel he was. She felt that she could gladly have died instead of him and been left with the joy of her memories of him to the last moment.

But, the happiest days of her life were punctuated with vicious, frightening telephone calls from an anonymous tormentor—sometimes male and sometimes female. And, the happiest days of her life were increasingly filled with humiliations—public and private—at the hands of the autocratic physician.

It is a quirk of the human mind—mostly male mind—that some of the most erotic sensations for some involve the degradation of a love object or degradation by a love object. Men of power often need to be demeaned in order to be sexually aroused: whipped, urinated upon, forced to perform humbling acts, or endure the threat of castration.

By the reverse token, men often find the power to transmute a beautiful, desirable woman into a love slave whom they can force to be and do any imaginable sexual act upon command is the ultimate arousal. To a limited extent, the overbearing Tarnower did that to Jean Harris by subjecting her to public embarrassments and humiliations so he could demonstrate to the world that this jewel of a woman was his willing and abject chattel. He broke dates with her, stood her up, withdrew invitations to affairs that everyone knew she had counted on attending with him, and was cruel and rude to her on the phone and in person. Worse of all he flaunted his sexual romps with Lynne Tryforos.

In December, 1976, she accepted the position of Head Mistress of Madeira School across the Potomac River from Washington, D.C. It meant being two-and-a-half hours further from Tarnower and perhaps would make an ultimate break with him easier. It didn't. It just added two-and-a-half hours to her drive. The distance did, however, cut down the number of visits she would make to Tarnower's Purchase home.

To the students and wealthy parents of the prestigious Madeira School for Girls in northern Virginia, she was the impervious iron maiden, demanding the best from her girls and enforcing strict discipline to get it. Madeira was the closest thing to a cloistered nunnery out of the Middle Ages that the spoiled daughters of the Protestant rich would find in the Washington area. It is so private that it has no sign and you can't find it without specific directions.

Begun in 1906 by Lucy Madeira, it occupies 700 acres of very expensive suburban forest in lush northern Virginia. The Eugene Meyer family, of *Washington Post* fame, had been Madeira's patron saint almost from the beginning.

It would have astonished the intimidated student body and parents of Madeira to see the transformation of relatively new Head Mistress Jean Harris in the five-hour drive she took some weekends up I-95 through Maryland, Pennsylvania and New Jersey to the home of Dr. Herman Tarnower.

The ice queen of prep school discipline and high standards turned into the sweet, submissive, lovesick girl who had been Dr. Tarnower's lover for fourteen years. He had uncovered the desperately lonely little girl inside her.

Now, he had discarded her, but wouldn't let her go. He toyed with her and ridiculed her by flaunting other women at her—particularly his work assistant, Lynne Tryforos, who waited on the egotistical doctor literally hand and foot. Lynne was entranced by the eighty-year old doctor and was his nurse, housemaid, lover, assistant, and anything else he wanted whenever he wanted.

Jean Harris, who accompanied him on TV interviews and to important public dinners, remained submissively on the sidelines as, to quote one friend, "a middle-aged geisha." She and Lynne both doted on every crumb of acknowledgement from the tyrannical doctor. Both women knew of the other with one often coming to Tarnower's bed while it was still warm from the other and each discarding lingerie, douches, cosmetics, and other intimate artifacts left behind by the other in

Tarnower's bathroom.

The extent to which Lynne was taking Jean's place was symbolized by an important medical association dinner where Tarnower first agreed to take Jean and, then, changed his mind and decided to take Lynne. This, to Jean was an open announcement to all their mutual friends that she had been dumped after fourteen devoted years. Then, the doctor changed his mind again and decided to take both of them with each seated at a different table while he sat at the head table.

At Madeira, Harris was under pressure as a relatively new head mistress who had the support of only part of the Board of Trustees. Discipline problems mounted among girls yearning to leave the medieval convent for the boys, bars, and booze of swinging Georgetown across the Francis Scott Key Bridge spanning the Potomac River.

And, there were those phone calls that usually came in the middle of the night with sometimes a male voice and sometimes a female voice describing in graphic detail how Hi was fucking Lynne at that very moment in the same bed he had screwed the haughty ice mistress, Jean Harris. The caller told her that she wasn't up to the sexual skills and tricks of the younger Tryforos woman who really knew how to pleasure a man in bed with her body and her mouth. The caller urged Jean to take some sex lessons and learn what to do with her body even though she was a pitiful old crone who ought to die. When Jean wasn't there, the caller would leave a contemptuous message on her answering machine along with a return phone number.

The return phone number was often Lynne Tryforos's home number and, when the outraged and distraught Harris phoned, Tryforos would scream at Jean to stop harassing her. Convinced that Lynne was behind the obscene phone calls, for a time Jean would repeatedly call Tryforos's home number every night at two or three o'clock. Most of the time, the phone rang, but there was no answer which conjured up visions of the naked young woman cavorting in Tarnower's bed as, indeed, she usually was.

The blinding pressure built week after week and month after month fed by Jean Harris's love obsession with Tarnower until it wanted to explode. On Monday, March 10, 1980, it did.

She had written Tarnower a long, whiny letter a few days before recounting her years of love and loyalty and the humiliations she had endured over Lynne and the troubles that beleaguered her at Madeira as she tried to prove herself to doubting trustees. She mailed the letter over the weekend.

Monday, she decided the letter was a mistake. It might force the end of the relationship. As demeaning as it was, it was the only love relationship she had. She called Tarnower several times during the day and he refused her calls until finally she got through and begged him to let her come up that evening. She had to talk with him, she said, and promised she would only stay a little while. Begrudgingly, he allowed it.

In despair, she pulled her car out of the gates at Madeira later that day and headed up the long concrete ribbon of an Interstate 95 shrouded in mist and rain to her destiny. It was just like every other time she had made this trip except this time she was armed with a determination to end the pain in her

212

heart. She was also armed with a .32 caliber Harrington & Richardson Model 732 handgun she had purchased the previous November 20, 1978, at Irving's Gun Shop in the Tyson's Virginia Shopping Mall.

It was after dinner when she pulled into Tarnower's Purchase home and went into the darkened house. Everyone, servants and the master, seemed to be retired for the night.

Entering the house through the garage as usual, she climbed the narrow iron spiral staircase to his bedroom and found Tarnower asleep. Her flipping on the three-way bedside lamp woke the doctor and he began grousing about the lateness of the hour. Jean got up and went to the bathroom where she found a greenish-blue satin negligee and gold slippers hanging. They were Lynne's. This bedroom which had once been an oasis of delight and ecstasy for Jean Harris was now a symbol of her lover's infidelities.

Only two people know exactly what happened next and one of those is dead, but clearly the gun was produced and a struggle ensued. The gun spat out four hot wads of lead from its .32 caliber muzzle and all the arrogance and all the money and all the fame of Herman Tarnower suddenly meant nothing anymore as his life bled out of him on the floor.

In the notorious trial that followed, Jean Harris tried to plead that it was an accident and that she had intended to commit suicide in front of him to punish him for what he had done to her. A jury thought otherwise and the genteel, controlled head mistress was convicted of murder and sentenced to fifteen-years-to-life in Bedford Hills Correctional Facility where she became prisoner #81G98.

Obsessed by her love, Jean Harris set out on a journey in 1980 to confront him and destroy herself. She ended up destroying him and confronting herself.

Jean Harris is one of three notorious love-obsessed women murderers who had been caged in the Bedford Hills Correctional Facility. All three have had television specials done on their cases and each seems to have been peculiarly appropriate to the subject.

Amy Fisher's was a juvenile electronic orgy of record setting proportions in which the television creature outdid itself in childish excess and banality as we will see later in this book. Carolyn Warmus's TV epic was the standard tsk-tsking, head-shaking attempt to draw Nielson ratings while pretending to probe a troubled woman's motivations.

The December 14, 1992, telecast of, *A Question of Justice: The Trial of Jean Harris*, was a documentary written and produced by two distinguished journalists, Cynthia McFadden and Martha Elliott, and has been shown only on the very limited Court TV cable channel. It is a more dignified venue as befits Jean Harris, but it also keeps her story from the minds of the general public which is unfortunate.

Two weeks later in the chilly, fog-enshrouded prison near the Hudson River, inmates hurried about their routines with a warm feeling in their hearts. As Joseph Berger of the *New York Times* characterized the mood:

"There was cheer among many that came from

knowing something glaringly wrong, at least in their minds, had finally been set right.".

The warmth had been ignited by Governor Cuomo's announcement of clemency for Jean Harris that would set her free, if the parole board agreed, within a few days.

"There will be people who say you should have done it sooner," said Mario Cuomo, "People who say you shouldn't have done it at all. People who say it's a great thing. There are no criteria. Everyone will apply their own. I did." The criteria he applied apparently related to her ill-health—she was at the hospital being readied for a quadruple heart bypass when she got the news—and her charity work inside the prison.

The saturnine Governor had rejected Jean Harris's pleas for clemency three times before: in 1986, 1988, and 1990, even though he had been inundated with 25,000 letters supporting mercy for Harris.

These included an appeal from Russell Leggett who felt she had not been given a proper defense at her trial. Instead of pleading that the shooting was an accident, Leggett thought the defense attorneys should have claimed it was an act committed under pressure of an extreme emotional state.

Leggett's view had more than ordinary significance since he was the judge—now retired—who presided over Jean Harris's trial and knew she would have gotten a shorter sentence if the jury had found her guilty of manslaughter instead of murder. The murder sentence was fifteen years to life whereas the manslaughter sentence would have been four to twelve years of which she probably would have served six years inside. At the time of the clemency grant, she had already been imprisoned for eleven years.

"I'm happy that the governor corrected a mistake that Mrs. Harris made in her own defense" was Leggett's reaction to the grant of clemency. "The only person to whom she constituted a threat is long gone."

The praise for the decision echoed from within the walls of Bedford.

"She helped everybody. She loved children. She was a wonderful woman," said the prison warden's secretary.

Among the imprisoned women who had children, Jean Harris was a beloved figure, teaching poor and abused women of all races parenting skills to improve the lot of their children — some of whom had been born behind the concertina wire-topped walls of Bedford.

Mary Bostwick, the children's center coordinator, said the staff was ecstatic at the Governor's clemency benevolence and spoke of Harris's work. "She is an educator at heart and the more you work with children, the more you realize you have to start with the parent."

Every day she would come to the children's center in the prison run by Sister Elaine Roulet for the Catholic charities and would work with the inmates. The women who come there are given the Hobson's choice of giving up their children at birth or keeping them for one year in Bedford before they are farmed out to relatives or foster homes.

These women include a woman and her baby both of whom are dying of AIDS and another who bore her first child as a consequence of being raped at age ten. This woman has borne thirteen more since then.

Up every morning at 5:30, Jean Harris spent two to six hours a day schooling these anxious and frustrated mothers on how to nurture, provide nutrition, and mete out punishment without physically striking the child. In addition, she helped with other work at the center, showing videos and doing administrative chores.

In addition, she visited and chatted with the mentally ill among the inmates once a week as she spent time fixing their hair to raise their self-esteem.

While the State of New York had imprisoned Jean Harris's body in a six by eight foot cell with cot, toilet, sink, and locker, it could not contain her spirit or her mind. She would watch the gulls swooping, soaring, and sailing over the prison beyond its depressingly drab and daunting walls.

"If you don't think you're a prisoner, then maybe you aren't one. The trick is just to keep looking up."

Her other escape was through reading everything and anything she could get her hands on and watching a little television—notably the *MacNeil-Lehrer NewsHour* after she and two other inmates fixed their dinner in a kitchen shared with up to fifty other women. The other two were the real cooks because, if left to her own culinary skills, Harris would eat cereal and toast.

She had frequent contact with friends and supporters, including her two grown sons who spent much time outside circulating petitions for their mother's release. Thirty-eight-year-old Jim Harris

217

has a property management firm on Long Island while his older brother, David, forty-one, is a banker in Connecticut.

In addition, she has been comforted by the thousands of letters of support she has gotten from everywhere. These are more than she can ever answer and many from women telling of similar experiences to her own at the hands of abusive men that they loved. All of them living some variation of the theme characterized by Kenneth L. Woodwind and Elizabeth Ann Leonard of *Newsweek*, that Jean Harris was.

"Engulfed with jealousy when Tarnower, sixty-nine, rejected her for his much younger medical assistant. The public and the press were fascinated by the sudsy pathos of a snobbish, Smith-educated socialite driven to abject self-debasement by a playboy physician who had once promised her marriage. Some saw her as the embodiment of the rejected older woman."

After reading her letters, Jean bundled them up and sent them to her alma mater in Northampton, Massachusetts, where the library takes charge of them. Her wry observation is that the very fancy Smith College hasn't had a lot of alums who are murderers and regards her with some special attention.

In prison, she coped and endured well enough to complete three books about her experiences and thoughts, the first of which was *Stranger In Two Worlds*.

"Prison is a place where good is bad and black is white and decency and truth are held laughable."

Still, Harris quickly concluded that feeling sorry

for oneself made the hard time harder to bear and adopted a positive attitude and determined to spend the time as best she could.

Stranger In Two Worlds earned $100,000 and, typically, she donated the money to set up the Children of Bedford, a foundation that has paid for the education of five other prisoner's children.

Her other books, *They Always Call Us Ladies* tells of her time in Bedford and thoughts on women's prison reforms and *Marking Time: Letters From Jean Harris to Shana Alexander*, a collection of Harris's correspondence with Alexander, the author of one of several books on the case, who became close friends with Harris.

Alexander says of her friend, "Jean's emotional strength is so powerful. She didn't have that in the beginning. She just cried all the time."

January 20, 1993, the three-member commission from the nineteen-member New York State Board of Parole voted to concur with the Governor's act of clemency and released Jean Harris from prison. She had appeared before the three so they could examine her for appropriate remorse and assurances that she would not be a danger to society if released.

Once again she testified for herself as she had done for eight days in 1981 when she told the hushed courtroom that she had driven to Dr. Tarnower's plush estate in Purchase, New York on a dramatic mission of self-destruction.

She said then that she had gone so she could spend a few still minutes with the man she loved before she slipped out to the pond near the house to shoot herself. Instead, the dramatic moment went awry as dramatic moments tend to do. She found the negligee of her hated rival, Lynne Tryforos, in the bedroom which triggered her decision to kill herself right there in the room where Tarnower had made love to both her and Tryforos.

Tarnower, she claimed, tried to stop her and, in the course of the fatal struggle for the gun, was accidentally shot. The jury interpreted what happened as cold-blooded murder by a woman wronged.

Jean Harris is out of her physical prison now so she can retire to her cabin in New Hampshire where friends planted crocuses and tulips every autumn as a symbol of their hope that she would be there the following spring to enjoy them. This spring she will be alone with a dog she is planning to get to keep her company as she thinks of her life and what it might mean.

The answer shouldn't be too hard for a woman schooled in the classics as she is. The story of Jean Harris and many of her love-obsessive sisters is the ancient Greek tale as told by Euripides 2,400 years ago. It is the tale of Medea, the wife of Jason, who sacrificed everything for Jason even to the point of murdering her own brother to help Jason recapture the Golden Fleece.

In the end, Medea herself is betrayed by her lover, Jason, when he abandons her for a younger woman, Glauce. It is a tale oft-told, but rarely learned.

Twelve
Love and Death at Wicky-up

Missy, Laura, Karen, and Eva are characters who appear to have walked right off the pages of a Stephen King horror story. The only difference is that they are real and so is their horror story.

Certainly, their story will be grist for the abnormal psychologist's case study book for years to come.

We are talking about four teenage girls growing up in a lower-middle and working class neighborhood of the north side of the San Fernando Valley in the city of Los Angeles. Three of them, Michele or Missy as she was called, Laura, and Karen, are the closest friends that teenage girls can be as they mature during a hormonally difficult time unsure of whom and what they are.

Missy Avila was a strikingly beautiful girl with blue-green eyes, dark hair, 5'2", 90 pounds with a lovely figure and pleasing smile. Her closest friend was Karen Severson, a 5'2", 200-pound girl who was much less attractive, but who had bonded indivisibly close to Missy. Missy's high school folder awash in adolescent doodlings had significant references to her friendship with Karen.

"Missy & Karen, friends till the end . . . Missy. Energetic, small, young, inpatient. Friend of Karen."

Missy's beauty stirred vehement jealousy among some of the other girls in the intensely competitive arena for the attention of boys. In times of tension and trouble, the bigger, more intimidating Karen stepped between Missy and some of the other girls.

Some thought it was overly protective and others suspected that Karen was securing her own agenda with Missy. "She wanted Missy to herself," Missy's mother would later observe. "She was jealous any time someone else got too close to her."

One boy who knew them both, John Arnold, described the relationship as a variant of love-hate:

"Karen was definitely jealous of Missy. Missy was prettier and she had a lot of friends. Karen was always fighting. She always had to prove something. Missy just had to be herself."

Ryan Augustine also knew them both and saw it as a possessive addition on Karen's part.

"If Karen didn't go anywhere, she didn't want Missy to go anywhere. She didn't want her to have other friends."

Karen's room at home was covered with pictures of Karen and Missy together.

It wasn't all sweetness and light because the boys at San Fernando Mission High School were drawn to Missy and she was friendly and responsive and, perhaps, not discriminate enough. In time drugs came into their crowd and Missy and the rest of the young people were part of it.

Other girls didn't like it that Missy was willing to sit on the boys' laps and kid around with them. They saw her as a threat. Even Karen was hurt by the ease with which Missy mesmerized the boys because, one day, it involved a boy Karen considered hers.

"I walked in the room and saw Missy sitting on his lap. I was a good friend so I didn't really care until she moved in on my territory and then I couldn't handle it."

Arleta and San Fernando, the communities where the activities of Missy, Karen, Laura, and Eve's group centered, lie along the northern rim of the San Fernando Valley section of Los Angeles that is a semi-arid valley with some forty percent of the population of Los Angeles. Hot and desert dry in the summer, it is the butt of many Angelino jokes such as, "The difference between hell and the Valley in the summer is that one place is unbearably hot, sweaty, and uncomfortable and the other place is where some people go when they die."

Known throughout southern California simply as, "The Valley," it spawned the Valley Girl culture of hormonally active, snotty, overly made-up, arrogant teenage girls. Its early days and corruption were also the subject of an award-winning movie, *Chinatown*, starring Faye Dunaway and Jack Nicholson showing how the publisher of the *Los Angeles Times*, General Otis Chandler, and his downtown cronies made a fortune buying up arid Valley acreage and transforming it into lush farmland.

The Valley became a productive agriculture basin created by stealing water from the High Sierra's Owens Valley to the north through a 300-mile steel straw called the Great Aqueduct. Its second rebirth came with its transformation into the quintessential bedroom suburb of post-World War II America, as over a million new residents poured into the orange and walnut groves that were converted to housing tracts by the G.I. Bill.

The richer suburbs were nestled against the Santa Monica Mountains that formed the southern boundary of the Valley and the lower class tracks pushed up against the San Gabriel Mountains forming the northern rim of the Valley. Free running streams are a rarity and along the few that lazily trickle down from the San Gabriels into the Valley, public drives and parks have been created snaking up into the canyons from the Valley floor.

The kids of Missy and Karen's group used to hang out in one of these in Colby Canyon about forty-five minutes from where they all lived in the community of Arleta. It was a pleasant area with grassy meadows and stands of woods with a modest creek running along the bottom. The girls had given it their own code name so strangers would not know about their favorite secluded rendezvous. They called it "Wicky-up."

Their friends would drive up the narrow one-lane road to Wicky-up to drink beer, flirt, play Frisbee, and make love in their cars or out in the shaded park. They parked their cars off the road and crossed a small footbridge to a clearing by the creek.

Although it was littered with the trademarks of their parties, beer cans, cigarette butts and other trash, this was their place—their hideaway—to which they would retreat. They often branded the many aspen trees that surrounded the place with carved announcements of relationships and devotion to each other.

One tree is carved with the romance of Randy and Karen and says " '85 Karen and Randy," while another speaks about another relationship, "Missy + Karen 4 Ever." It didn't work out that way.

After the chubby and emotionally dependent Karen had a tiff with Missy over her sitting on Karen's boyfriend's lap, the two stopped speaking even though they could hardly avoid seeing each other. The boyfriend, Randy Fernandez, had previously gone out with Missy before he and Karen connected and started living together. Ryan Augustine, a longtime friend of the girls, particularly Karen and Laura, described one of the encounters during this tense period.

"I remember a bunch of us were in the park having a couple beers and playing Frisbee. Karen saw Missy pull up in a car and walk over and she got up to meet her halfway.

"They started yelling and Karen slapped Missy a couple times and pushed her around. Then Karen picked up a beer bottle. . . . That's when we broke it up.

"Karen got into fights a lot. She had a bad attitude and a big mouth. A year ago she got into a fight and I had to pull her off some woman. I just think she was jealous of Missy because she was prettier and more popular."

Adolescent jealousy suddenly seemed meaningless on October 4, 1985 when about noon two hikers enjoying a trek up Colby Canyon spotted something in the nearby creek. Going over to inspect more closely, they discovered it was the body of a young girl with chopped off dark hair and held face down in the water by a log over her neck. Since this was part of the Los Angeles National Forest, the Forest Ranger station was notified at 1:10 p.m. and Ranger Bob Libershal soon arrived on the scene and summoned the Los Angeles County Sheriff.

The hikers and the ranger had found the body of a young girl wedged face down in the creek by a rock. Nearby on the sandy shore was clumps of dark hair that seemed to have been chopped off her head.

Within hours, the Los Angeles Sheriff's Department had identified the dead young woman as Michele "Missy" Avila who had been missing from home for three days. The whole school and community were stunned by the murder of this petite, popular girl and the police began the vain search for the killer.

Mystically, Irene Avila, Missy's mother, reported that she had been frantic and depressed about Missy's being gone from the minute of Laura's call which alerted her to Missy's disappearance. Whatever it may mean, Irene said, "I dreamed on the night she disappeared that they found her in a canyon. Somehow I just knew that something terrible had happened."

Backtracking and interviewing Missy's family and friends, they learned that her redheaded girl friend, Laura Doyle, had picked up Missy at her home on October first at 3:30 in the afternoon with both girls laughing and in a good mood. Missy told her mother Irene that they were going to the park and she would call home at eight. Three hours later, Laura telephoned Irene, asking to speak with Missy.

"What are you talking about? She's with you."

"No, I left her at the park."

Laura said she dropped Missy at Branford Park where she was talking with two boys in a blue Camaro while Laura went to get some gas for her car. When she came back, Missy, the boys, and the blue Camaro were gone. This was the story also given to the sheriff's deputies, Melinda Hearne and Bill Patterson, who were investigating the murder, questioning scores of Missy's friends and classmates. Laura was the focus of intense questioning by the sheriff's investigators because she, apparently, was the last person to have seen Missy alive aside from her killers.

A few days after they buried Missy, Irene got a sympathy card from Laura on which Laura had written:

I'm sorry she's gone, but she's not really gone. She's right here with all of us. Irene, you were Missy's mom and you were mine.

Michele's brother, Mark, had a small apartment near his mother's house where he lived with his

227

girlfriend, but after the funeral he was so shaken by what happened that he took off for a week with another man he knew to Hawaii to settle himself down.

That's when Karen and her two-year-old baby, Christine, moved into Mark's apartment and Mark and his girlfriend moved in with his mother to be there to comfort her. In the months to come, there was considerable moving around and Karen would live for a time with Irene Avila, too.

Mark, Karen, Laura, and all the rest of them continued to hang around together and, after Missy's death, they went as a group up to Wicky-up to look at the place and see if they could find any clue as to who murdered her.

Karen played a strong motivator in this because she wanted to find Missy's killer. Soon, she became convinced that her ex-boyfriend, Randy, was the killer and she began to spread that word among their group. Randy and she had lived together in a trailer for a time until shortly before Missy's death when they had a big fight and she had slapped him across the face. He responded by punching back and that's when she ordered him out of the place.

He dropped out of the group and got a job in the nearby community of Reseda as a front end auto repairman. One day a few weeks after Missy was buried, Karen had Mark get on the extension phone while she called Randy at work. She asked if he had heard about Missy and Randy said he hadn't. Then, she told him she had been murdered and kept him on the line trying to get him to admit that he had hated Missy and probably had something to do with her death. He hotly denied it and the conversation ended with Karen hanging up on him.

Several weeks later, a bunch of the gang were hanging around drinking a lot of beer, including Mark, Karen, and some of their other friends. That's when Karen again claimed she was sure that Randy had killed Missy and proposed that they, as an informal posse, capture him and force him to confess.

The plan they hatched was that Karen would go to her father's house with another girl and they would take some of the pool chlorine that he had there. Meanwhile, a group of the boys led by Mark and Victor would take a van and find Randy. When they spotted him, they would scoop him off the street and kidnap him.

When they brought him back, Karen planned to use the chlorine to torture him and make him confess. If that didn't work, she proposed that they should cut off one of his fingers. Fortunately, the boys couldn't find Randy that night and the plot fell apart.

The deputies and Irene Avila spent the next two years searching for a blue Camaro. Whenever Irene located one, she called Laura, who came and helped Irene check it out. Nobody ever found the missing blue Camaro during those two years and there was a good reason for that—there was no blue Camaro. Laura had lied.

"Basically, they've all made fools of me and the police," said Irene Avila in retrospect about Laura and her friends. "I don't know how many times

I've spent days and weeks following bits of information about blue Camaros. They really had us going."

The detectives were just as frustrated. Melinda Hearne expressed their feelings.

"We both held out amazing amounts of hope for this case. Everytime someone gave us even the slightest bit of information, we were off and running until we hit another brick wall. The whole thing hit us pretty hard. It's been on our minds every day since her body was found."

Then, the focus shifted. Laura changed her story after two years of futile investigations. It was late one night that she and Karen Severson came to Irene's door with a serious admission.

The two came into the modest home and sat in the living room grim-faced and told Irene the search for the blue Camaro was a sham and that Laura had not dropped Missy off at Branford Park that fateful day in October. Instead, Laura said that Missy had been using and dealing drugs for a while and she had to meet her supplier secretly. Laura claimed that Missy got her to drive to a church and drop her off to meet this guy whom she owed $500.

When Laura came back later to pick up Missy as scheduled, no one was around. Not wanting to get involved with a drug dealer's vengeance or to tell Irene that her sweet-but-not-so-sweet daughter was into the narcotics scene, Laura made up the blue Camaro yarn. She figured it would protect Irene's feelings and the memory of her best friend Missy, and save them all from problems with violence-happy drug suppliers.

When told the new story, Sgt. Bill Patterson followed his instincts and sensed there was something more to Karen and Laura's story that they weren't telling, but he still didn't have it quite right.

"The stories never fit. We felt they knew something, but didn't think they were involved."

Just as Laura wanted to protect Irene and wanted to shield Missy's memory for those two years, Karen had moved in with Irene to comfort her and keep her from being lonely. Her divorce from her husband and Missy's father, Ernie, had become final just three months before.

The two women cried together and shared memories of the dead Missy who had been so important to both of their lives. In some ways it was also therapeutic for Karen Severson, too, because she took Missy's death particularly hard.

Irene recalled that initially, the day that Missy's water-sodden body with the butchered haircut was fished out of the stream, Karen went hysterical with grief. Karen lapsed into an obsessive reverie over her dead friend.

Friends said that Missy was all she seemed to talk about and think about. Karen visited Missy's grave every few days, leaving notes and letters on her tombstone and plastering pictures of her all over where she lived in the Avila household.

Karen soon enrolled in the Modern Beauty Academy in Panorama City, a community in the center of the Valley with some pretty tough elements in it, including the infamous Blythe Street which is an open all-the-time drug-dealing market. At Modern,

231

Karen was trying to get her life together and learn enough to get a decent job. She struck up a friendship with another student, Sharon Walker.

Sharon knew that there was some trouble in Karen's immediate past life. "When I first met Karen, she told me that her best friend had been murdered. I understood because I lost a friend who committed suicide, so I thought I could help her and we became good friends."

Sharon and Karen would visit Missy's grave several times a week.

"She would cry and cry and tell Missy she loved her and missed her and that it shouldn't have happened to her."

Afterward, they would go back to where Karen lived and listen to audio tapes that Karen and Missy had made together when they were younger girls and before times went bad. At Christmas time, Karen went out to the cemetery and set up a small Christmas tree for Missy to enjoy during the holidays.

"Karen would get hysterical. I felt sorry for her. Once she told me about drinking a beer while standing on Missy's grave. When her car wouldn't start after that she told me that Missy was holding her back. Missy wouldn't let her leave the cemetery."

There were other disturbing things for Walker in connection with Karen and Missy. Karen would talk about how visions of Missy would come to float in her room or Missy would come sit down and they would talk in the night.

And, the threatening phone calls.

Sharon began getting threatening telephone calls from a girl who identified herself as Missy and warning Sharon to stop asking so many questions about Missy. The caller warned that, if she didn't stop all those questions, she [Sharon] would be next.

Nor was Sharon the only one swept up in Karen's grieving rituals. Ryan had known Karen since they were in elementary school and he was part of Karen's coming to terms with Missy's death. She often wanted Ryan to take her up Colby Canyon to party in tribute to the dead Missy.

"There were lots of times when Karen would ask me to take her up to Wicky-up to go drinking. She was always wanting to go up there where they found Missy."

Karen, Laura, and Missy had grown up together, going to the same schools, living in the same neighborhood and sharing the same kind of lives. Missy was the outgoing, popular one while Karen was less attractive, but more aggressive and loud. Laura was more intense and seemed to be a definite love obsessive with boys being the core of her life and the validation of her to the point that she would brand herself as belonging to a current boyfriend by cutting his initials into the palm of her hand with a knife.

August 10, 1988 was a day that traumatized forty-seven-year-old Irene Avila almost as much as the day they found Missy drowned in the creek. The phone rang and a voice on other end announced that Karen and Laura had been arrested for the murder of Missy.

"It was like somebody punched me in the stomach. I was shocked. I walked toward my room and passed out.

"I don't trust anybody anymore. My nerves are so bad. I can't eat. I can't sleep. I haven't even mourned my daughter. I haven't even got to the point where I can completely let go."

The two were arrested on the basis of new information about the slaying that Eve Chirumbolo gave to the police after remaining silent for almost three years. Eva said she had remained mute about the murder for that long because she was afraid something would happen to her if she talked. The reason that she finally came forward was that her eighteen-year-old brother had committed suicide some months before and she finally understood the impact of such a tragedy on Michele's family.

Eva said that she and Karen had driven to Stonehurst Park in the community of Sun Valley where they met Laura and Michele who had driven there from Michele's house. Then, the four of them in the two cars drove up the narrow road to Wicky-up where the murder was committed.

Both Laura and Karen were charged with first degree murder with Karen also being charged with kidnapping, false imprisonment, and being an accessory after the fact to murder. Both pled innocent.

"I trusted Karen so much," said the stunned Irene. "We all trusted her. She was my daughter's best friend. They grew up together. That girl was part of this family. In fact, I think Karen wanted to be part of the family. She wanted to be Missy.

234

She wanted to take her place."

Karen talked frequently about getting vengeance on the monster who killed her best friend and Irene's only daughter.

"Oh, the minute we find this animal who did this to her, I will be sitting right by you in the courtroom."

Her arrest left Laura drawn and pale and totally withdrawn. She spoke little and refused interviews. She was eighteen at the time of Missy's murder and, if convicted of first-degree murder, could be sentenced to twenty-five years to life. She was being held in lieu of posting $1 million in bail while Karen was being held without bail.

Karen's reaction to her arrest was that she was the innocent victim of a conspiracy of silence in which she took part, but felt deeply guilty about.

"I'm being framed for murder. I need a lawyer. I don't know if I should say this, but Laura always said if she got caught she was bringing me down with her.

"I know the details about what happened to Missy, but I'm not going to say. I know who did it, but I can't say."

Karen later expanded on that a little by alleging that there were four girls and three boys involved in Missy's murder and that jealousy over her trying to move in on somebody's boyfriend was the motive. Someone, by implication Laura, was so obsessed with love for a boyfriend that she would murder for it. The stunned Irene was left bewildered by the sudden turn of circumstances.

"She moved in with me, cried with me, and

made me less lonely. Now, it seems like she just wanted to stay one step ahead of me.

"I took her in and treated her like a daughter. What kind of cold-blooded person would live out a lie for three years? She was Missy's best friend."

But, what happened didn't surprise Karen's mother, Paula Severson, who said she understood about her daughter keeping the facts of Missy's murder buried inside herself.

"She has kept this inside her for a long time. I don't know why she kept it inside her. She would never hurt Missy. But she has kept this inside her like a cancer for the last three years."

Karen's behavior even surprised seasoned prosecutor, Deputy District Attorney John Bernardi who said it was normal for somebody who was connected with a crime to obscure their involvement.

"But going to the extent of living with the victim's family and trying to assist them in efforts to locate the murderer, that I don't believe I've seen before. It seems to be very unusual."

For investigators Patterson and Hearne it was the end of a long and frustrating road during which they interviewed scores of people—more than either of them had in the previous five years of investigating murders. Yet, no one talked. That was the eerie thing about the case. A lot of people in that subculture of kids and young people peopled by Karen, Laura, Ryan, John, Randy, and Eva had to know something—some maybe knew everything and, some of the others may have been involved in the killing as Karen's statement suggests. Yet, no one talked for three years.

Deputy District Attorney Bernardi wondered about the code of silence practiced by these young people.

"It's hard for me to believe that over a three-year period, these girls didn't reveal some or all of what occurred to others. They must have kept it a secret because they were afraid of ruining friendships or fearful of reprisals."

In spite of all the adoring worship of Missy since her death, it became clear with the arrest of her alleged murderers that she had not been any goody-two-shoes and that she had probably slept with several of her friends' boyfriends as part of her and her group's credo to party, party, party with drugs, beer, and boys until you drop.

"I didn't know it at the time," a saddened Mrs. Avila looked back, "but Missy was in with some bad people before she died. She trusted people too easily."

She stared at a picture of her family in the living room showing Missy with her three brothers and her sister-in-law.

"I look at that picture of Missy and I can't help but think about how she must have struggled. Karen knew about it all this time. She was right there and didn't help her."

An integral part of the partying ethic was to do all kinds of recreational drugs as available including a generous consumption of beer. Equally important was something that was almost an addictive opiate in this subculture, sex. Everybody had sex. The more sex with the more people, the better.

Yet, it was a subculture that also lived by the

mores of the dominate culture and everybody was judged by the kind of sex party and girlfriend or boyfriend their attractiveness could command on the social market. For girls, in particular, their value as human beings was certified by the kind of dude they could get and hold on to as their guy.

When Missy either actually did have sex with other girls' boyfriends or they thought she did, she was the target of retaliation. The year before she was murdered, for example, she was set upon by several girls and beaten up for sleeping with their boyfriends. Karen claims she knew that Missy was doing it even though Missy wouldn't admit it to other people.

"Missy got beat up because she was sleeping with another girl's boyfriend. She wasn't that innocent."

Missy had invaded Karen's territory, too, and it hurt and angered the pudgy teenager. She and Eva went over to Missy's house in mid-September, 1985 to tell Irene that Missy was playing around with everybody's boyfriends and that she had better stop or there would be more trouble. Irene ordered the two girls out of her house.

Even though Missy had treated her badly, Karen was still deeply linked with her emotionally.

"But no matter how bad she hurt me, I could never kill her. And, truthfully, this is killing me. I didn't do it, I didn't touch Missy, and I'm not going to take the rap for murder."

That apparently was not the attitude of Laura. It was, again, this love obsession that steeled Laura to take revenge on Missy. Laura was very angry with Missy because Laura's boyfriend, Victor Amaya, had left Laura and was having sex with Missy. Laura voiced her threats to kill Missy twice in the weeks preceding the murder and they were made in front of Victor.

After keeping silent for three years, Amaya finally testified in Glendale Municipal Court to those threats which he had originally dismissed as jealous talk. His testimony was the hottest evidence presented on the first of a two-day preliminary hearing for Laura, who is charged with Missy's murder.

He said he had known Missy for five years and been involved romantically with her before he connected with Laura. He had a romance with Laura for nine months and, then, decided to drop her and go back to Missy. Laura discovered what was happening when she walked in on Victor and Missy in Victor's home in Arleta and was almost uncontrollably angry at the betrayal. Forty-five days later, Missy was dead.

Amaya's testimony was attacked by Laura's lawyer, Ellery Sorkin, on the grounds that Victor was a self-serving, unreliable bum who was deep into drugs and alcohol and who had been convicted of felonious assault on his own mother and was now back in jail for violating his parole.

In the nearby community of Pasadena, the Juvenile Court was deciding on August 29 whether or not Laura's co-defendant, Karen Severson, should be tried as an adult or a juvenile since she was sixteen days short of being eighteen at the time of the murder. Mitigating facts for trial as an adult is the fact that she was so close to being eighteen, the horrendous nature of the crime and the fact that, even at age seventeen, Karen was the mother of a two-year-old child.

The tragedy saturated the lives of all the families involved, but the trial may be therapeutic in that it brings down the curtain.

For Irene, "I'm going to feel good that finally my family can get on with their lives. We won't have this hanging over us. I won't have to see my sons and my daughter-in-laws suffer anymore."

And, for Barbara Doyle, the mother of Laura, "It's been a hardship on all of us. But you have to feel what other people are going through. I just wish they understood, too. Like the Avilas, they love their daughter, I love my daughter, too. But no matter if she's found innocent or guilty, there has been a lot lost already."

When the four of them arrived at Wicky-up, Eva, who had been riding with Karen, could see Laura and Missy in the car ahead of them and she could see from the gestures that they seemed to be arguing. Karen told Eva that she and Laura planned to give Missy a good scare that afternoon.

When they parked their cars, Laura and Karen got out of their respective cars and were yelling at each other pretending to be mad at each other. Missy stayed in the car crying and Eva got out gingerly because she didn't understand what was going on, but it seemed like a potentially explosive situation.

After a few minutes Laura and Karen stopped cursing each other and turned on Missy, proclaiming that they weren't really mad at each other, they were really angry with Missy and this seemed to frighten her more and make her cry even more.

Then, Laura ordered Missy, "Let's go for a walk," and grabbed her wrist hauling her out of the car. All four of them walked around a barricade single file and went over the footbridge to Wicky-up with Laura and Karen now cursing the crying Missy and Eva apprehensively tagging along.

Through her tears, Missy said the worst that they could do was just to leave her there and make her walk home. That wasn't what Laura and Karen had in mind.

They forced Missy to sit on a big rock with her back to the stream and Laura and Karen on each side of her while Eva hung back a little distance away. Laura and Karen began shouting the names of boys Missy had had sex with and cursing her out in particular about sleeping with each of their two boyfriends, Randy and Victor.

Things were getting too rough for Eva and she asked Karen for the car keys, saying she would be right back. Karen tossed her the keys and Eva got out of there and back to the cars which were some distance and out of sight from where the three girls were by the creek.

Laura stepped into the running water of the creek and Karen, who was taller and weighed twice as much as Missy, had hold of Missy and pushed her to Laura. At the cars, Eva heard a single scream, but didn't leave the car because she didn't want to know what was going on or to be a part of it.

Then, Laura grabbed Missy by the wrist and pulled her into the water. As the girls struggled

241

with each other, Missy's face was forced down into the shallow stream in about eight inches of water until she passed out from lack of oxygen.

Once Missy was limp, one or two of the girls hauled a log over and put it on top of Missy's neck to hold her in place. Then, they all left Colby Canyon, Karen driving away in her car and Laura in her car with Eva. That's when Laura said to Eva, "We killed Missy," and added that Missy deserved to die for having sex with Laura's boyfriend, Victor.

Laura drove fast and erratically and Eva wanted her to stop and let Eva drive, but Laura wasn't listening. All she could do was speed down the canyon road and repeat that she had killed or they had killed Missy. She occasionally gave a little laugh that Eva would later describe as evil. Once Laura wondered out loud if they had really killed Missy and briefly considered going back to make sure.

Laura was in an exhilarated, vicious mood and Eva was scared. She was scared of what had happened and how she might get dragged into it and scared of what Laura and Karen might do to her. She was grateful when Laura finally brought Eva back to the place which she shared with Karen and her two-year-old child and Eva's boyfriend, John. She was even more grateful that John was home.

Once there, Laura turned on Eva and they got into a fight that spilled over into Eva and John's bedroom. When John came in to break it up, Eva ordered Laura out of the room and, steaming, she left. A few moments later she came back through

242

the door with a butcher knife in her hand still angry. John leapt to the head of the bed, pulled out a hand gun he kept there and spun around to confront Laura.

As he pulled back the hammer and cocked the gun, he ordered, "Drop the knife, bitch."

Laura dropped the knife and retreated out of the place and drove off in her car.

From then on Eva was terrified of talking about what happened that afternoon on Wicky-up because she knew Laura would kill her, too. In fact, the whole thing motivated Eva to dissociate herself from that crowd and, after drifting around the Valley for a few months, she left Los Angeles and moved to Las Vegas for a time.

Family problems and the suicide of her brother brought her back to the Valley and in time to the sheriff's station to tell what she knew about the murder of Michele Avila.

The jury in the Pasadena Superior Court had the case for only four hours on January 30, 1990, before it returned to the courtroom of Judge Jack B. Tso. They returned a verdict of guilty of second-degree murder in the cases of both Laura and Karen.

Prosecutor Deputy District Attorney Tamia Hope had argued that the women had committed first-degree murder, but the jury—while convinced that Laura and Karen murdered Michele "Missy" Avila—weren't sure it was premeditated. One juror said there was no question that the two women murdered Missy, but thought it might have been that they got carried away and didn't know when to stop—that it wasn't planned in advance.

Also, Eva's testimony didn't come across as completely sincere and candid to some of the jurors who felt she was just trying to save her own skin and didn't tell everything that happened at Wickyup that October afternoon.

Irene and her three sons thought that Laura and Karen got off too easily, but Irene was at least glad that the horror was over.

Five weeks later, Laura and Karen stood stoically staring forward before Judge Tso who pronounced their crime a vengeful murder and deserving of the maximum sentence he was allowed to render. He sentenced them to fifteen years to life in prison.

Adults often don't appreciate that adolescents and younger children have the same social characteristics and feelings that grown-ups do and are frustrated in their ways of expressing them. Missy's friends and acquaintances have the same spectrum of feelings as they will have about a similar tragedy should it take place later in their lives. If the young people in Missy's social group were older, they might have held a mass and erected a granite tombstone. They couldn't do that, so they did what they could.

Carved high on one of the aspen trees of Wickyup that mutely stood and watched Missy being murdered by her two life-long best friends is, "We love you Missy."

Thirteen
Not Her Sister's Keeper

So, as far as everybody was concerned, the messy death of John Cassidy, with much of his head blown off by a shotgun blast, was going down as a suicide.

John Cassidy lived in the Pennsylvania town with the jaw-testing Indian name of Monogahela and, for reasons that were not immediately clear, he committed suicide on February 12, 1991, in the home he shared with his wife, Mary Kay, twenty-nine, and near the home he shared with her sister, Bonnie McKinley, thirty-seven. He chose a messy way to go: a single blast of his shotgun to end it all. Everybody in town including the local police thought it was suicide.

Well, actually, not "everybody" thought that. In the process of doing the autopsy, Coroner Jackson got an anonymous telephone call from a woman saying it hadn't been suicide.

When he asked her to identify herself or to come to the coroner's inquest to present her information, she refused. He explained that, without some other proof to the contrary, it looked like suicide to him and that's the way he was going to rule it. The woman hung up and the coroner's inquest was held and the final report established the death of John Cassidy as a suicide.

The coroner's hearing ended with a closing statement by Assistant District Attorney of Washington County Paul Petro, known locally as "The Singing D.A." who began his conclusions by singing an excerpt from "You Always Hurt The One You Love."

One curious twist in the case at this point was that the coroner had been at his job for some forty years and had examined a number of shotgun suicides. The shotgun is a common weapon in mountainous western Pennsylvania of which the Monogahela Valley — or Mon Valley or even simpler "The Valley," as the natives call it — is a part. So, he had, over the years, inspected a lot of shotgun wounds both self-inflicted and inflicted by others.

The shotgun blast that blew out the back of John Cassidy's head was *NOT* consistent with a self-inflicted shotgun wound. The normal self-inflicted shotgun wound to the head was the muzzle of the gun against the side of the head with the damage to the head being from one side to the other.

In John Cassidy's case, the muzzle had been shoved under his chin and against his throat, with the head damage being from lower front to upper back. In this position, it is also harder to reach the trigger than in the usual suicide position at the side.

Nevertheless, there was a predisposition to declare Cassidy's death a suicide because of what happened the previous year and, for that matter, for a number of years leading up to that fatal moment when his life ended.

Monogahela is a community in a region of independent-minded people dating back to the beginning of the United States when western Pennsylvania farmers rebelled against the new U.S. Congress's tax on one of their economic mainstays: whiskey. The tax triggered the Whiskey Rebellion, which was put down by troops under George Washington and marked the only time in our history that an American president ever led American troops against Americans.

Although the Rebellion of 200 years ago was suppressed, the spirit and the spirits that prompted it have not been, and people in the Mon Valley still believe in leaving others alone to live their lives as they will. However, even in this climate, John Cassidy had a lifestyle a bit beyond the ordinary.

He had known the two sisters Bonnie and Mary Kay for a while and had raped both of them when they were teenagers.

In some ways, he probably thought he was making some amends for that when he married the petite, dark-haired Mary Kay after she turned seventeen. But then he, Mary Kay, and Bonnie entered into a novel living arrangement. The three all moved in together and the two sisters simply shared John as their joint husband.

Over the years that followed, John would have five children by Mary Kay and four by Bonnie. In addition, he picked up a spare with an outside woman who wasn't part of this cozy arrangement.

Trying to keep things manageable, after the trio had produced the first children, it was decided that Bonnie and her kids should be set up in a separate house. So when John was at the original house, he was Mary Kay's husband and, when he was at the other house, he was Bonnie Jean's husband.

Complicating matters even more if that's possible, John had developed into a heavy drinker and cocaine freak. This meant he often became unruly, abusing his family, and, alternately, apathetic and in the doldrums. He had wide mood swings between violence and depression.

This was the environment in which John Cassidy became a suicide victim. John C. Pettit, the District Attorney for Washington County, Pennsylvania related the setting.

"What made it easy to go by as a suicide was about a year earlier at least one of the same police officers from Monogahela had responded to a domestic disturbance call and found John Cassidy sitting on the couch of his living room with a shotgun in his lap threatening to commit suicide.

"The officer and his partner disarmed Cassidy and, then, took all the firearms in the house with them. Since that time, they continued to have a number of domestic disturbance calls to the Cassidy house the rest of that year.

"So, when they were called again on this occasion, it seemed to make sense as a suicide."

They buried John Cassidy at a funeral attended by his friends, the two sisters who were his wives, and the ten children he had sired. It was a sad day that many there had known was a long-time coming, but inevitable. However, at least one person left that graveside with a heart colder than the winter wind whistling down Mon Valley.

After the funeral, Bonnie had a bitterness growing and gnawing inside her not understood by most of the other people who had watched them lower her de facto husband into the ground. It was a bitterness which, nurtured by a dark secret and lonely nights ahead, led her to make a deadly decision.

She had made the anonymous phone call to the coroner. When the coroner refused to act on her call, her inner conflict became more troubling. For, were the truth to be known, she would have to expose herself as what many people in their small western Pennsylvania town would regard as a traitor. She would have to betray one of her own blood.

Finally, four weeks after burying her man and her sister's man, Bonnie McKinley drove over to Belle Vernon State Police Barracks along with her brother, Edward Hill, and told Trooper Roy Fuller what had really happened to John Cassidy. Showing the proof of what she was saying, Bonnie fished into her purse and handed Trooper Fuller a small audio tape cassette that she said she had retrieved from John Cassidy's home.

Some time before, John and Bonnie had gone to the local Radio Shack store and bought a telephone tape recorder which he went home and installed on his own telephone line in the basement. He suspected that Mary Kay was cheating on him with a much younger man, David Bowers, and he wanted to hear what she was saying on the telephone from home. Only he and Bonnie knew about it. The tape cassette from this machine was what the four relatives brought to the state police.

This cassette was one of the most explosive bits of nonevidence State Trooper Roy Fuller had ever handled in his years as a Pennsylvania State Trooper and became something very dicey for the authorities by putting them on the horns of a legal dilemma. In Pennsylvania, surreptitiously recorded conversations cannot be used as legal evidence or justification for police action.

Christopher Buckley, local journalist who covered the story, related what happened next.

"What the state police did when they got the tapes was called Mary Kay Cassidy and asked her to come to the state police barracks in Belle Vernon which is about a fifteen or twenty minute ride from Monogahela and the closest state police barracks to where she lived.

"They brought her into the room and asked her to retell her story and she retold the suicide story. Then, they said to her, 'We have a tape. We have a tape.' She, of course, was not aware that John had bought the machine and that he had taped their own telephone line. They told her the tape had a conversation between her and David Bowers.

"She asked to hear a few seconds of the tape, but they wouldn't play it for her right then. Instead, they suggested that she get an attorney, but she kept pressing them to play the tape for her. So, they finally played a few seconds of the tape for her.

"She broke down and told them the whole story. What had occurred that night was that . . . he had threatened her on many occasions, one time putting a knife to her throat and another time he was going to cut off all her hair because she wanted to go to a Christmas party with the people she worked with.

"On the night that she killed him, she came home from the twenty-four-hour convenience store where

250

she worked and he was there and threatened her again. He forced her to drive to the community of Clairton which is a third-class city, about a twenty-five minute drive out of Monogahela toward the city of Pittsburgh.

"Clairton is very run down. It used to have a steel plant there, but it's been boarded up and the place is overrun with crime. Especially since the city no longer has a police department because they couldn't afford it and they have to depend on the already over-extended state police to patrol the city. Drugs, among other things, are pretty rampant down there.

"He forced her to drive him there where he bought some cocaine and then they went back home where he did the cocaine and drank heavily. Before long he passed out on the couch in the living room."

Mary Kay contemplated her life and knew that unless she did something, it would continue the way it had been. Besides she had a new, younger lover who offered her a brighter future. David Bowers was only seventeen, but she saw a renewed chance at happiness with him. That was one of the things they talked and thought about in person, on the phone, and while making love.

She went up into the attic and dug out a shotgun stashed away there and located a shotgun shell and slid it into the chamber. All the while she was rolling over in her mind what she was doing and the consequences of it all for the rest of her life and the lives of her children.

Then, she went downstairs and stood looking at her blacked-out husband, John, as he lay on the couch or sat in the chair [the stories disagree on this specific point]. She had put the butt of the gun on the floor and wedged the muzzle under his chin and against his throat. She was still weighing the right and wrong of what she was doing.

At that moment, John began to stir and that decided it for Mary Kay in an instance. If John woke up and found her about to kill him, he would most likely turn violently on her as it had before, but this time he would murder her.

The decision was made. She clutched at the trigger and pulled it.

Then, she called 911. The rest followed along with what the Monogahela police officers reported and with the coroner's verdict.

It was March 11 that Trooper Roy G. Fuller listened to a piece of the tape and got Mary Kay in for questioning. He said that, while he made reference to the tape, he only played a part of it for her after she insisted on hearing it and after he had recommended that she get a lawyer. When Fuller finally began to play it for her, she listened to only the first ten seconds of it.

"That's enough. You can turn it off."

Then, she took a swig of the soda she had been drinking and, according to Fuller, Mary Kay dropped her head in shame and tears began to creep out of her eyes and she confessed, "Yes." That's when the whole frustration of her life with John and her love for David spilled out.

With what little of the tape they heard and with Mary Kay's statement, the police realized what they had. They had evidence that John Cassidy had been murdered, but much of the evidence they had couldn't be used! Naturally, they called the District Attorney, John C. Pettit. The state police also called in the local Monogahela police because the case was in their jurisdiction.

Pettit told how he became aware of the case.

"They came in, as I said it was both the State Police and the Monogahela City police, and they told me what they knew about the circumstance and asked me to listen to the tape. I did, but only enough to verify that there was the taping of voices and that there was some evidence that it was not a suicide.

"The next step was a search warrant to search Mary Kay's residence. We felt there was probable cause to get a warrant to search Mary Kay's home and, I believe, she even permitted a voluntary search. Then, based on some information that was obtained there, it was used as further probable cause to search David Bowers's residence.

"That search provided us with additional evidence and we ordered the arrest of Mary Kay Cassidy for the first-degree murder of her husband. This was followed by her getting a defense attorney, Ray Amangello, who was experienced in defending murder suspects. A habeas corpus hearing was held in which the defense moved to suppress the evidence, saying that Mary Kay was being held unlawfully on the basis of unlawfully obtained evidence."

So, here was the quandary that often faces prosecutors. He knew that Mary Kay and David were lovers who had plotted to murder John Cassidy. All that had not been specifically settled was the precise moment and method and, when that serendipitously presented itself that night, Mary Kay carried out what had been their premeditated plan. However, the main evidence, as noted, couldn't be used in court.

So, should D.A. Pettit try them both for murder and take the chance of losing and both of them going free? Or, should he try to get them on *SOMETHING* so they would both serve some time and there would be at least partial justice done? It is a decision faced by prosecutors all over America every day. Most of them do what Pettit did—go for half a loaf.

Besides which Mary Kay was upset by the unaccustomed publicity about the murder allegation and her lifestyle with John Cassidy and her relationship with her sister and it was wearing abrasively on both her and her children. In one harrowing instance, a local TV reporter stuck his microphone and face right into hers and demanded, "Mrs. Cassidy, is it true that you blew your husband's brains out?"

Naturally, the relationship between the two sisters and other family members was quite tense because it was Bonnie and the two sisters' brother, Edward Hill who had turned in Mary Kay.

On the other side, from Bonnie's viewpoint, her sister was betraying their joint husband by her love relationship with David and she had no right to kill their joint husband. Just because she wanted to be rid of John and had David as a ready replacement, didn't mean it was okay with Bonnie. At one hearing when Bonnie was asked why she turned in her own sister, she replied, "She didn't have to do it. We could have continued to share him."

In the end, Mary Kay and her attorney agreed to the idea of a plea bargain. What everybody finally agreed on was that Mary Kay would plead guilty to

254

third-degree murder and take a five-to-ten year sentence and would turn state's evidence to testify against David Bowers. She could be out in about two and a half years.

As John C. Pettit explained it:

"So, rather than roll the dice, she pled guilty and gave full statement as to what she and David did. He was not involved in the actual killing, but he was involved in a conspiracy for the solicitation of murder. In Pennsylvania, if you encourage another person to commit murder, that's solicitation to commit murder."

The amorous relationship between David and John's wife, a woman almost twice his age with a husband [or, at least, half a husband] and four children, grew out of the times they were initially thrown together by John and David's hunting outings. However, before long, the platonic turned to the romantic and Mary Kay and David became secret lovers.

Based on Mary Kay's statement, the relationship quickly went from friendship to hugging to kissing and, then, to passion fulfilled at various times and in various places such as while they were out riding or in a motel room or at a friend's house. It was, she insisted, never at the house she shared with John mostly because they both feared his violent wrath.

Now, Mary Kay is in prison. She and her sister and brother are estranged and her children are with their maternal grandfather.

Said reporter Buckley, "When the police got that tape—and it's never been heard publicly—the state police allege that it ties David Bowers, Mary Kay's boyfriend, to the case and that they were allegedly talking about getting rid of Mr. Cassidy."

One curious twist is permitted comment, however. David was still a minor under Pennsylvania law at the time John Cassidy was murdered and, as such, might have gotten a reduced sentence since he didn't actually pull the trigger—Mary Kay did. But, for some incomprehensible strategy, David's lawyer decided to move that he be tried as an adult. Washington County District Attorney John C. Pettit concurred.

For Mary Kay, David became her hope of the future. A pure love without the exploitation and abuse she endured with John. A second chance at life with a man she loved.

That has all changed now. Even in death, John Cassidy has been able to reach out of the grave and smite her dreams of happiness.

Mary Kay was sentenced to prison on May 5, 1992 by Washington County judge John F. Bell after confessing to third-degree murder as part of the plea bargain deal she had worked out. Also, as part of that deal, she testified against David Bowers on April 1 at his preliminary hearing.

She said:

"I was more or less backed into a corner. I didn't have any choice and I'm telling the truth about the situation and what happened because it's the best alternative for myself and my kids. . . . I don't believe I could have gone too long without telling the truth."

Mary Kay's testimony was that teenage David was the one who originally came up with the idea of killing her husband, John, and told her she could murder him in ways that would make it look like suicide. Mary claimed that David's encouragement and support was a big part of her decision to kill John. The third full week in January 1993, the trial of David began on the charge of persuading Mary to kill her husband with Neil J. Marcus as his defense attorney.

At the beginning of the trial a key letter from Mary Kay to David was introduced as evidence:

Hi.

I hope when the time comes I can do what I have and want to do. Taking someone else's life is not up to me but he leaves me no other choice.

I will not put up with his behavior. It will only get worse. Slowly progress [sic] until he will do what he keeps saying he'll do. POW. Everyone around him will die.

I believe when he gets as drunk as he does that something snaps in his brain and no one can stop him. I don't want to wait around to see it when that day comes. It's like living on death row only no one has set the actual day yet. You don't know if it's today tomorrow or days or weeks from now.

I can't live like this anymore. This is not living in my book. I am convinced in my mind that he must be stopped because he will never stop himself. He is that sick. If I do and it's the wrong thing then I guess I will pay the price but if it's not then maybe I can pull my life and my kids lives back together where they should be.

The hurt and pain inside has turned to hate and resentment. I hate the fact that he can control my life and feelings. NO MORE . . .

What in the hell did I do that was so bad that I deserve this?? I know I have made mistakes in my life, but nothing to warrant this.

Everyday my feelings for you grow stronger. I can't get you out of my mind. I feel like a young girl in love. It feels good . . .

Have you ever been in love before?? Be honest.

Not to change the subject but it's 2:40 a.m. and I need sleep. See ya.

At the trial Mary Kay's sister, Bonnie McKinley, told of being the spare wife who started having sex with John in 1980 and having four children by him. She and the children set up a separate household nearby in 1986, but they continued to be lovers. "I was in love with him," said the grim-faced Bonnie at the trial and she described how John suspected Mary Kay was cheating on him and how Bonnie and John went to the Radio Shack store to get a telephone recording machine which they installed on John and Mary Kay's home telephone line.

Bonnie told how she called the coroner after John's death and anonymously tried to alert him that it wasn't suicide and, then, how she finally felt she had to take the tape cassette of David and Mary Kay's plotting to the state troopers.

Attorney Marcus's defense of David was simply that his accuser, Mary Kay, was a convicted liar and murderess and that David, his very religious young client who suffered from a learning disability, had been easily seduced by an older married woman.

For Mary Kay it wasn't that way. To her, apparently,

she and David were very much in love and she saw David as her one true love whose ultimate fulfillment was frustrated only by the existence of her husband, John. She testified at how David had instructed her in the technique of murdering her husband.

"He told me that if I would wait until my husband passed out [from drinking], I could shoot him and make it appear to be suicide. He told me to be certain that I wiped the bullet and the gun so there were no fingerprints, to wear gloves and to position the gun so it would appear to be suicide."

She testified that her relationship with Bowers began innocently in the mid-1980s when he came to her home to go hunting and fishing with her husband. Bowers was twelve years old at the time.

She said she and Bowers got closer when he would stay overnight so he and her husband could get an early start on their fishing and hunting outings. On June 27, 1990, Bowers called her on the phone and professed his love for her. She marked that day on her calendar with a star and continued to put a star on her calendar every day they saw each other from then on.

Mary Kay and David spent their nights together for six consecutive days after she murdered John. One can only wonder how this made Bonnie feel since the man she loved had been murdered by her sister and Bonnie was the only one who knew how to prove it with the secret tape.

On Saturday, January 23, 1993, the jury of six men and six women voted on the guilt or innocence of David Bowers for the second time in two hours. The verdict, announced soon after in open court, was "Not Guilty."

Later, one of the jurors, John W. Efaw, Jr., explained to the press.

"Her [Mary Kay] testimony was more like hearsay. And, she had lied to authorities on three different occasions about the death of her husband. She really manipulated him [Bowers] into the relationship. You could see that by the letters and cards she sent him. She came on to him instead of him coming on to her."

Another juror, Richard L. Frank, said the crucial defense exhibit was Mary Kay's letter to David.

The Bowers trial was really a trial of what began as two sisters' obsessive love for a man they had both loved at one time and whom Bonnie apparently still loved even in death. The electric anxiety of revenge, rape, love, hate, incest, betrayal, sex, violence, and murder that pitted blood relatives one against the other in the reticent culture of the Monogahela Valley was something straight out of the Greek tragedies of Euripides. The trial of David Bowers is over. The trial of the two sisters has just begun.

Fourteen
Semi-lethal Ladies

You couldn't have asked for a more beautiful day and the time was just right. It was a brilliant, sunshiny May morning by the waters of South Oyster Bay with the sounds of sail lines slapping against spars at the marina next door. Cawing gulls wheeled overhead, enjoying the May weather as much as the humans below them working on their boats, getting them ready for summer or toasting their skin in the bewitching warm sunshine.

Yes, you couldn't have asked for a more beautiful day and the time was just right — except for Mary Jo Buttafuoco whose life was about to change dramatically forever.

On the sun porch of her home in Massapequa, Long Island, Mary Jo was getting her deck furniture ready for summer by giving it another coat of enamel. Then, a few minutes after eleven, the doorbell on their Adam Road West home rang and she carefully put down her paint brush in a can so it wouldn't drip on the deck and strode inside to see who was at her door. Probably a salesman or

261

somebody soliciting for charity. Certainly none of her friends and it was too early for the mailman.

Peering out through the storm door that would soon be taken down for the summer, Mary Jo saw what looked like a young teenage girl. It was really a wife's worse nightmare come calling at her front door.

Yet, up until the last two seconds, Mary Jo regarded the adolescent female at the front door with a certain impatience. She wanted to get back to painting before it was too late and she didn't have a lot of forbearance for teen prattle.

The young girl asked if she was Mrs. Joseph Buttafuoco and, when Mary Jo acknowledged she was, nervously made an incomprehensible comment about rarely confronting a wife before she spilled what she thought would be a shocking secret to the older woman.

"You husband is having an affair with my seventeen-year-old sister."

"Really?"

"I think the idea of a forty-year-old man sleeping with a seventeen-year-old is disgusting."

Mary Jo acted with that disbelieving skepticism teenagers so often experience from adults and which infuriates the young person. For instant proof, the young girl who had identified herself as Ann Marie living on Dolphin Court produced a white polo shirt bearing the yellow racing car logo and name of Complete Auto Body and Fender, Inc. She claimed Joey gave it to her sister and she found it in her sister's bed.

Checking the size of the shirt as an extra large which was her six-foot, 235-pound husband Joey's size, Mary Jo momentarily glanced across the street at a young man seated behind the wheel of a red Thunderbird.

"Who's that?"

"My boyfriend."

Returning the focus to what Ann Marie had claimed about her younger sister and Joey, Mary Jo essentially dismissed the story as the figment of some teenybopper's mind saying her husband's company gave out the polo shirts all over town. She thanked Ann Marie for stopping by and said she was going inside to call Joey.

For Mary Jo that ended the conversation. The only thing missing was dismissal of this meaningless little girl with a wave of the hand.

Then, came the last two seconds.

Mary Jo's head detonated with a thunderous sound and sharp pain as a .25 caliber bullet bored its way into her head entering by the right ear burrowing downward to splinter her jaw, slice her carotid artery, and rest at the base of her skull.

"Shit. The little bitch got me." Mary Jo blacked out and the rest of her life was put on hold.

Mary Jo didn't die, but the story of Amy Fisher who called herself Ann Marie is properly included in our collection because Amy fits the profile of the erotomaniac. The fact that a freak chance of a woman being shot in the head and surviving does not change the intention or the circumstances that make this clearly a case for our book.

Certainly, there are a number of love-obsessed women who fantasize about murdering someone standing in the way of their love fulfillment, but they are constrained from acting by other forces within themselves and their stories wouldn't find their way in this volume. But, Amy Fisher did more than fantasize. She planned and she acted and only chance or ineptness kept Mary Jo from having her brains tattooed all over the outside of the Buttafuoco's storm door that morning in May.

Amy Fisher ran out to the parked red Thunderbird, leapt in, and the car sped away, leaving Mary Jo sprawled on the floor of her front porch. Fortunately, the houses in the waterfront community are close together and neighbors, Joe and Josephine Slattery, were alarmed by the sound of the shot. Joe Slattery ran over to see what happened and saw the life oozing out of Mary Jo as she lay crumpled in her blood on the porch floor.

Joe Slattery didn't need a second look to understand what had to be done. He sprinted back to where Josephine waited and hollered, "Call 911." Josephine was on the phone in a flash punching up 911, summoning the police and medical help for a shooting victim. Mary Jo was blessed with such neighbors otherwise she might have simply bled to death before anybody found her.

Next, Josephine touchtoned Joey at work.

"Come home. It's an emergency."

"What's wrong?"

"Why all the questions? Move yourself!" Josephine thought. Into the telephone she yelled:

"Just get home!"

It penetrated. Joey thought about the fact that Josephine had never called him at work before.

"Oh, God. Dad, I got to fly out of here. My neighbor said there's an emergency."

Joey leapt into his car and his brother Bob came along with him. The Buttafuoco brothers would face whatever was wrong. Joey floored the gas pedal in a cold-sweat panic for the whole eight miles to the house. It's a miracle he didn't kill them both getting there and his mind was racing with all the horrible possibilities even faster than the rear-drive wheels on his car.

They had to stop short of the house because the area was cordoned off with yellow police strips. Ducking under them they heard the gathered neighbors murmuring, "Joey's here, Joey's here," but nobody came over and told Joey or Bob anything as they ran forward toward the house.

The first thing Joey saw was the blood stains. Bloodstains on the house, bloodstains on the steps, bloodstains on the front door. He turned toward the ambulance, but there was no one and then he began to run to the helicopter on the beach.

He got there in time to see his wife of fifteen years lashed to a stretcher with her hair frazzled, darker than usual and wet. He knew it was from blood. He knew instantly she had been shot in the head and began rushing to reach her when a wall of cops piled on top of him and pinned him to the sand until the helicopter rose and the spinning rotor blades were clear. They just wanted to keep him from getting sliced by a rotor blade.

The cops got off him one at a time and most said nothing and those that had any comment told Joey simply that it didn't look good for Mary Jo and then drifted away in the normal bewilderment even the most seasoned cop has at the senseless brutality we humans visit upon each other.

Then, came the long drive to Nassau Medical Center and the grim meeting with the hospital surgeon to weigh the odds in the grisly chess match with Death. The doctor pulled no punches—he didn't have the luxury or time or reasoned deliberation—he was faced with that kind of critical test he had trained for all his career. The odds would have unnerved even Nick the Greek.

"If we don't operate on her, she'll be dead within twelve hours. If we do operate, there's no guarantee that she'll wake up. And, if she does wake up, there's no guarantee that she won't be paralyzed."

If Joey Buttafuoco lives to be a thousand years old, he will never forget those words.

The surgery began about three hours after she had been shot. Again, had it not been for the quick response of the Slatterys, she might have still been lying and dying on her front porch. She came out of the operating room eight hours later alive, but with the bullet still in her, very close to the spine—too close to be removed.

For the rest of the night Joey stayed nearby, coming into her room every half hour to check on her. Finally, about four in the morning he came in and made a stunning discovery. On the yellow doctor's pad hanging near her was written, "Was I shot? Why?" It was in Mary Jo's handwriting and written neatly on the line.

Even though she was only partially awake and seemed dazed, Joey began to talk to her because of the written questions she had managed to write. He asked her several times who did it? Who shot you? Who did this thing to you? And, gave her the yellow pad and pen.

Slowly, painfully, the answers were written:

"Nineteen-year-old girl."

"Are you sure?"

"A nineteen-year-old-girl."

"Do you know her? What's her name?"

"Ann Marie."

"I don't know any Ann Marie. Where does she live?"

"Dolphin Court" [which was the false address that had been given Mary Jo that morning at the front door].

Joey called the police and they were there a few hours later along with Joey and Bob when Mary Jo was able to speak in a halting, raspy voice. When she got to the part about the polo shirt, Joey knew who it was. They were new and he had only given one away so far—to the daughter of Elliot Fisher. It was Amy.

It was Amy Fisher, a seventeen-year-old high school senior he initially said he had been sleeping with for over a year. Soon after telling the police this, Joey's memory lapsed again and he claimed he had *NOT* been sleeping with her.

The police got Joey to cooperate in trying to lure Amy out of her home away from her mother and father. They wanted to question her immediately. Joey called her, but she wouldn't meet him. Instead, she got into her car and took off. The police then cornered her and arrested her.

They held her at police headquarters in Mineola for twenty-four hours without notifying her parents or anybody she was in custody.

Amy Fisher didn't have any trouble with her memory of events and after night-long questioning, she admitted to holding the gun at the time Mary Jo was shot, but claimed it was an accident.

"I showed her the shirt Joey had given me. I felt she didn't believe me and she kept asking me questions like where I lived, who I was with. At this time, I felt she was dismissing me and didn't care about what I was saying. I saw her turn to go back in the house, at which time I took the gun out of my pocket and hit her on the back of the head. I saw her stumble. I had my finger on the trigger. I went to hit her again because I was so angry. I then raised the gun again and it went off. I heard a pop sound and saw blood coming out of her head."

Detective Sergeant Daniel Severin told reporters Amy was obsessively in love with Joey who had been sleeping with her every day for a year or more and she sensed he was trying to break it off and go back to being only with Mary Jo. Amy hated Mary Jo for taking back her man.

Where does a seventeen-year-old high school girl

get a gun? Well, it apparently wasn't as hard as a lot of people might think. Besides, Amy was a spoiled only child whose well-to-do parents had rarely denied her anything.

Her father, Elliot, fifty-six, had a heart condition and spent his time at home managing the family's investment portfolio while her mother, Rose, thirty-nine, ran the family Stitch-N-Sew shop in Freeport, not too far from their home in Merrick.

To her parents, Amy was every mother's dream. The perfect child of a Jewish father and Italian mother raised as a regular, decent girl who matured at a time when cars and perfect bodies were the criteria of success.

At sixteen when she got her first driver's license, her parents bought her a 1989 white Dodge Daytona with careful pink detailing pinstripes and *AIMEE* on the door. She soon became more difficult for her parents to keep track of or to control.

Ironically, her doting father made Amy's initial connection with the beefy Joey who worked at the body repair shop founded by his racing car driver and mechanic father, Casper, decades before and still overseen by the seventy-seven-year-old patriarch. Amy had several accidents in the Daytona beginning in December of 1990 and Elliot took the repairs to Complete Auto Body and Fender, Inc. It was near his wife's shop.

That's where she first met Joey Buttafuoco and his brother, Bob, and their father, Casper. Buttafuoco was an arm-wrestling champ who worked out regularly, was muscular and big, but wore a pinky ring and a diamond stud in his right ear along with a gold medallion of the Blessed Mother from Medjugorje. He went to work for his father right after graduating from Massapequa High School and married Mary Jo Connery in 1977 when he was twenty-one and she was twenty-two. The years since then have produced two children, Paul in 1980 and Jessica in 1983.

The next phase of the relationship between Amy and Joey was muddied by conflicting recollections. As already noted, Joey first told police that he had been turned on by Amy and she by him and they started having an affair. Amy started hanging around the shop a lot and, in fact, apparently staged a series of "accidents" to give her an excuse to bring the car in for repairs. In the end, Joey said her bill totaled $13,000 to $14,000.

Then, Joey said his first story was wrong and that he and Amy were just friends who would share a slice of pizza now and again although he did call her frequently. He would call her beeper number and leave his code for her to call back, "007." In October, her parents bought an even more trendy car, a black LeBaron convertible in which to tool around.

Meanwhile, Amy would brag to her girlfriends at school that she was such a sex maniac that she drove her lovers wild. Among adolescent females in this era that is a mark of achievement surpassing all others. She claimed Joey was so crazy in love with her and with her having sex with him that he insisted she have a beeper so he could summon her for his sexual pleasure upon demand. A coworker at Complete Auto Body and Fender, Inc. would later tell reporters that Buttafuoco bragged about giving Amy her first orgasm.

To the jaded New York news media another non-fatal shooting out on Long Island was hardly worth a yawn much less any significant space and, when the police arrested Amy on May 21 for attempted murder, that was the level of news attention it got. Peter De Rosa changed all that.

Peter De Rosa was a twenty-eight-year-old customer of ABBA Escort who had three sessions with Amy and video taped the second one at his house. Right after Amy was arrested for attempted murder, Peter was on the phone peddling his now hot video tape. A *Current Affair* was first in line with $8,000 cash on the barrelhead and eleven days after her arrest, little Amy Fisher became a television star.

A *Current Affair* aired the fourteen and a half minute tape on June that opened with Fisher sitting on the edge of De Rosa's bed:

"Let's take care of business. Then we don't worry about this when we take care of pleasure. I don't like to think of business and pleasure at the same time," said Amy in a routine that is as old as the trade of prostitution itself. One of the three basic rules of prostitution being to get the customer or john to pay out front because, once he's screwed you, you can't repossess the merchandise.

"Ahh, I think I know what you're saying."

So, Peter produced $100 and the two began cavorting on the bed for a few minutes until Amy asks Peter to turn off the light. Peter complied and seven minutes of dead screen followed with millions of Americans frozen staring at their dark screens like a people transfixed.

The lights came back on the sex scene as Amy was pulling herself together to leave and Peter asked her to go with him to a bachelor party. Amy uttered what would become her signature, defining self-assessment, "Anything. I'm wild. I don't care. I like sex."

That was the line that transformed the back page, minor, out-of-town crime incident into the "Crime of the Month" for the Manhattan Media Mavens.

"Long Island Lolita" became the identifying label. The *New York Daily News* and the *New York Post*, neither noted for tasteful restraint on any occasion, shrieked, "The Lolita Tapes" and "High School Student by Day . . . Call Girl by Night," which was inaccurate since Amy would have sex with men day or night. Even the somewhat more subdued *New York Newsday* couldn't help itself and finger-wagged, "Oh, Amy, Oh, Amy, Oh, Amy."

Meanwhile, District Attorney Fred Klein had his hands full because a tawdry little local love obsession and attempted murder had now become the linch pins of sweeps week on the local news and he was dancing in the center of the spotlight with a lot of people he didn't know and he wasn't sure he could trust. Missteps in delicate situations such as these can pull the plug on a public career.

For example, was he dealing with a pathetic little

272

girl adrift in the sea of love or a brazen home-wrecking whore? The media made the situation more intense, but hardly more enlightened. Some would say he decided that the voting strength would go with the wives who said home-wrecking whore. He asked Nassau County Court Judge Marvin Goodman to set bail for this dangerous criminal who threatened the moral fiber of every family in America at $2 million. The Judge agreed. It was the highest bail ever set for any criminal in the history of Nassau County.

Defending himself against charges of excess and ingratiating himself with all those worried wives out there in TV land, Klein patiently explained to the court.

"The defendant's conduct after the shooting is completely inconsistent with an accident. She did not call for help. Students, friends, even her own family who saw the defendant within minutes and hours and days of the shooting, have confirmed that they saw nothing unusual in the defendant's conduct during this period of time after the shooting, hardly, hardly an indication of a woman who accidentally shot a stranger in the head.

"Your honor, I suggest to the court that the likelihood of flight of this defendant in this case is astronomical. One might describe this defendant as a seventeen-year-old girl who lives at home with her parents and goes to high school. That would be about as accurate as describing John Gotti as a businessman from New York City. This is not your typical seventeen-year-old high school student. I

273

emphasize that to the court. She is completely beyond the control of her parents, of the school, or this court."

Presto! Within two weeks of her arrest, Amy Fisher had been elevated in the annals of American crime from a minor love-hate attempted murder in the 'burbs to the peer of the most dangerous Mafia boss in New York.

Another Amy spoke out for the first Amy, *New York Post* columnist Amy Pagnozzi wrote, "Amy Fisher will be made to pay as much for her sexuality as for any crime she may have committed while the men will get off—they always do." If Carolyn Warmus, Jennifer Reali, Jean Harris, and many others in this book read Pagnozzi's column, they would all nod in sad agreement.

But, wait. The TV circus had other rings in which to perform.

Elliot and Rose, well off as they were, couldn't raise the $2 million bail and were despairing about getting Amy out of prison until her trial, when defense attorney Eric Naiburg came up with an inspired and, in this media enraptured age, a quite logical alternative.

Standing before the same television cameras as his opponent Klein had two days before, Naiburg announced:

"If this child has to utilize the only asset she has left—the publicity surrounding this case—she's going to utilize it."

He then said they were inviting film companies to bid on the exclusive rights to the Amy Fisher story with the minimum bid being the $2 million required for bail.

This enraged Joey Buttafuoco's lawyer, Marvyn Kornberg, but it brought Amy's lawyer, Eric, more than a dozen offers within the next twenty-four hours. By July, the Fishers had raised the bail money with an assist from a film company.

Curiously, Joey's lawyer, Marvyn Kornberg's outrage at the concept had cooled considerably which might have something to do with the Buttafuoco's sale of the rights to *THEIR* story to Tri-Star Television for a few hundred thousand dollars.

And, the media wars continued to milk the story for all it was worth with Joey creating another moment in media history by calling in to the Howard Stern radio talk show to rebut another caller. The first caller claimed to be Buttafuoco's landscaper who had witnessed Joey and Amy cavorting in his swimming pool. The only difficulty with the story being that the Buttafuoco house doesn't have a pool.

So, Joey called in to straighten that out and to plead his case of unceasing, eternal love for Mary Jo. She was released from the hospital at the end of May, suffering nerve damage to the right side of her face. She's left with permanent hearing loss, dizziness, trouble walking, and double vision, and the right side of her face is partially paralyzed. Mary Jo responded in another interview with, "The story is pretty simple: I love my Joey. My Joey loves me."

From his public statements, it seems that

Naiburg depicts an entirely different situation and history than Mr. Innocent Blissfully Married to High School Sweetheart and In Love Forever. Apparently, Naiburg thought Buttafuoco was a Teflon Bum and classic pimp who turned a loving, obsessive, naive young girl into a disposable plaything and, finally, a whore.

He said Buttafuoco was "screwing" Amy every day in every way and in every place for a year. Sometimes it was in the two-story Freeport Motor Inn and Boatel with the turquoise drapes and doors, knotted pine paneling and blue-and-white patterned bed spreads. Naiburg had room receipts signed by Joey. Sometimes it was at her parents gray two-story home on Berkley Lane with the white shutters, the brass trim, and the neatly trimmed little curvy lawn in front. In fact, he says that's where on July 2, 1991, Joey took her during the day to do it in her own bedroom. Later, that night, he had sex with her again at the Freeport Motor Inn and Boatel. Sometimes it was in the apartment over the body shop. Sometimes it was on Joey's powder blue and white thirty-one foot speedboat, the Double Trouble, moored in the marina. It really didn't matter. According to Amy, Joey wanted sex all the time and she wanted to give it to him all the time.

She loved him. That's the one theme that keeps getting lost in all of the legal jousting and media tumult. She was obsessed with this knowledgeable, irreverent, confident male hulk. She told her acquaintance, Stephen Sleeman, who would play a role in the shooting of Mary Jo, "He loves me and we have great sex." She wanted him. She needed him. She told Sleeman, "I'd do anything to see Mrs. Buttafuoco die, because I want Joey . . . he's the only person I love." She loved him and Mary Jo was in the way. Not too novel and not too complicated.

This apparently started happening in August of 1991 and Amy saw Joey was slipping away from her. She was not a passive girl accustomed to accepting whatever cards fate dealt her. She had been the focus of two doting parents who wanted to and were able to give her most of what she wanted when she wanted it. She would fashion her fate — not be ruled by it. Or, at least, that was her inclination.

So, when Joey started drifting, Amy decided it must be because of the only rival she knew about, Mary Jo. Eliminate Mary Jo, and Joey was hers.

As the police reconstructed the sequence of events starting in August, Amy went to another student at John F. Kennedy High in Bellmore, Christopher Drellos, with an offer to trade sex and money for a gun. That wasn't something Christopher was willing to do, but he did take her to a nearby restaurant and introduce her to somebody who was, Stephen Sleeman, a twenty-year-old waiter at Michaels, a seafood restaurant in Freeport.

Sleeman was a diminutive Vietnamese young man who originally bought into the program with Amy because Christopher told him she would give him lots of great sex if he played along with her.

Sleeman was into the early planning stages of the hit from what the available evidence shows. He staked out the Buttafuoco house to plot the residents' routine comings and goings. He followed Mary Jo to the grocery store and the mall and associated places and then met with Amy to report on what he had learned.

His compensation was $600, paid in bits and pieces and a blow job every time they met. She told him that she got the $600 by sleeping with men for money and, beyond that, she needed a lot of sex because she got bored easily. Except with Joey. She had the greatest sex with Joey.

At the end of October, Amy and Stephen knew the Buttafuoco routines well and a plan of action had formed in Amy's mind. Amy would go up and ring the doorbell and pretend to be selling candy for charity. At the moment Mary Jo appeared, Stephen was to leap from hiding in the bushes and gun her down with his .22 caliber rifle. At the last minute, the money and the sex wasn't enough and Stephen chickened out.

He refused to shoot Mary Jo and wanted to know why it was necessary anyhow if Joey was so in love with Amy. Amy had the easy rationalization of every obsessed woman that Joey didn't hate Mary Jo and wouldn't do anything to hurt her.

At the beginning of November, Amy forced the issue and she rang the Buttafuoco's doorbell and pretended to be selling candy for charity. When Mary Jo went inside to get some money and return, Sleeman was supposed to jump out and cut her down with his .22 rifle. Instead, he panicked and ran back to the car.

Furious, Amy decided men couldn't be counted on in a tough situation such as this and she decided she would take care of her rival herself. In some ways, she thought, that was really the way it ought to be anyhow. Mujer y Mujer just like the guys do it to settle a feud or dispute when they go Mano y Mano.

It took five months more, according to the police, but she finally made the acquaintance with Peter Guagenti, a twenty-one-year-old Brooklyn auto parts store clerk and premed drop out from Fordham, with slender Levantine looks and very dark, curly hair. Amy bought a shoddily built Italian Saturday Night Special — a Titan .25 automatic — from him. Peter delivered it to the Fisher home on May 19, 1992, and she gave him $800 which was about twenty-five times what it sells for on the street and no sex and, then, he drove her to the Buttafuoco house in his red Thunderbird and waited outside.

Within forty-eight hours she would be arrested and under intense questioning.

Finally, in late July, Naiburg was able to put together a bail deal with KLM Productions, an independent film company created by three Long Island men, and Amy's parents put up $100,000 cash between them. This, coupled with a lien against the parents' $900,000 home and life savings convinced a bail bond company to post the bail.

Amy was released July 28 with the warning to

stay away from Mary Jo and the rest of the Buttafuoco family. The rejoicing Naiberg promised the press he was going to take Amy out to a fine Italian dinner that night and toast her temporary freedom. A bitter Mary Jo replied through the media that she couldn't have a fine Italian meal. She was forced to subsist on baby food because of what Amy had done to her.

"I won't feel safe again until she's behind bars. I just know what this girl did to me in cold blood. She's a sick girl."

With the passage of time and the loss of media interest, cases such as these tend to simmer down into the mundane routine of pedantic law not unlike conflicts of much less intensity. So, attorney Eric Naiburg had a quiet lunch with prosecutor Fred Klein at a restaurant near the Nassau County Courthouse. By the time the coffee came, the basic deal was struck and it would stand the case on its head. The two men agreed that Amy would plead guilty to reckless assault with a five-to-fifteen year sentence and the possibility of getting out on a work-release program in only three years.

Was that the complete deal? No.

Klein had to give up more than the reduced charge. Klein agreed to assemble a grand jury to consider charges of statutory rape, and conspiracy to commit murder against Joey Buttafuoco and Amy would agree to testify against Joey.

Fred Klein met with the Buttafuocos and their attorneys to discuss the details of a plea bargain. He said that Mary Jo would have agree to an even lighter sentence for Amy if the statutory rape charge against Joey was dropped. They compromised by having it put to a grand jury to decide.

By September 22, the deal was agreed to by everybody involved and the next day Amy was before Nassau State Supreme Court Justice Marvin Goodman to seal it. She briefly told what had happened when Mary Jo was shot. She still maintained that it was an accident and that Mary Jo had fallen on top of her after being hit.

"I tried to get her off of me and I hit her, I think twice, and then I left. I ran away."

He set sentencing for December 1.

The *New York Daily News* headlined what should have been the end of the lamentable story in early October 1992 with "Amy Cuts Deal."

Amy indeed had cut a deal with the prosecution that could see her back on the street by the time she's twenty-one. Given the ferocity of the prosecution's allegations against Amy and the enormously high bail based on her alleged criminal viciousness, many people were surprised that the State would agree to a plea bargain. Unless, of course, its case was not as solid and clear cut as it claimed against Amy.

But Prosecutor Klein again defended his actions and suggested that he had also had in mind going after Joey all along but couldn't do anything without her testimony. He told reporters the plea bargain deal was:

". . . one of the most difficult decisions that I

have had to make in over thirteen years as prosecutor and I did not make it lightly.

"We got one fish. Now we are going to look for more fish."

Mary Jo lashed back immediately.

"She tried to kill me and now she is taking my husband and she's trying to destroy us. It's frightening that one person can do so much damage.

"This girl is an attempted murderer, a liar, and a prostitute. Something's wrong here. Something's real wrong."

Seventy-seven-year-old Casper Buttafuoco was understandably confused over the latest turn of events involving his son.

"How does this go from a $2 million bail to a three-year minimum sentence? That's what you get for crossing the street wrong."

Casper was not the only citizen bewildered by what was going on in what seemed to have become Long Island's endless soap opera of a woman obsessed with love who tried to murder.

The day after Amy and the State of New York cut a deal, a video tape of a visit to Paul Makely by Amy was broadcast on *Hard Copy.*

It showed Amy visiting Makely at his gym, kissing and hugging him and him fiddling with her breasts. She did not seem at all like a repentant, remorseful little girl. Instead, she asked Paul to marry her so she could have conjugal visits with him while she was in jail which is permitted in some New York prisons.

Then, she said she quite liked getting all the publicity she's had since the shooting. When Paul asked her why, she replied to him and unknowingly to millions of TV viewers.

"Because I can make a lot of money. I figure if I have to go through all the pain and suffering, I'm getting a Ferrari."

"Pain and suffering?"

"I don't want to go there [to prison], but I figure I'm being a good sport about it."

Obviously, Amy's latest love Paul Makely had betrayed her. He made the tape deliberately, sold it to *Hard Copy* for something reputed to be between $10,000 and $50,000 and immediately dropped out of sight. It couldn't change her plea bargain deal made the day before, but it could destroy her usefulness as a witness in any future trials.

Amy watched the program in attorney Eric Naiburg's office and was devastated by this treachery by yet another man in her life. One of Naiburg's associates said she viewed the program with total disbelief and sobbing, "And I loved him. I loved him. I loved him."

In the next fourteen hours Amy tried twice to commit suicide — first by swallowing ten to fifteen Xanax and later by taking fifteen to twenty Lorazepam. She was saved and admitted to the psychiatric ward of Huntington Hospital suffering, the doctor said, from severe depression.

The predictable result came almost instantly when Denis Dillon of the Nassau County prosecutor's office announced that the contemplated charges against Joey were dropped because the

283

State now had no "credible supporting evidence" because all depended on what had now become Amy Fisher's "virtually useless and unbelievable" word against Joey's.

The end? No.

On Sunday the twenty-seventh of October, *Hard Copy* and the infamous Paul Makely struck again. This time with an audio tape Amy had given Makely before her videotaped visit to him. The implication of sexual abuse by her father was clear.

"I just don't understand why my mom ever had me. I mean, she let my father do such terrible things to me. And I feel like she just looked the other way. She didn't do anything to stop it. And now all she can say is that she's sorry. And all my father can say—the pathetic person that he is—is that he's sorry, too. And he keeps saying that he never meant to hurt me. He actually thinks that will make it better."

Then, on October 30 came another round in the Contest of the Dueling Tabloid Medias as Amy did several hours of interview for *Inside Edition*. During this she essentially restated her previous story again.

November 4, her attorney Naiburg rushed her into court and asked that her sentencing date be moved up so she could start her prison term immediately. He told Justice Goodman that Amy and her family were captives of the media and every aspect of their lives besieged by reporters, camera crews, and vulturish interviewers. Goodman agreed to revoke Amy's bail and put her back in custody to protect her from the press. Amy's sentencing was still set for December 1, 1992.

Just so there wouldn't be a titillation lull, *Inside Edition* aired its exclusive interview with Amy as a three-part series November 9, 10, and 11, while each of the three major networks set a movie of its own on the Amy-Mary Jo-Joey triangle.

Like a mother going to visit her daughter's future college to check out the cleanliness, food, suitability of accommodations, and attitude of the administration, Rose Fisher had defense attorney Eric Naiburg take her on a tour of Bedford Hills Correctional Facility in Westchester since that's where she learned Amy will most likely be sent. Coincidentally, her prison mates at Bedford Hills would have included Carolyn Warmus and Jean Harris.

And, then, Mary Jo could not be contained either. She filed a formal request with the court that she be permitted to address Justice Goodman before he passed sentence on Amy.

On December 1, 1992, Amy Fisher stood facing Justice Marvin Goodman again and, for the first time since May 19, she also faced her victim, Mary Jo Buttofuoco whose formal request to address the court before sentencing was granted.

Supported by more than ten of her family and friends—but not by Joey Buttafuoco who decided to stay away for fear that his presence would make him the target of a verbal attack by Amy and distract from the proceedings—the permanently partially paralyzed Mary Jo said.

"On May 19, Amy Fisher rang my doorbell and viciously and deliberately assaulted me. I was left for dead with a .25-caliber bullet lodged in my head about one inch from my spinal cord. As a result of this violent act, my life and the lives of my family have changed completely."

Mary Jo wanted to urge Justice Goodman to impose the maximum sentence on the Long Island Lolita who had almost succeeded in being a lethal lady, murdering for the love of Joey Buttafuoco.

Justice Goodman really didn't need any encouragement in spite of what Amy said before he sentenced her. It was actually less important what she said and more important what she still was: a strong-willed, seemingly unrepentant woman obsessed by love and willing to do whatever she had to do to satisfy her love obsession.

The only reason that Amy was not at that moment facing sentencing for attempted murder was because of the plea bargain deal Eric Naiburg had made for her.

"I realize that what I did was terribly wrong," Amy told the court of Mary Jo. "I put Mrs. Buttafuoco and her children through so much pain and for that I am deeply sorry. If I could take the pain away, if I could change everything, I would.

"I had an affair with a married man. And it's also the truth that Joey knew of my intention toward his wife and he encouraged me. I feel the truth, and only the truth, can help heal the wounds for everyone involved."

Then, it was Justice Goodman's turn:

"You are a disgrace to yourself, your family, and your friends," he said, setting the tone and going on to say he believed that Amy was a wild animal that stalked its prey, motivated by lust and passion.

Then, concluding by mixing his metaphors, Goodman passed sentence. "You were a walking stick of dynamite with the fuse lit and this court believes that, under the circumstances of the case, any lesser sentence than the maximum would make a mockery of the criminal justice system."

With that he gave Amy five-to-fifteen-years in the state prison. She could be out when she is twenty-two on a work-release program or eligible for parole when she is twenty-four.

The end? No. Again.

Amy Fisher became a media cottage industry overnight with the spectacle of all three major television networks rushing a TV movie into production. The mind-spinning result was that NBC aired, "Amy Fisher: My Story," on December 28, 1992, with the CBS version—"Casualties of Love: The Long Island Lolita Story"—pitted directly against the ABC version, "Beyond Control: The Amy Fisher Story," on January 3, 1993.

The results? Each of the movies may have set records for the television season. The NBC movie got a viewer rating of 19.1 compared to the average network show rating of 12. The CBS movie got a 15.8 and the ABC version got 19.4. All three will end up being among the highest-rated movies on television in that season!

In the forty-plus years of network television,

there has never been a movie on all three networks about the same subject or criminal case. Nor, has there ever been an instance when two major networks put on such a movie in the exact same time slot.

Ruth Slawson, CBS senior vice president for movies, was dazed by what happened,

"I was stunned. I don't know anyone in the business who wasn't stunned."

An estimated 25 million homes watched the syrupy, sophomoric saga of Long Island's Amy Fisher. That probably works out to about 75 million people or a third of the entire population of the United States.

Clearly the significance of this is that it doesn't tell us as much about Amy Fisher as it tells us about ourselves.

In early April 1993, Joey was indicted for statutory rape — a charge hardly ever prosecuted and rarely proven.

How to end this drama? It is another story of a love obsessed woman willing to murder for her man and it refuses to end. That is, of course, logical and in keeping with human history since this same story has been repeated and continued for thousands of years since at least the ancient Greeks. The story remains the same — only the names change.

Fifteen
Erotomania and Murder

As we have seen, many of the people described in this book are suffering from a little understood aberration, noted at the beginning, known to psychologists and psychiatrists as "erotomania." It has only recently been surfacing in the popular press, but it has been known for a long time in the therapy community of professionals.

In plain English, erotomania is a love obsession with another person whom you believe is wildly in love with you in return and there is some outside obstacle keeping the two of you apart.

Sometimes this obstacle is money or age difference or relatives or career. For example, priests and men in powerful political, business, and military positions have careers that virtually prohibit open affairs, divorce, and scandal. Most of the time, however, the obstacle is a husband or a wife. The solution to the unwanted husband or wife is often murder.

A specialist in erotomania, psychiatrist Dr. Jonathan Segal, believes that there are tens of thousands of erotomanics in the country and most of them are women. That is not a sexist observation, that is simply the reality of the situation.

Writing in the American Journal of Psychiatry [October, 1989] Dr. Segal explained erotomania in specific detail.

"The erotomanic . . . becomes convinced she or he is passionately loved by another person. [They] are usually women from modest backgrounds while the objects are generally older men of distinctly higher social and financial status who are almost inevitably married or unavailable for other reasons."

These erotomanics often follow an interesting pattern. They start by becoming love obsessed with a person—usually a man—whom they can't normally have; someone unattainable. They then weave a set of dreams and hopes around this person that says, "If I could only have him as my lover and husband, my life would be secure and beautiful."

In some sense, this helps the person with the love obsession explain away her own failures and unhappinesses. Namely, she has been blocked by an external barrier from being the happy person she can be. She shifts the blame for her unhappiness to someone or something else: the barrier keeping her from her lover.

As part of the dream the erotomanic is weaving, there is the unsubstantiated fantasy that her love object also feels desperately in love with her in return.

To prove this, she picks up on little clues that seem irrelevant to the rest of the world: "He's wearing a green tie to signal me that he wants me," or "He smiled as we passed in the parking lot to tell me that he is dreaming about being with me," or "He had that news conference where he touched his earlobe as a special, secret message meant only for me."

Experts seem to agree that, the popular TV movies and tabloid stories addicted with the "Fatal Attraction" theme to the contrary, erotomania is not primarily about sex. It is about love, nurturing, caring, protecting, fulfilling, and being in a loving—not necessarily sexual—relationship.

Erotomanics may be either male or female, but the experts say that the majority of them are women. Sometimes, the erotomania climaxes in murder as we have seen and as is further illustrated by the infamous American case of "Tiger Woman" Clara Phillips.

It stunned Clara Phillips to discover her rich stockbroker salesman husband was sexually involved with the gorgeous twenty-two-year-old widow, Alberta Meadows.

Even worse, she knew and had befriended Alberta and, now, her rage at having her man stolen was beyond bounds. Picking a day they knew Alberta would be shopping at Bullock's, the tony department store formerly in the mid-Wilshire district of Los Angeles, Clara and a friend, Peggy Caffee, followed Alberta through the store as she moved from department to department. When she was preparing to leave, the two women raced outside and wheeled Clara's car around to the door.

When Alberta appeared, the two in the car hailed her as friends and enticed her inside for a ride home. Once the car was moving and they were chatting gaily, the two women convinced Alberta to stay with them while they took a ride in the country.

Only when they had reached a lonely stretch of country road in the rural San Fernando Valley did Alberta become apprehensive as the conversation turned mean with illusions toward her affair with Clara's husband—first veiled and then, as Clara's anger rose anew, open and threatening.

On a deserted segment of the pepper-tree-lined dirt road, Clara suddenly jammed on the brakes and Alberta, now in terror for her life, leapt from the car and began running. Clara wrenched open the tool box in the car and seized the handle of a ballpeen hammer and sprinted after the retreating Alberta like a carnivorous cat running down its prey.

Catching up to the screaming Alberta, Clara sprang upon her like a tiger in blood lust, knocking the doomed Alberta to the ground where Clara began cursing and yelling as she wildly smashed the woman's head, crushing the skull and sending spurts of blood over herself and her victim.

Peggy sat transfixed in horror as she watched the deadly tableau with her hand over her mouth and a million thoughts racing through her mind as to what she should do. This was more than she

292

had bargained for and, now, she was part of a murder.

Clara continued to slam the deadly ballpeen hammer into the lifeless head of Alberta several times before she rose to her feet with a serene smile of vengeance and walked back to the car, the bloody, dripping hammer still in her hand.

The conclusion came soon after that. Clara dropped the frightened Peggy off near her residence and drove home to her philandering husband. She entered quietly and went directly to him to announce that his affair was over. She relished telling him the grotesque details of what had happened to his lover and warned him that fate awaited any other woman who took her man.

Falling back on a classic male stratagem, he immediately confessed, claimed Alberta had seduced him, and begged Clara's forgiveness with a promise of eternal fidelity. Then, he shifted to concern over Clara's safety once Alberta's body would be discovered. He proposed putting her on a train at Union Station in Los Angeles to Tucson where a friend of his would take care of her until things quieted down.

Clara accepted the newly found affection and concern and let him put her on the Santa Fe train to Arizona. When he was certain the train had left the station, the husband rushed to the telephone and revealed all to the police. When Clara arrived in Tucson, there was, indeed, someone to meet her and take care of her: the police.

At the trial, Peggy didn't hesitate a moment to

turn state's evidence and describe in detail the murder including how Clara leapt upon her victim like a tiger and smashed her head in with a hammer. The press instantly dubbed Clara "The Tiger Woman" and she was convicted of murder and sentenced to California's Tehachapi Prison for Women. She has since been released and is now living a quiet spinster's life in Los Angeles.

Like the case of "Tiger Woman" Phillips, only about twelve percent of the murder or manslaughter cases that go to trial in this country involve women according to Mimi Hall, reporter for *USA Today*, but they get a disproportionate amount of attention.

"Sexism and racism play a role in the fascination, partly because the public is especially curious about seeing the seedy side where they don't expect it . . . [moreover] . . . they're domestic disputes revolving around love, sex, and money."

Movie producers and network executives explain the public fascination is largely due to the fact that they are good stories. While they may not be classic literature, they have all the elements of Greek drama, Shakespeare, and O'Neill. They are morality plays in which a crime is committed, sometimes as the result of a person's evil side coming into control, and the perpetrator is tried, convicted, and punished.

Fortunately, not all erotomanics resort to violence, but they suffer from the disorder nonetheless. Whether they do something violent or not may only be a matter of time or a matter of degree.

In some notorious cases, it has not progressed

to actual violence. For example, the woman who is constantly stalking and invading the Connecticut home of David Letterman probably sincerely believes that she loves him and he loves her back in spite of his having her repeatedly arrested and put on the train to someplace else.

A classic example of erotomania was reported in *Vanity Fair* by Marie Brenner in the case of Diane Schaefer who is a chic woman in her early forties who appeared at her trial in designer clothes to answer her eighth misdemeanor charge of aggravated harassment. Well-educated with an extensive formal vocabulary and tastefully groomed, Marie Brenner described her as "a brainy blonde who had seen better days, . . . totally out of place being brought into the courtroom in handcuffs."

Yet, here she was testifying about the impassioned love affair she had been having with Dr. Murray Brennan, world renowned chief of surgery at the Sloan-Kettering. It was an affair the doctor categorically denied had happened or was happening. To him it was what Marie Brenner called, an "odd fixation and psychological terrorism."

For eight years Diane had haunted the doctor's life and she almost gleefully told the court about their romantic rendezvous in such graphic detail that the judge had to keep admonishing her to tone it down. The intimate sexual details of her illusionary romance with Brennan were symbols of their love for each other and she wanted to proclaim it to the world.

For example, she once talked her way past the

295

doorman of Brennan's apartment building and was waiting for him when he arrived home. She told of fondling and caressing him and sitting on his lap while his wife fumed in rage in the next room. Predictably, the doctor's story in court of the incident was vastly different.

In his version, he walked and found her awaiting him in see-through lingerie and immediately called his wife on the phone to tell her what was happening. As he was doing that, Diane was trying to unzip his fly, but he resisted and made her leave.

The unsettling thing about Diane's erotomania is that she was extremely clever and inventive in showing up at places the doctor would be whether it was in New York or at conferences in cities around the world. She was able to get access to his apartment, his calendar, private phone numbers, and addresses. She knew every detail of his family and his life. She also seemed to know details of his itinerary when he traveled and managed to put herself on the same planes and in the same hotels with him. On occasions, she would be right behind him at an airport and try to force her way into the same cab so she could be next to him.

Schaefer's phone calls to Brennan were constant both at home and at the office forcing him to change his home numbers repeatedly. His secretaries were besieged by her calls and so was his answering machines on which she would leave licentious messages.

Coupled with that were the peppering of him

everywhere with adoring love letters. All of these messages demonstrated that she knew every intimate detail about his life, his wife, his children, and family. She even extended her investigation of her love object to contacting his mother in New Zealand to find out things about him.

Although Murray didn't tell his wife about his encounters with Diane for several months, he ultimately did when letters from her started arriving at the house. Susan's first reaction was to write Diane back, woman-to-woman, telling her to leave her husband alone. Diane not only rebuffed that, but took to attacking Susan whenever she had the chance. For example, Diane showed up at a medical association convention in Boca Raton in the spring of 1983 and went directly up to Susan and announced that she was going to marry Murray Brennan.

Susan then became agitated and pushed for legal action against Diane and worried that Schaefer might suddenly decide to kill what she thought was the only thing standing in the way of everlasting happiness with Murray: Murray's present wife. She appeared at airports and meetings involving Brennan in Salzberg, Milan, New Haven, Washington, and San Francisco. When he showed up in Milan to give a lecture, for example, Diane was sitting in the front row smiling adoringly.

In association with her trial, the prosecution sent some of her letters to Dr. Park Dietz who specializes in analyzing obsession cases that lead to violence. Dietz became exercised about what he found in her letters and warned the prosecution that most of them betrayed the kind of emotional/mental condition that led to violence in other cases.

On the flip side of that assessment, Ms. Schaefer's lawyer, Joyce David, related to her feelings about Dr. Brennan. She has had those same feelings about a man herself and she knows scores of other women who have too.

When Diane says she isn't crazy, just in love, Joyce understands. All Diane wants to do is be Mrs. Brennan and the only barrier to that, she believes, is the present Mrs. Brennan who is also a medical doctor.

Ms. Schaefer's love obsession is well known to the Manhattan District Attorney's office because there were a series of complaints about her going back a number of years including one where the fixation of her attention was the judge in one of her early stints in court.

Schaefer graduated from New York University in education and began hanging around medical facilities and conferences in Manhattan. She earned some money doing occasional medical articles for magazines. The first recollection that both Dr. Brennan and Ms. Schaefer agree on was their initial meeting, related to a conference he attended in Chicago in October of 1982 when she came up to him at O'Hare Airport in Chicago and introduced herself while he was waiting to get a cab. She says and he denies that they sat next to each other holding hands and touching on the plane enroute

298

to Chicago.

Either way, they both agreed that they shared a cab into Chicago from O'Hare airport. At that point, their stories differ again. He said that he didn't see her in Chicago beyond the shared cab. She said that the shared cab graduated into dinner and lovemaking in his hotel room.

They both agreed that he had dinner with her back in Manhattan later. She said it was because he was falling in love with her. He said it was because she was a medical writer to whom he thought of giving some work, but changed his mind during the dinner because she was coming on to him so strongly.

About this same period is when Dr. Brennan was shifting from Bethesda, Maryland, where he lived with his physician wife, Susan, and their four children to Manhattan and the Sloan-Kettering Institution. The family moved to a suburb of New York, Susan stopped practicing medicine for a time and Dr. Brennan kept a small apartment in Manhattan for those nights he worked late at the medical center.

One of the things that Murray Brennan did not know at the moment Diane Schaefer came into his life was that she was already into somebody else's life—his new boss's, Dr. Jerome J. DeCosse, Chairman of the Department of Surgery when Brennan came to Sloan-Kettering.

He had met her late in 1978 and she immediately focused on him and invaded his life from then on with messages, letters, meetings, and other harassments including following his wife, Sheila, when she went on errands or went shopping. Diane claimed that she and Dr. DeCosse had a passionate affair that began when, at twenty-eight, she lost her virginity to him.

Demonstrating her ingenuity in insinuating herself into DeCosse's life, Schaefer got an ID card from the hospital so she could move freely about his domain; had herself listed in the New York phone directory as "D. DeCosse" to get calls from people trying to reach him; and, got hotel rooms with connecting doors next to his at out-of-town medical conventions. In this latter situation, she would write him notes urging him to unlock his side of the connecting door.

When he and his wife went to visit family in Bozeman, Montana, and were greeted in the small airport by his wheelchair-ridden mother and his brother, there was Diane Schaefer lurking, and staring at them all.

Through all of this, Dr. DeCosse maintained that he fended her off and tried to get her out of his life. On December 14, 1981, he alerted his superior, Dr. Edward J. Beattie, Jr., the Chief Medical Officer, that he was being harassed by Diane Schaefer and had concluded that she was dangerous and wanted legal advice. This was the start of legal attempts at getting rid of Ms. Schaefer's harassments.

Unfortunately, Dr. Brennan didn't know about any of this at the time he first had contact with Ms. Schaefer. And, neither of the two doctors understood what type of delusionary behavior they were dealing with in Diane. The one advantage of the situation for Dr. DeCosse was that Schaefer would shift her love obsession from him to Murray Brennan.

In time the two doctors did compare notes and the link was made. They then went to the District Attorney who interviewed Schaefer and tried to get her to accept counseling. She refused and continued to harass Dr. Brennan. The Manhattan D.A.'s office cautioned the Brennan's that prosecuting for harassment is not as easy as it sounds and, even if they won, it was still a minor crime with a minimum penalty.

The amazing thing about Marie Brenner's investigation of Diane Schaefer was that she learned that Diane had another side to her life entirely — one where she used names such as Susan Brennan and Jerry DeCosse. She was a burlesque dancer and porno girl in sex shops and nude bars around Times Square and along West 42 Street.

Putting that aside, the D.A. turned the case over to Linda Fairstein who headed the sex crimes unit. She tried to get Diane's family to intervene and see that Diane got psychiatric help, but they didn't seem able to do that. Her parents pleaded that Diane not be arrested. And, in fact, the Brennans really didn't want her arrested. They just wanted her out of their lives. None of those good intentions worked. The harassment got so bad with no therapeutic solution in sight that Diane was arrested.

On the first arrest, Diane was let go without bail and without being required to get counseling. Angered that her make-believe lover would do this to her, she intensified the harassment and a second arrest followed. This time there was no bail and therapy was required after which she appeared before Judge Stephen Crane representing herself and the judge was sufficiently persuaded by her presentation that he let her go.

That was a mistake as the judge soon found out because Diane immediately began stalking him and his wife including the usual letter writing barrage with notes proposing lustful assaults on Crane in his courtroom. At the same time she continued to appear where Dr. Brennan, her true love, appeared professionally or socially. At the next opportunity, Brennan had Schaefer arrested again for harassment. That was the fifth time she had been arrested for the same crime.

In spite of all this, no order forbidding Diane from harassing the Brennans was be issued by the court for a year. As slow as the wheels of justice grind, they do — in fact — grind and Diane finally appeared in court facing seven charges of aggravated assault represented by her attorney. The jury was out nine hours deliberating the life and behavior of this woman. When it came back, it pronounced her guilty on all seven counts and the judge sentenced her — a woman broke and broken — to the maximum of two years in prison on Riker's Island by Hellsgate in the East River.

Doctors Marie Rudden, John Sweeney, and Allen Frances have extensively studied and analyzed erotomania, "the delusional belief that one is passionately loved by another." It seems sadly true that the women we describe in this book appear to suffer some degree of erotomania over which they seem to have little control.

For Diane Schaefer, Carol Warmus, Elisabeth Broderick, Jean Harris, Laura Doyle, Amy Fisher, Beth Meyerson, Libby Holman, Jennifer Reali, Lucille Miller, Lawrencia Bembenek, and the thousands of other erotomanic women—some of who murdered—it is a pathetic and bewildering outcome.

They really don't understand why the world has turned against them when, as the song from "Chorus Line" says so poignantly, all they did, they did for love.

About the Author

Educated and raised in California, George Mair has been a teacher and soldier, CBS broadcaster, and *L.A. Times* nationally syndicated columnist, chief press officer to the Speaker of Congress, and a radio talk-show host.

A veteran of the Korean War, his undergraduate and graduate work was done at UCLA where he earned a teaching credential after which he ran the family development and banking business for ten years.

As Editorial Director at CBS Radio in Los Angeles for ten years, he wrote and produced 3,000 plus editorials, 100 documentaries and won thirty-two awards.

Moving to Washington, D.C., as *L.A. Times* nationally syndicated columnist, he became editor-publisher of America's oldest daily newspaper, *The Alexandria Gazette* in 1982 and chief Public Relations counsel for HBO in 1985.

He returned to Washington in 1987, finished his tenth book and became Press Officer to the Speaker of Congress. He left Federal service mid-1989 to become a radio talk host on station WPGC. He is currently working on two more true crime books.

**ORDINARY LIVES DESTROYED BY EXTRAORDINARY HORROR.
FACTS MORE DANGEROUS THAN FICTION.
CAPTURE A PINNACLE TRUE CRIME . . . IF YOU DARE.**

LITTLE GIRL LOST   (593, $4.99)
By Joan Merriam
When Anna Brackett, an elderly woman living alone, allowed two teenage girls into
her home, she never realized that a brutal death awaited her. Within an hour, Mrs.
Brackett would be savagely stabbed twenty-eight times. Her executioners were Shirley
Katherine Wolf, 14, and Cindy Lee Collier, 15. *Little Girl Lost* examines how two
adolescents were driven through neglect and sexual abuse to commit the ultimate
crime.

HUSH, LITTLE BABY   (541, $4.99)
By Jim Carrier
Darci Kayleen Pierce seemed to be the kind of woman you stand next to in the grocery
store. However, Darci was obsessed with the need to be a mother. She desperately
wanted a baby — any baby. On a summer day, Darci kidnapped a nine-month pregnant
woman, strangled her, and performed a makeshift Cesarean section with a car key. In
this arresting account, readers will learn how Pierce's tortured fantasy of motherhood
spiraled into a bloody reality.

IN A FATHER'S RAGE   (547, $4.99)
By Raymond Van Over
Dr. Kenneth Z. Taylor promised his third wife Teresa that he would mend his drug-
addictive, violent ways. His vow didn't last. He nearly beat his bride to death on their
honeymoon. This nuptial nightmare worsened until Taylor killed Teresa after allegedly catching her sexually abusing her infant son. Claiming to have been driven
beyond a father's rage, Taylor was still found guilty of first degree murder. This grip-
ping page-turner reveals how a marriage made in heaven can become a living hell.

I KNOW MY FIRST NAME IS STEVEN   (563, $4.99)
By Mike Echols
A TV movie was based on this terrifying tale of abduction, child molesting, and
brainwashing. Yet, a ray of hope shines through this evil swamp for Steven Stayner
escaped from his captor and testified against the socially disturbed Kenneth Eugene
Parnell. For seven years, Steven was shuttled across California under the assumed
name of "Dennis Parnell." Despite the humiliations and degradations, Steven never
lost sight of his origins or his courage.

RITES OF BURIAL   (611, $4.99)
By Tom Jackman and Troy Cole
Many pundits believe that the atrocious murders and dismemberments performed by
Robert Berdella may have inspired Jeffrey Dahmer. Berdella stalked and savagely
tortured young men; sadistically photographing their suffering and ritualistically pre-
serving totems from their deaths. Upon his arrest, police uncovered human skulls,
envelopes of teeth, and a partially decomposed human head. This shocking expose is
written by two men who worked daily on this case.

---

*Available wherever paperbacks are sold, or order direct from the
Publisher. Send cover price plus 50¢ per copy for mailing and handling to Pinnacle Books, Dept.735 , 475 Park Avenue South, New
York, N.Y. 10016. Residents of New York and Tennessee must
include sales tax. DO NOT SEND CASH. For a free Zebra/Pinna-
cle catalog please write to the above address.*

HE'S THE LAST MAN YOU'D EVER
WANT TO MEET IN A DARK ALLEY . . .

THE EXECUTIONER

By DON PENDLETON

PINNACLE BOOKS AND *TRUE DETECTIVE* MAGAZINE TEAM UP TO BRING YOU THE MOST HORRIFIC TRUE CRIME STORIES!

BIZARRE MURDERERS	(486-9, $4.95/$5.95)
CELEBRITY MURDERS	(435-4, $4.95/$5.95)
COP KILLERS	(603-9, $4.99/$5.99)
THE CRIMES OF THE RICH AND FAMOUS	(630-6, $4.99/$5.99)
CULT KILLERS	(528-8, $4.95/$5.95)
MEDICAL MURDERERS	(522-2, $4.99/$5.99)
SERIAL MURDERERS	(432-X, $4.95/$5.95)
SPREE KILLERS	(461-3, $4.95/$5.95)
TORTURE KILLERS	(506-7, $4.95/$5.95)